This book is both an exposition and a defence of a social scientific approach to conflict in international relations. Professor Nicholson addresses two central questions. To what extent can we usefully discuss behaviour in violent or potentially violent international conflict as rational? How do we formulate and test theories in international relations so that we can rationally believe in them?

After outlining social scientific approaches to international relations, the author describes the problems of rational decision making in conflict situations. He shows how rationality is in many strategic situations hard to define and often leads to paradoxes such as the prisoners' dilemma. Psychological stress can further result in the distortion of decision processes in times of crisis. Professor Nicholson pays particular attention to such distortions and also analyses how unconscious motivation relates to the rational choice framework. In the following part, the author explores rational beliefs about the international system. He examines theories of arms races, alliances and the international problems of ecology. Here he is critical of the classical school of international relations for a lack of rigour in dealing with the problems of evidence and belief. Finally, he discusses the philosophy of science, policy and ethics.

With its emphasis on social scientific approaches, theory building and testing – and above all its clarity and accessibility – *Rationality and the Analysis of International Conflict* provides students with a key to understanding the complex field of conflict analysis. This book will therefore be core reading for courses on international relations, and it will also be read by students and specialists of political science and economics.

CAMBRIDGE STUDIES IN INTERNATIONAL RELATIONS: 19

RATIONALITY AND THE ANALYSIS OF INTERNATIONAL CONFLICT

Cambridge Studies in International Relations is a joint initiative of Cambridge University Press and the British International Studies Association (BISA). The series will include a wide range of material, from undergraduate textbooks and surveys to research-based monographs and collaborative volumes. The aim of the series is to publish the best new scholarship in International Studies from Europe, North America and the rest of the world.

CAMBRIDGE STUDIES IN INTERNATIONAL RELATIONS

RATIONALITY AND THE ANALYSIS OF INTERNATIONAL CONFLICT

MICHAEL NICHOLSON

*Professor of International Relations and
Director of the University of Kent's London
Centre of International Relations*

CAMBRIDGE
UNIVERSITY PRESS

Published by the Press Syndicate of the University of Cambridge
The Pitt Building, Trumpington Street, Cambridge CB2 1RP
40 West 20th Street, New York, NY 10011–4211, USA
10 Stamford Road, Oakleigh, Victoria 3166, Australia

First published 1992

Printed in Great Britain by J. W. Arrowsmith Ltd, Bristol

A catalogue record for this book is available from the British Library

Library of Congress cataloguing in publication data
Nicholson, Michael, 1933–
Rationality and the analysis of international conflict / by
Michael Nicholson.
     p.   cm. – (Cambridge studies in international relations: 19)
ISBN 0 521 39125–3. – ISBN 0 521 39810 X (pbk.)
1. International relations – Psychological aspects.
2. International relations – Decision making.
3. War.
4. Social sciences – Methodology.
I. Title. II. Series.
JX1391.N5 1992 91–3780 CIP
327.1′6′019–dc20

ISBN 0 521 39125 3 hardback
ISBN 0 521 39810 X paperback

CE

To Christine

War is waged by men; not by gods. It is a peculiarly human activity.

Frederic Manning, *The Middle Parts of Fortune*

CONTENTS

PREFACE

Though there are exceptions, most of us pride ourselves on being rational. Political leaders are particularly eager to be seen as such. Because of this, it is important to consider the whole concept of rationality in international relations and see whether the decision makers and students of the area are justified in their beliefs in their own rationality, in particular as regards their beliefs and decisions about violent conflict. This is what I attempt to do in this book. Despite its academic, almost clinical analysis, it is about violence, wars and rumours of wars.

I discuss the problems in terms of the field which is sometimes known as 'Conflict Analysis'. I give an account of some aspects of this fascinating discipline, though I have tried to go beyond an account and give an interpretation of the field, putting it in the broader context of the nature of a social science and the concept of rationality. It is a vast and developing field, and I do not pretend to be comprehensive. To illustrate my argument, I have described some of its more important aspects, giving some flavour both of the work done in the field and the way in which social scientists work. Above all, I wish to convey the notion that social scientists, like natural scientists, are very concerned to ask what the grounds are for believing in the various propositions they make in their disciplines. It is this which basically characterises science and is at the core of the developments towards a more scientific approach to the discipline which have occurred over the last three decades or so.

Originally I set out to write a revised edition of my *Conflict Analysis*, long out of print, which was published in 1970 and gave an account of the field as it existed then. However, the developments have been so extensive that a complete rewrite seemed more appropriate, so this is essentially a new book. I have deliberately made it as much an interpretation of the field as an exposition, though I hope it does service as both. It follows that most of what appears here is an account of the work of other people which I have fitted together to argue a case

xv

not necessarily implicit in the work of any of them. The book is intended to be intelligible to the novice in the field but still of interest, at least in part, to my professional peers. A few paragraphs remain, nearly untouched, from the earlier book, where I have felt that the work still stood and I could not improve them, but most of the book is freshly written with some topics omitted and several new ones introduced. There is not a great deal of overlap with my book *Formal Theories in International Relations*, apart from a small amount here and there, in particular the first section of the chapter on arms races. This is emphatically not a simplified version of *Formal Theories*. Even when it deals with some similar topics, it is dealing with some of the conceptual issues which there were more or less taken for granted.

Some readers might wince at the diagrams and numbers which appear in the text. No mathematical knowledge is required except for a very basic understanding of graphs, and even this in only a few places. I have tried to be as clear in my arguments as possible. Readers unaccustomed to this style of argument will find that it comes quickly after puzzling through a few of the examples.

I have depended on my family and friends to prevent me making too much of a fool of myself in public. I particularly want to thank Tyrell Harris (Bedford and Royal Holloway College, London), Martin Hollis (University of East Anglia), Ian Rowlands (London School of Economics), Hugh Ward (Essex University) and Keith Webb (University of Kent at Canterbury) for these services. I owe an especial debt to Steve Smith of the University of East Anglia for encouragement in writing this book and a very detailed reading of the manuscript which has resulted in many improvements. His help has been far beyond anything one could reasonably expect of the editor of a series.

My family, Jane Castrillon, Paul Nicholson, Caroline Nicholson and Geoff James I want to thank for reading the manuscript and making extremely useful comments, particularly on presentation, which I have altered considerably in view of these comments. My brother Philip Nicholson, formerly of the Westminster Hospital Medical School, also read the first version of the manuscript and gave a large amount of help with the proofs.

Christine Nicholson helped throughout by reading the text in its various drafts with patience and encouragement – the latter a particularly self-sacrificing act, as it only resulted in further drafts. The clarity I strive for, however unavailingly, is at least in part due to her insistence.

INTRODUCTION: RATIONALITY AND THE ANALYSIS OF CONFLICT

A traveller on the back roads through northern France near its borders with Belgium is struck by the number of cemeteries. These do not contain the mortal remains of the elderly and unfortunate of the region, but those of many young men from all over the world who had little reason to want to go there in the first place. However, between 1914 and 1918 many did go, to live for a while in misery, discomfort and terror, and a tragically large number died there. Small and unimportant towns like Passchendaele, Verdun and Mons, small rivers like the Somme, are now symbols of the wastage of young men's lives by societies which, by many other criteria, were highly civilised. The whole area seems a colossal monument to doomed youth, and indeed was seen as such by many of the generation who went there and survived it. Poets and writers such as Siegfried Sassoon, Robert Graves and Wilfred Owen have made the experience vivid for later generations. It may be the literacy of the participants as well as the sheer scale and horror of the events which has made the First World War[1] so particularly vivid for so many people who have no direct memories of it. If this were one isolated event in history, we would look at it with horror. Unfortunately it is not. Barely twenty years after the men had crawled out of their trenches, their successors were involved in an even more destructive war. Nor does the habit seem to have been broken. War still appears to be an absorbing occupation for human beings.

As far back as we can tell, people have devoted some of the best of their minds and bodies to the problem of killing their fellows. Humans are the only animals which take the business of killing other members of their species with such seriousness. Other primates kill members of other species, usually for food. Members of the same species fight amongst themselves for mates, territory and so on, but they rarely

---

[1] The First World War was given its title as early as the Armistice in the title of a book by Repington (*The Great World War*) 'to prevent the millennial folk from forgetting that the history of the world is the history of war' (A. J. P. Taylor 1965). A bleak comment.

fight to the death. Killing amongst the non-human primates is equivalent to murder rather than to war. War is a predominantly human activity. Despite its frequency, it is an activity which conflicts with the aims of most other human activities, such as the quest for wealth, knowledge, a happy family life and so on, all of which are much better pursued under conditions of peace. The paradox is apparent. As Thomas Hobbes remarked, 'Avoid the "state of warre" in order to pursue the "Arts of Peace".'

War is not universally abhorred. People's attitudes towards violence culminating in death and suffering are ambivalent, combining horror for its obvious miseries with fascination for its splendour and the opportunities for gallantry and even for a noble death which war provides. People's ambivalence towards violence, I shall argue, is one of the problems we have to face. Attitudes to war during the twentieth century seem to have altered somewhat, and common belief seems to regard it as a regrettable necessity rather than as something desirable in itself. The vast slaughter of the First World War may have had something to do with this. Perhaps more important is our greater belief in the prospects of controlling society. War at one time was regarded as inevitable – it still is by some. However, slavery was once also thought to be part of the natural order of things, though now it is an almost defunct institution. Hence, despite the many horrors of social life such as those caused by poverty as well as war, we are less inclined than our ancestors to see the 'natural order of things' as being quite as natural as they did. Even if we cannot necessarily form utopias, we can at least see society as to some degree malleable and open to constructive change. Once war is seen not to be an inevitable feature of human life, there is the prospect of working to stop it rather than making the best of a bad job. Despite this change in attitudes, we have so far had very little success in stopping wars being fought. It is still the case that societies get into positions where, to many people, the only way out seems to be to fight. Why should this be?

War appears as the supreme example of irrationality. It is the wanton destruction of life and the general conditions of human happiness. War may well destroy the human race in its entirety; it will almost certainly still cause much misery and suffering in the future as it has in the past. To link it, then, with rationality would seem unusually absurd. I aim to show the contrary; far from being absurd, it is the rational analysis of the dilemmas posed by wars and the threats which holds out some hopes for the future.

There are two basic aspects of rationality which will be explored in this book, rational conduct and rational belief. The two involve rather different problems. The first is a question of action: what is 'rational conduct' or 'rational behaviour' in the sort of situations which arise in international relations? The second is a question of belief: what can we rationally believe about the behaviour of people in the international system? Rational behaviour presupposes rational belief, but, as will become clearer later, there is more to it than that. Further, we consider rational beliefs about the international system without being too directly concerned with behaviour even if at some stage, though possibly a much later one, the issue of behaviour becomes significant, unless curiosity alone is what motivates our enquiries.

In practice we believe what we believe for a whole range of reasons, including habit and laziness. In the minutiae of everyday life this may not matter too much, and indeed may save us a lot of trouble. However, if we are to look at serious issues such as what causes wars, it is crucial that we consider carefully the grounds for our beliefs. If we believe that the balance of power or the control of the arms race reduces the risk of war, we must ask ourselves why we believe such things. Further, belief is not an all or nothing business, but commonly involves belief with some degree of doubt, a factor which raises some further complications.

In general the classical study of international relations[2] has been casual about the bases for belief. Scholars such as Hedley Bull, Martin Wight and Hans Morgenthau make generalisations about behaviour but take little interest in why we should believe in them other than by referring to some haphazardly chosen examples. They seem to regard as peripheral what I hold to be central – namely the question of what are appropriate reasons for believing in such generalisations. There is now no excuse for neglect. There has grown up a whole new aspect to the discipline which, however crudely and awkwardly at times, places the testing of hypotheses as central to its endeavours. Much of this book, though particularly part IV, is an implicit or explicit criticism of the more recent exponents of this classical point of view. This is not a criticism of the 'historical method'. These authors' use of historical examples as illustrations of their generalisations – in the case of Wight with an extraordinary breadth of historical knowledge – does not mean that they are using the historical method as it is generally used. Historians are not typically interested in formulating generalisations,

[2] By the 'classical' or 'traditional' school of international relations theorists I mean such relatively modern writers as Hans Morgenthau in *Politics amongst Nations*, Martin Wight in *Power Politics* and Hedley Bull in *The Anarchical Society*. All were opposed to the social scientific approach to international relations and conflict, Bull and Morgenthau explicitly and Wight implicitly. I discuss such views in greater detail in chapter 12.

whereas these writers are trying to justify their generalisations but without being clear about the nature of such justification.

Though the problem of why we believe what we believe is a basic philosophical problem, we shall attack it only from half way through and, even then, bear in mind that we are illustrating the problem rather than justifying it from first principles. Essentially we start with the assumption that our methods of understanding the natural world are broadly right and look at the consequences in a number of cases of assuming whether social behaviour can be looked at in broadly the same way. In this book I do not justify it more than superficially. Anyone who wants a fuller justification of this approach should consult my *Scientific Analysis of Social Behaviour: A Defence of Empiricism in Social Science* (London: Pinter, 1983).

Rational conduct is conduct which results from choices based on rational belief. However, while to base action on rational belief is a necessary condition for rational conduct, it is not a sufficient condition. Under uncertainty, criteria for rational choice become less clear, while in conflict they are frequently downright ambiguous. Rational choice and rational conduct become far from clear-cut concepts in conflict, a point which is central to the discussion in chapter 4. 'Rational choice theory', as this style of theory is not unnaturally known, normally assumes that people are consistent and coherent about what they want. There are good reasons to doubt this, and I try to broaden the approach by analysing the nature of preference in greater detail, particularly in chapter 6 and I discuss the problem of crises as an extension of rational choice theory in the following chapter. I see rational choice theory as a part of a tradition, or a 'scientific research programme', in Lakatos's terms, rather than a body of accepted theory. It is inadequate by itself but is invaluable as a basis for analysis.

Though war is in some general sense irrational, there are two immediate ways in which rational belief and rational conduct relate to its analysis. First, if a war breaks out, it can be waged in rational ways. Totally against our will we might find ourselves forced into considering wars or threats of wars. Strategy is the study of how to act rationally in the use of and in the face of violence. It may, though it does not necessarily, presuppose the approval of violence.

Secondly, because some form of behaviour is irrational, it does not mean we cannot analyse it by rational means and act rationally, taking the irrationalities into account. Medieval witch-hunts were not rational – they were doubtfully so even in terms of the beliefs of the day (Cohn 1975). It is not only possible but necessary to analyse such phenomena by rational means in order to avoid some repetition of similar sorts of behaviour. The emphasis of this book is similar. Central to it is the notion that we cannot answer the question 'How can war be stopped?' without going back to the question 'Why are wars fought?' The second question will not give an automatic answer to the first, but it is a necessary prerequisite. This can be done only by means of a rational analysis.

Of particular interest is the question of how best to avoid a danger of war. Often in human behaviour we find ourselves caught in 'rationality traps' where the only thing to do seems to be to declare war or carry out some other act which in the broader scheme of things appears manifestly irrational. The conditions where war breaks out seem prime cases of such rationality traps. However, reason can perhaps help us to avoid these or even show us how we can extricate ourselves from them if we fall into them. Simply to argue that war is irrational and that therefore it is pointless to think how one should act for the best within it is to assume an ideal situation.

In this book I stress three themes. The first is that of rational choice and the resulting rational conduct. I show that rationality is an inherently ambiguous concept when applied to conflict situations and is an area amply provided with paradoxes. Even in those cases where it is straightforward, there are considerable pressures which suborn people away from rational behaviour. This is the subject matter of part II of the book.

Secondly, in conflict analysis (as in any other field) we should constantly be self-conscious and self-critical about the grounds we have for believing things. This is the issue of rational belief, which is illustrated by four topics in conflict analysis discussed in part III which illustrate how the social scientist works. The problems of part III are rather different from those discussed in part II, but still problems subsumed under the general heading of 'a rational approach to the problem of international conflict'. In conflict analysis, we have learnt, are learning, and, we hope, will continue to learn, a great deal through systematic analysis of behaviour by the application of the methods of the social sciences. The process of analysis is not merely the assertion of prejudice and counter-prejudice, though this is not to deny that prejudice still plays a disproportionate role in the study of international relations, as in all other areas of human behaviour.

Finally, as a general background to many of the issues in this book, I argue throughout that conflict is a general phenomenon in social life. An understanding of one manifestation of conflict, such as industrial conflict, can often have significant implications for the understanding of forms such as international conflict. There are various generic conflict processes which make it legitimate to use quite homely examples to illustrate patterns of conflict which appear in many different and often much more serious forms. A major distinction, however, is between conflicts which are violent or which threaten violence and those which do not. There are still links and parallels which may be very useful, but, as I argue later in the book, and in particular in chapter 6, issues can be raised in violent conflict which are absent when violence is absent.

These two central parts are sandwiched between two parts which essentially justify this mode of analysis and relate it to a broader intellectual context. Many of the disagreements about international relations and conflict analysis are disagreements in the philosophy of science – again the basic problem of why we believe what we believe.

Two contrasting errors tempt scholars. First, there is the error of exaggerated dogmatism. For example, consider two statements. The first is a common assertion of conventional wisdom: 'Deterrence has preserved the peace for the last forty years.' The second is the expression of radical wisdom: 'At least since the death of Stalin, peace in Europe has existed because neither of the power blocs particularly wanted to disturb the status quo. In particular, the Soviet Union has not attacked the West because it did not particularly want to.' Both are asserted with vigour and conviction, but there is no clear way of deciding between them. I do not mean this in the sense that it is an inherently undecidable question. To answer it, though, we need an advance in our theoretical knowledge of human behaviour and not just an addition of further facts about these particular situations.

The second error is the error of exaggerated humility. Some writers seem to imply that, ultimately, all we say about the international system is an account of our prejudices (Frankel 1988). On this view, we believe one of the above two statements about the USSR according to our temperamental dispositions so that, even in principle, we can no more decide between them on rational grounds than we can decide whether the works of Bach are a supreme manifestation of the human spirit or a collection of curious noises. I argue that this view is mistaken. We can analyse conflict through the methods of the social sciences, and our knowledge can increase. We therefore must pursue the discovery of theoretical propositions about the behaviour of human beings, tested by evidence, which will suggest whether the above propositions are true or false. In the case of the propositions about deterrence, we need fuller and better-attested theories about deterrence in order to discriminate between the hypotheses suggested. We are acquiring such a knowledge. Our ability to make reasoned arguments is much better now than it was twenty years ago, but there is still a long way to go. The points I wish to emphasise are that it is possible to acquire such knowledge, that we have acquired some already, and it is rational to suppose that this will continue. It will be most disappointing if this book is anything but an interim report.

PART I
CONFLICT

In this part the basic concepts are discussed. Two features appear and reappear throughout the book. The first is the concept of conflict itself and the issues involved in its definition and analysis; the second is the concept of a social science. Conflict is looked at as a generic process which is involved in all social behaviour. However, it is war and violent political conflict which are central to the analyses of this book, though not to the exclusion of other significant issues in conflict analysis. I approach war from the point of view of a social scientist and argue the legitimacy of this mode of analysis and, indeed, its necessity if we are to be able to have the sort of understanding of it which would help reduce its incidence. The reasons for holding this view are discussed at some length.

1 CONCEPTS OF CONFLICT

1 THE DEFINITION OF CONFLICT

This book is primarily concerned with international conflicts, and in particular with those which erupt or may erupt into violence. However, conflict is a general feature of human activity, and it is towards its more general aspects that we turn first.

'Conflict', as it is used in everyday speech, is a vague term and associated with it are many vague concepts. While in principle the issue of definition is a question of decision about how to use words, in practice definitions are already located in a linguistic context and have prior associations. Thus we need to be careful in our definitions, and take care to note where a disagreement which appears to be merely a question of linguistic taste hides some more basic division about how we should conceptualise the underlying characteristics of the discipline.

Conflict is an activity which takes place between conscious, though not necessarily rational, beings. If two astronomical bodies collide, we do not say that they are in conflict. A conflict is defined in terms of the wants, needs or obligations of the parties involved. These wants may be relatively practical, such as in a conflict over fishing limits, where one would hope negotiation would end in a settlement. It may concern fundamental beliefs and attitudes such as over the status of Jerusalem, where attitudes are not readily altered.

A conflict exists when two people wish to carry out acts which are mutually inconsistent. They may both want to do the same thing, such as eat the same apple, or they may want to do different things where the different things are mutually incompatible, such as when they both want to stay together but one wants to go to the cinema and the other stay at home. A conflict is resolved when some mutually compatible set of actions is worked out. The definition of conflict can be extended from individuals to groups (such as states or nations), and more than two parties can be involved in the conflict. The principles remain the same.

11

Because conflicts involve wants or needs which are states of mind, there is a sense in which they are subjective. However, what a person (or collective, such as a state) wants is an objective characteristic of that person. Wants are subjective in the sense that an answer to the question 'Why do you want to do X?' can be given ultimately only in terms either of 'Just because I want to' or 'Just because I ought to'. (Admittedly X may be something basic like stay alive – it is nevertheless a want, though a very urgent want.) There is an extension of the latter principle to an assertion 'You ought to' – that is, according to my moral principles you are under some obligation even though you would deny it. Such justifications where there are conflicts of beliefs are common in religious conflicts. While these are the ultimate justifications, there may be a whole set of intervening stages such as 'I want to do Y, and X is the means of achieving it.' However, having gone through a chain of reasons, one ends with a statement of either desire or obligation. There is no external justification for these final statements of wants. Thus, the desires of a state (more strictly its decision makers) which motivate its actions are based ultimately on needs or obligations which are justifiable only within a self-contained system. In this sense they are subjective. The desires of, say, the Spanish government concerning the status of Gibraltar can be justified only in terms of other desires, or obligations. However, these desires of the Spanish decision makers concerning Gibraltar are an objective, though not thereby an unalterable characteristic which they possess and are thus quite 'real' as far as the analysis of behaviour is concerned.

We are still left with one terminological point. We use the word 'conflict' in two different ways, as in a statement such as 'Britain and Argentina had a conflict over the status of the Falklands/Malvinas.' This can mean (and since 1843 has meant) that the two governments have opposed interests which they may be trying to reconcile. For a lot of the time, neither side was willing to put many resources into resolving the conflict in its own favour. Neither side was trying to damage the other in order to persuade it to accept its point of view. Indeed the conflict was often dormant, when neither side did much about it. Nevertheless, in 1982 it finally resulted in war, and again 'Britain and Argentina had a conflict over the status of the Falklands/Malvinas', only now the statement means something rather different – namely that there had been some conflict behaviour – people were devoting resources to damaging each other. This is stronger than the former meaning. Unfortunately the sentence asserted and repeated above does double duty in many analyses of conflict to describe these two different situations (and to a degree which goes surprisingly unremarked, as it does at times lead to confusion). Where there is ambiguity, 'conflict behaviour' can be used to refer to damaging action taken by the parties to induce a settlement in their favour such as a strike or a war, and 'a conflict exists' or a 'conflict of interests' to refer to the situation where the parties perceive an incompatibility between their views, and are prepared, at least in principle, to use conflict behaviour to solve it. A 'disagreement' is where the earlier conditions for a conflict were met but where the parties are unwilling to use conflict behaviour to resolve it. On this definition, the dispute between Britain and Spain over the sovereignty of Gibraltar is a disagreement rather than a conflict.

Conflicts abound in all forms of social behaviour. In industry there are strikes, in international politics there are wars and threats, in marriages there are quarrels, and, when people tire of acting out their conflicts in these fields, they can always turn to sport as a highly institutionalised and constrained form of conflict. While these forms of conflict are very different from each other, they are all recognised as conflicts and hence have some common attributes. It is thus appropriate to look at conflict as a general form of conduct to see what insights are to be gained from looking at the activity as a whole. There may be none, but there will probably be some. Though our interest is primarily in war and its causes, the more general analysis of conflict provides, if nothing else, a set of concepts which will be of use in tackling the prime problem of the causes of war.

Consider the issue of bargaining. In general, bargaining is a process whereby two (or more) parties, whose aims at least partially conflict, endeavour to find some mutually satisfactory agreement. When a trade union and a firm bargain over the wage rate, the union wants the highest rate possible and the management want the lowest. Both start off with demands which are incompatible with each other and then bargain until they reach a level which both will accept and which is normally in between the two original starting-points. It is not just a matter of talking, however. If the management appear recalcitrant, the union can call a strike. The firm can have a lock-out. This, however, is relatively infrequent, not because the management have a stronger social conscience than the unions, but because the firm performs the positive action of handing out the wages – the workers are involved only in the passive action of receiving them. The union cannot directly force the management to hand out a higher wage and, prior to an agreement, the situation in general favours the employer. The union can break this *status quo* positively only by calling the strike. Thus, it is natural that the hostilities in an industrial dispute should normally be initiated by the union. The strike will end at some time with a concession by one or the other party or, more commonly, by both.

This situation has some parallels with international conflicts. Suppose two states disagree over the degree of influence which they will both exert over some third country. They might discuss the problem and arrive directly at some solution. In the bargaining, however, the prospect of fighting will come up, and indeed the situation might break out into war. The war may end in the submission of one party or some agreement.

Clearly there are some analogies between the two processes of industrial and international disagreement. In both cases there are incompatible goals, and in both cases there are threats. Consequently an analysis of industrial bargains might provide some hints for the analysis of international bargains. It is not difficult to spot breakdowns in the analogy, and the most such a procedure can do is to suggest ways of tackling the prime problem. However, this is by no means a trivial contribution.

The most serious way in which the analogy breaks down is with respect to the issue of violence. Most strikes today do not involve violence, whereas war, by definition, is a violent act. Even in the days and places where strikes were often accompanied by violence, this was not the primary element in the conflict. The threat to the employers was usually the withdrawal of the work force, only rarely the possibility of riots.

Our attitudes to violence are curious and by no means completely consistent. When war breaks out, it is not infrequent for the populations of the warring states to become enthusiastic. Even the suggestion of negotiation becomes the suggestion of treason. The only acceptable alternative for each opponent is the subjection of the other. Even in more limited wars, victory in the limited sense becomes the requirement, as was demonstrated in the Falklands/Malvinas War. This is not true in the non-violent conflict. Even in the midst of a strike, negotiation is a proper activity, and a solution involving a compromise is often acceptable.

2 DEADLY QUARRELS

In his studies of war and violence, Richardson introduced the useful term 'Deadly Quarrel' (Richardson 1960a). The term is virtually self-explanatory, referring to any conflict which intentionally results in the death of some of the participants. It neatly encapsulates the core of a set of intellectual, political and moral concerns of these studies. One of the virtues of this definition is that it directs our attention beyond international wars alone and suggests that any deadly quarrel is within the ambit of our analysis, whether it is a war as commonly understood between states, a civil war, violence between criminal bands, guerrilla war or murder. While these manifestations of violent conflict clearly have their own particular characteristics, they also have many things in common. The grouping together of deadly quarrels is useful for two different sets of reasons. First, for intellectual or scientific purposes: there is some presumption that violent (i.e. deadly) conflicts have some characteristics in common which are not shared with non-deadly conflicts such as strikes or trade wars. Thus in the scientific analysis of conflict we can usefully group them together to examine these similarities. Most scholars would accept this point, though they would differ on its significance. I shall argue that this is a crucial division which is often underestimated. Secondly, quarrels which result in death involve moral issues of a different order of magnitude from those which do not. Thus, at the individual level, murder is regarded in most societies as the worst, or one of the worst, crimes. At a larger social level, peace is an ideal which captures most people's imagination. Even ardent free-traders, who would regard competitive tariffs with great dismay, would rarely put them in the same moral category as war. This association of the intellectual and moral (and hence political) is accidental. It is fortuitous that the two classes are co-extensive.

The concept of a deadly quarrel categorises under one heading phenomena as diverse as the world wars of this century and murders. This obscures one division which is important from a scientific point of view. Consider the case of murder. Of course, murders themselves come in very different forms. In some, primarily the domestic murder, the victim is already well known to the murderer – this indeed being the point. (In many countries, family murder is the largest category.) Others are committed against a person who is acting in a particular role, such as a policeman who is trying to stop an armed robbery. The murderer would have killed whoever was there irrespective of their particular identity. Nevertheless, even this 'anonymous' form of murder involves as an essential attribute the killing of an individual who can be recognised as such. This makes the act different from, and more personal than, killing in a large-scale conflict. For this reason, an analysis of the causes of murder is not likely to be very helpful in an analysis of the causes of war and vice versa. They probably involve totally different sorts of psychological processes among the actors. The state of mind of a murderer – whether this is a crime of passion, or a murder committed in pursuance of a robbery – is likely to be very different from that of a soldier going into battle. This point applies to other forms of social violence where the size of the social group is an important determinant of its behaviour. I shall call 'face-to-face groups' those groups which are small enough for the individuals within them to recognise the other members. In them behaviour is different in a great many respects from that in a larger group which I shall call 'anonymous' or 'political', where the other members are just people in a general sense and not recognised as individuals. A deadly quarrel between two small groups such as small criminal gangs is more like murder than war, and we should be careful about over-stressing the relationships between them.

We can now gather together a few of the main types of conflict and relate them. There are two main features. First is the issue of violence, and secondly is whether it is a face-to-face group, in which people can individually recognise each other, or a political group, where most other members are anonymous. This can be presented in a two-by-two matrix with an illustration of each as follows:

Matrix 1.2

	Group characteristics	
Nature of conflict	Face to face	Political (or anonymous)
Violent	Murder	War
Non-violent	Family quarrel	Strike

War is a central social problem. Along with threats of war it is the core, though not the exclusive, interest, of this book. Its definition, unlike many of the others, is not unduly problematic. I shall define it as any situation of large-scale deadly violence between anonymous or political groups, and for the most part there is little ambiguity. How we subdivide wars into international war, revolutionary wars, wars of national identity and so on raises many problems, but the categorisation of the basic phenomenon is not unduly difficult. The definition of war is essentially behavioural, but only a legal pedant would insist on legal declarations, a definition which would exclude many acts of mass violence in this century. While the activity of war or warfare is not hard to define for the most part, the unit of 'a war' is sometimes difficult to specify. Thus, we talk of the Second World War, as if it were a single entity, but it could equally well be represented as a whole collection of wars loosely connected together. This is a common problem and troublesome for our statistical analysis.

3   VIOLENCE AND STRUCTURAL VIOLENCE

The normally understood meaning of 'violence' is the deliberate infliction of physical injury or death on one person or group by another. When two parties use violence against each other, we refer to it as 'fighting' and, anticipating a distinction to be made below, call it 'somatic violence'. In the case of two states or other political groups, we call such fighting 'war'. Sometimes, as in the case of football hooliganism, the fighting appears to be almost for its own sake. Sometimes, however, it is to achieve some particular goal. Thus people use violence in the pursuit of a robbery, where the violence is used as an instrument. There are other more amorphous goals such as revenge, honour, pride and so on. For states, violence is normally interpreted as an instrument with which to achieve something else, and most of the theory of international relations is based on the notion that violence is used instrumentally for the rational pursuit of goals. However, in the rhetoric of war, the concepts of honour and pride *et cetera* are just as freely used as in individual violence, and it is not clear that international relations theory has fully encompassed the significance of these notions. This is an issue I shall return to.

The core of the concept of violence is that it is the *deliberate* use of physical force to injure or kill another human. War is the extreme case of this, where the organised use of violence results in the death of some of the participants and bystanders, often in very large numbers. This indeed is the point of war.

However, violence is not the only cause of avoidable death. Take, for example, road accidents. A true 'accident' is unavoidable. However, by rebuilding roads, relighting and so on, the accident rate could be brought down very substantially. A decision not to redesign roads is not made deliberately to induce death. It involves a passive attitude to life rather than an active attitude to death. Nevertheless, people die prematurely because of it. Provisionally, then, we can introduce another category besides that of violent death, namely the category of 'avoidable death' characterised by the couplet:

> Thou shalt not kill; but need'st not strive,
> Officiously to keep alive.
>
> Arthur Hugh Clough, *The Latest Decalogue*

17

Some scholars such as Galtung (1969) have argued that avoidable death should be regarded as a form of violence. They define 'structural violence' as the avoidable deaths caused by social structures of society. They are particularly concerned with the issue of inequality either of income or the relevant resources of society such as medical services, which, of course, are usually closely correlated.

Let us consider the issue in terms of the problem of famine. Famines have frequently been responsible for a large number of deaths. For example, the Bengal famine of 1943 probably resulted in about 3 million deaths (Sen 1981); rather more than half of these deaths took place after the famine itself in the recurrent cycle of diseases directly attributable to it. This is some five times the number of British deaths in the 1939–45 war of 618,000 (Beer 1981), and substantially greater even than the Japanese deaths of 2,179,000 in the same war, so clearly we are dealing with something of great significance as a cause of premature death.

The conventional notion of a famine is that there is an overall short-age of food and because of this a large number of people die, either directly through starvation or indirectly because of the diseases which accompany famine. Thus the explanation of the Irish famine from 1846 onwards is that the potato blight devastated the basic crop of the Irish, resulting in a horrendous number of deaths. It was believed that it was an Act of God and that there was nothing much which could have been done about it, though its effects might be ameliorated. In the case of the Irish famine this was done only with great political torment. The Irish were the unhappy victims of conflicting ideologies and self-interest. Initially the Corn Laws were protectionist measures which kept out foreign corn from the starving country. They were repealed by the Prime Minister, Sir Robert Peel, in 1848, but at the cost of his career at the hands of the outraged protectionists. From the other side the passionate belief in the free enterprise system and private initiative hampered the development of major government relief programmes. Throughout the famine, there was a substantial net *export* of food from Ireland to England – courtesy of the market forces of the day (Woodham-Smith 1962). Much of the Irish peasantry had nothing to offer to the market and hence could get nothing from it. The most enlightened and knowledgeable government of Ireland would have had trouble dealing with a desperate situation. However, it is also clear that, even with the knowledge of the day, much more could have been done to relieve the Irish if many of the people involved had not viewed the world through ideological spectacles which deprived them of common sense. A lot of people died in consequence.

We should therefore try and see why famines occur. This is often regarded as unproblematic. It is normally assumed that for some reason or another – commonly the failure of a crop – there is a serious cutback in the food supply. However, the closer analysis of a number of famines, including the Bengal famine of 1943, by A. K. Sen has shown that the question is less clear. The reduction in food supply per head in 1943 in Bengal was not in fact particularly marked. Although the supply of food grains in Bengal was low compared with neighbouring years, it was in fact 9 per cent higher than 1941, which was not a famine year. What happened in 1943 was that certain groups lost their 'entitlements' – that is, basically, their income – and were unable to buy any food. In effect what had happened was that there was a sudden redistribution of income which left significant parts of the population essentially without an income; so they starved. If in some way the entitlements to food, effectively the distribution of income, had been the same as in 1941, there would have been no famine. Sen's work has shown that this was not unique to the Bengal famine but also characterised various other famines.

This makes it less clear that we can regard famines as something out of our control caused by a malignant, or at least indifferent, providence in causing an abrupt shortage of overall food supplies. In part, they are the consequence of the income distribution and hence of the social structure of society. They can, of course, be ameliorated by bringing in extra supplies of food. There is little doubt that the death toll in Bengal could have been reduced by this. The extent of the famine had been underestimated, but there was a clear understanding that there was a famine and that food importation would save life. Despite pleas by some of the British administrators, shipping space was not made available, as it was being used for other purposes in the war. However, to what extent could the entitlements of the desperately poor have been increased and could interventions in the market have been made? A significant aggravating factor in the famine was the perverse operation of markets. Probably something could have been done even with the knowledge then available. Certainly more could be done in any future famine, with the greater understanding of the nature of famines as a failure of entitlements and the market mechanism, as much as a failure in actual total quantity of food.

However, while we can in part attribute a famine such as the Bengal famine to the social structure, can it properly be regarded as a form of violence? Galtung argues firmly that it can and should, taking as the core of the definition of violence the notion of avoidable death. Galtung would not want to restrict it to famines, but to include all the

19

situations in which there is avoidable death due to maldistribution of income, and conceivably to all forms of avoidable death whatever. Clearly, many deaths in poor countries could be avoided if income distribution were less unequal. Even in wealthy countries such as the UK, there are marked differences in death rates between social classes for many forms of disease. To what extent this would be improved by making the income distribution more equal is unclear. For example, in the UK there is a differential death rate attributable to smoking-related diseases, but this is not due to a lack of income as such. The appropriate ways of stopping this would be an increase in the taxes on tobacco (a well-established mechanism) or advertisements against smoking. However, we can accept the basic argument that more equal income distribution would cut down the mortality rates of the poorer section of society without causing corresponding increases in the formerly richer parts.[1]

Against Galtung, I would argue that structural violence should be distinguished from somatic violence, and show why its characterisation as violence is unfortunate and misleading. The main reason is scientific. The causes of somatic violence such as war are very different from the causes of poverty. Further, poverty itself is not caused just by unequal income distribution. It can also be caused by low average income per head, no matter how it is distributed. The problem of poverty is related to the whole problem of underdevelopment which has occupied economists for many years. We do not fully know the answers, but it is unlikely that it will help if we confuse the problems with another set of even more intractable problems. Of course, it may be that poverty causes war, though this is by no means clear. Certainly there is some relationship between poverty, the rate of growth and revolution, but this is not to say that they are the same thing. To do so is to confuse a cause with an effect (Cohan 1975). Further, even if poverty is a cause of war, it is certainly not the only one. There are plenty of wars for which poverty cannot be reasonably adduced as a cause.

My second objection to the Galtung formulation is that it involves an emotive definition which can be confusing rather than illuminating in other moral and political contexts. Poverty is deplored, but to identify it as a form of violence also can invoke greater degrees of blame than might be appropriate. Thus, one might readily espouse the view that a leading political goal would be the reduction in violence. If structural

[1] It can be argued that such a change would be short-lived in that the greater increase in equality would reduce the rate of economic growth by reducing incentives. While I am sceptical of this argument, it is as yet by no means decided either way.

and somatic violence are added together, then in principle one could decide when acts of overt, somatic violence reduced poverty to the degree that such acts would actually decrease the amount of violence. Indeed this sort of argument could well be used in the case of some revolutions. However, to regard a revolution using violence as 'peaceful' in that the total amount of violence (structural plus somatic) is reduced seems at best paradoxical and more designed to soothe the conscience of a pro-revolutionary pacifist than to advance the cause of clear analysis. It would seem much better and clearer to argue that certain goals are worth the use of violence. This assumes, of course, that revolutionary violence actually brings about the goals which were claimed at the beginning of the revolution, which is also an issue of contention.

Not all mass violence is war or revolution. Genocide, where one group deliberately attempts to eliminate another, such as the Nazi genocide against the Jews, is another form of mass violence. The Nazi genocide was not historically unique or even unusual (Kuper 1981). There is an appalling record of this sort of behaviour. The point about genocide is that it is one-sided. The violence is inflicted on one group by the other with very little reciprocal violence by the weaker side. Thus it is to be distinguished from asymmetric wars, in which one party is clearly the weaker but, nevertheless, violence is inflicted both ways. There are other cases of heavily asymmetric violence which would nevertheless still not be regarded as genocide. A classic example is the slave trade between Africa and America during the seventeenth and eighteenth centuries. While the aim of the slave trade was not to kill people, indeed the opposite, the methods of transportation inevitably involved a high death rate, as was clearly known at the time. Further, the whole idea of slavery is based on the idea of coercion. It is possible to argue, then, that this is a form of violence. However, if this is accepted, are the one in six who died on the voyage from Ireland to the United States in the 1840s (Woodward 1938) likewise to be regarded as the victims of violence? They were not slaves, and in a sense had a choice about whether to go or not, with a general awareness of the dangers. However, the choice was largely theoretical, being between starvation at home and emigration with its attendant risks; they may well have chosen the safer option. Clearly we are reaching a point where the definitions are difficult. We can plausibly argue for different conventions, though always remembering that our classifications have to serve a role in both scientific and moral discourse. It would seem that for both purposes there is a useful distinction between the deliberate intention to kill on the one hand

21

and the indifference to the death of others on the other, where in the latter case one might, on balance, prefer people to be alive rather than dead, but be unwilling to incur any costs to achieve it. The distinction between the two is justified by two empirical speculations. First, the causes of the two phenomena are very different. The explanations for the slave trade do not seem to have much to do with the causes of war, and can be analysed in economic terms. Secondly, the psychological attitudes of people either involved in or organising the two processes are likely to be different. Slavery involves the total denial of humanity to the victims in a way which war sometimes does, but need not. If we are to understand these phenomena with a view to avoiding them, we must be careful that we are asking the right questions and avoid mixing up disparate phenomena. While such careful analysis of language might appear to be a typical academic's approach and to the sceptic appear like the precise definition of a problem one has little intention of doing anything about, it is, in fact, important. In the case of famines, the increased understanding of them should in the future give us a better idea of how to ameliorate them. However, this has nothing much to do with war.

4   CONFLICT ANALYSIS AND ITS RELATIVES

It is useful, if dangerous, to distinguish between 'social science' and 'social engineering'. The former is a description of how social groups actually behave, and the second is a prescription for achieving specified goals in the light of the propositions discovered by the social scientists. The concept of a 'scientific' and an 'engineering' aspect of a discipline is common. The civil engineer, in building a bridge, makes use of the propositions of physics and metallurgy concerning the behaviour of materials under specified conditions – the scientific propositions being utilised to alter the environment in some specified way. Similarly, medicine is the adjusting of the behaviour of the human body when, for some reason or other, it starts malfunctioning. This is done by reference to a large body of scientific theory and factual information about the operation of the human body, and its reaction to various inputs such as viruses and drugs.

The area of study outlined in this book is often known as 'conflict analysis', though the term is used loosely and there is no generally accepted definition. I shall define conflict analysis by two criteria: first, conflict is seen as a generic activity, properly analysed in many different contexts from the inter-personal to the international; and secondly, conflict can be analysed as a social science. Three other fields of study share some of these characteristics and examine many of the same phenomena. These are 'peace research', 'international relations' and 'strategic studies'. Of the disciplines, international relations and conflict analysis are, at least in principle, disciplines which analyse the world as they find it and are not directly concerned with making recommendations. Thus they are 'scientific' disciplines. They differ in that international relations deals with only a part of the material that conflict analysis does – namely international conflict. Quite what 'international' should mean is a contentious issue. By some it is restricted to the interactions between states (another term which arouses controversy). However, such a definition is unduly restrictive and arbitrary.[2] States, or governments, are significant actors where violence is concerned, but they are by no means the only ones. Nor are a state's attentions completely taken up with the issue of war and how to prosecute or avoid it. For many scholars conflict analysis and international relations are disciplines which overlap completely, as international relations is regarded as a social science and therefore a sub-set – though a very important one – of conflict analysis. Most of the material in this book would be looked at as international relations by those who see international relations as a social scientific discipline. It would not, of course, by the critics discussed in chapter 12.

Peace research and strategy are normative or 'engineering' disciplines in that they are explicitly concerned with making recommendations, and working out how to achieve specific results. They differ in that their practitioners would emphasise different values – peace research being more concerned with the dangers of war and, in a broad sense, with the interests of all members of the international society; strategy is more concerned with the interests of a particular actor such as a state or an alliance. The strategist may be a 'revolutionary strategist' whose concern is with a revolutionary group, but who still has the interests of some specific social group at heart, where these interests are perceived to be in conflict with a broader group. Even the normative disciplines overlap. For example, the analysis of many sorts of international collaboration, such as arms control, concerns practitioners of both groups. Likewise both take note of the

---

[2] The significance of the state in international relations is very controversial. The 'realists' (a tendentious enough name which implies some prior insight into 'reality' which is obscured from others) hold, amongst other things, that essentially international relations is the study of the interaction of states where their predominant mode of interaction is power. This is criticised by many scholars, who argue there are numerous other significant actors in the international system (religious groups, political groups, multinational corporations and so on) and that the role of power is exaggerated. I add nothing to this controversy here, but draw attention to its existence.

23

findings of the conflict analyst and international relations specialist. However, the distinctions between the disciplines are vague, especially when it comes to values. Scientific disciplines are not carried out in isolation from values, and studies are often made with policy in mind somewhere. Even conceptually there are some problems in that the subjects of the scientific disciplines can become aware of the theories which purport to describe their conduct and hence alter it. The theorist has to be aware of this possible feed-back process in formulating the theory and be aware that the very act of formulation involves some impact on behaviour which blurs the distinction. These issues are discussed in more detail in chapter 2, section 6 and in the final chapter.

The different disciplines indicate a rough core of interests and emphases, but nothing more. All, in one way or another, have the problem of war and violence as a central question. This is also true of this book, where the underlying attitudes are that violence is to be deplored, which is a view about morality, and that it is likely to be reduced if we understand more about it and the contexts in which it arises, which is an empirical assertion which I believe to be true but is not, of course, certain.

2 SOCIAL SCIENCE AND THE STUDY OF CONFLICT

1 THE NATURE OF THE SOCIAL SCIENCES

Conflict analysis involves the study of conflict at all social levels by looking at it as a social science. I have been rather vague about what I meant by a 'social science', a vagueness I shall now remedy.

The social sciences are the study of the actions of people in relation to other people. Economics, social psychology and anthropology are all examples, though the divisions between them are often arbitrary. This much is agreed, but all else is controversial. There is a fundamental debate between those who argue that the social sciences can be constructed on a recognisably similar basis to that of the natural sciences, and those who hold that this is impossible as an issue of principle and not because of some practical difficulties such as the supposed greater complexity of social systems. Underlying this debate is a disagreement about the ways in which we can analyse social behaviour. Crudely there are those who argue that an investigation of human behaviour involves the reconstruction of how the actors in any situation viewed it. Proponents of the strong version of this view hold that this is all we know or can know about behaviour; this version leads directly to the view that social science in some sense akin to a natural science is impossible (Winch 1958). The alternative view is that such concepts as 'gross national product', 'arms level' or 'alliance' can be perfectly well understood without any close examination of actors' interpretations. Further such concepts as 'perceptions', 'hostility' and so on, which do involve some comprehension of states of mind, can still be looked at scientifically in the sense I elaborate below. I follow the second school of thought. This account treats some basic disagreements rather lightly. I outline a case rather than argue it in detail. Those who want a fuller justification should consult my book on the subject (Nicholson 1983).[1]

[1] There is a vast literature on the 'philosophy of the social sciences'. The view from which this book is written is standard amongst economists and widespread, but far

Unfortunately there is also disagreement about the nature of the natural sciences, so to model the social sciences on a picture of the natural sciences which is also disputed is to put the argument in further jeopardy. Again, I affirm a number of positions I should ideally argue. These arguments (or assertions) are part of the philosophy of science, or, more specifically, the philosophy of the social sciences.

Those who make claims for the possible scientific study of human behaviour argue that there are two crucial characteristics involved. First, generalisations in the sense of propositions which apply to classes of events, and not just to individual events, are central. Thus we are prepared to talk of the causes of wars (in the plural) and not just the causes of, say, the First World War. The second characteristic is that these theories should be testable against evidence, and that there should be some general, albeit rough, agreement amongst the practitioners concerning what is an appropriate test. This means that when a theory is postulated, it must be phrased in such a form that, when we can find data from the real world, we can establish whether the data are consistent or inconsistent with the theory. This defines the social sciences firmly as accounts of how people and society behave as a matter of fact as opposed to how people ought to behave in some moral sense. These two forms of enquiry are sometimes referred to respectively as *positive* and *normative* studies, a usage much favoured by economists but little by anyone else. The nature of 'facts' and their relations to 'theory' are discussed in section 4 of this chapter while the relations between facts and values are discussed in the final chapter of the book. The view that social behaviour can be analysed in this manner, elaborated below, is known as empiricism. While this is a widely held point of view amongst analysts of social behaviour, it is by no means universal. I argue the case for its legitimacy in Nicholson (1983) and discuss some objections to it in chapter 12. In this chapter I outline the general principles of such an approach, initially in terms of a picture of the natural sciences, reinterpreted to include the analysis of social behaviour.

2   THE LEVEL OF ANALYSIS

In the discussion of any problem, it must be decided in what particular framework the analysis should be conducted, and at what

from universal, in other social sciences. In international relations and conflict analysis it is much more common in the United States than elsewhere, including Britain, where there is widespread scepticism. The *locus classicus* of the opposing point of view to mine is Peter Winch (1958). In international relations, Charles Reynolds (1973) also writes from an opposing point of view.

level of generality the questions should be posed. Conflict and war are no exceptions to this. Prior to a more detailed discussion of the methodology of the social sciences I shall show the relationship between generalisations and individual events. A whole range of questions can be asked about any social issue, and it appears that many misunderstandings of the purposes of the study of conflict arise simply because the answers produced are assumed to be answers to another set of questions, for which the answers given are either inappropriate or irrelevant.

Divisions of the level of analysis are arbitrary: however, the following scheme is convenient. After describing it, I shall illustrate it in terms of the analysis of suicide, where such a division is relatively uncontentious, before applying it to the problem of imperialism, an issue more relevant to this study but where contention abounds. However, if one accepts such a scheme for the first sort of problem, it is hard to see why one should not for the second.

It is convenient to divide the levels of analysis into three. The first level is that of the individual act or event, in which the analysis is in terms of the peculiarities of the individual. It stresses the uniqueness of the individual event. The second level of analysis is to recognise the particular events as individual, but endeavour to relate them to broader categories of similar events. Though each event is still seen as unique, the stress is on its connections with other like events. The final level is the most general of all, in which we seek to understand the general behaviour of classes of events and are uninterested in the idiosyncrasies of the individual units. The first two levels concern the behaviour of individuals, though from different perspectives; the third is concerned with the study of a different sort of phenomenon, namely the group of events, as opposed to the individual components.

This approach can be illustrated by reference to the analysis of suicide. Every suicide is a unique event, and the result of a whole set of complex interactions of pressures and influences on an individual who has his own unique personality formed from his lifetime of experiences. A particular suicide can be described in terms of the individual alone, and as an event peculiar to that individual. If one were to examine an individual suicide in a very personal sense, then one would despair of formulating a theory of suicide. It would all appear too particular and special. The understanding of suicide would seem to be more the concern of literature than science.

However, a psychiatrist would view the problem somewhat differently (and for these purposes we must assume that the suicide had either failed, or was still in the ranks of the suicide-prone). The problem would still be one of examining an individual, but the basis of the examination would be what the patient shared with others and not in what ways there were differences. The psychiatrist has a body of theory which states that, when individuals are placed in various types of situation, some develop certain characteristics. People can be divided into various classes – manic depressive, paranoid and so on – and their responses to various situations classified. This suggests what sort of therapy would bring about an improvement in the patient's condition. A psychiatrist uses knowledge of the behaviour of classes of events in order to classify patients and relate the individual to the theories in order to explain behaviour in their terms. The psychiatrist is not denying that the patient is an individual whose particular situation will deviate from the 'pure' case of whatever condition is the appropriate condition. Indeed, the patient may have a combination of symptoms which the psychiatrist has never seen before in quite that form. However, the behaviour of the individual can usefully be considered in terms of propositions derived from the observation of large classes of individuals.

Clearly, these two levels of analysis overlap with each other. However much an event is described as unique, it is nevertheless placed in a context of other events, and indeed it is only in relation to other events that it can be referred to as unique. The two classes represent the different ends of a spectrum rather than a dichotomy.

The third form of analysis of suicide is the sociological approach. Here the behaviour of groups of individuals is the dominant concern. We are more interested in explaining, say, why the suicide rate in Norway is very much lower than in either Sweden or Denmark, despite the apparent similarities between the societies. We are not trying to explain particular cases. Each suicide in each country is a unique event, explicable in terms of a unique set of personal circumstances. However, it is hard to believe that the differences in suicide rates between the two countries are completely accidental, and, in default of finding any differences in the statistical definition of suicide, we have to assume that there are factors absent (or present) in Norway which make these individual events less likely there. The propositions made in the analysis of this problem will be propositions about groups. Contrary cases will be found readily in all the countries concerned, but this is not a problem for the type of investigation in view.

Again, classifications are not absolute, and there is a clear overlap between an analysis on the group level and an analysis on the individual level. The propositions made by the psychiatrist about the individual owe their origin to propositions about groups, while the propositions about groups are likewise not divorced from propositions about the individual. There is an overlap, but nevertheless there are distinct problems.

The problem of the level of analysis similarly appears in the study of international relations. Consider the problem of imperialism. During the nineteenth century there was an acceleration in the expansion of the European powers into less developed parts of the world. Sub-Saharan Africa, which, apart from South Africa and the slave-trading stations was largely untouched by Europeans, became quickly overwhelmed and was largely under the political control and occupation of the various European powers by the end of the century. This was accompanied by further expansions in most of the world and a tightening of control in various parts already under European control, such as the consolidation of the British control of the Indian subcontinent. Each colonial power and each colonial territory had its own peculiarities. Portugal was very different from Britain, and an analysis of the Portuguese domination of Angola would look very different from an analysis of the British consolidation of its control in India. There are many interesting questions which can be answered only at the level of the individual case. However, it seems unlikely that all these acts of expansion were independent of each other; the presumption is that there are some common causes somewhere. For this we need a theory of imperialism under which the particular instances can be subsumed. Such a theory relates to particular instances in much the same way as the individual patient would relate to the psychiatrist's general theories of mental conditions. There have been attempts. In Hobson's theory (Hobson 1902), later developed by Lenin in a Marxist framework, expansion was attributed to a particular state of capitalist development where the rate of profit in the domestic economy declined, making the capitalists search for more lucrative opportunities abroad in what would now be called Less Developed Countries (LDCs). This might apply to that particular stage of imperialism, but ideally we would like something more general still which would explain the Roman Empire, the Iberian Empires in the American continent, and the British Empire prior to the later stage of capitalism which came with the Industrial Revolution. However, the principle, followed by Hobson, of trying to find a theory of the general process and not just an account of individual instances is entirely on the right lines. The general theories of imperialism would then represent the third level of analysis, providing the theories in which one can study phenomena at the second stage.

3   A PRELIMINARY VIEW OF SCIENTIFIC DEVELOPMENT

It is now time to turn in more detail to the nature of a theory in the social sciences.

A common approach in both the social and natural sciences is known inelegantly as the *hypothetico-deductive method*. The procedure consists of assuming, for the sake of argument, the truth of a few hypotheses and deducing their logical implications. There then emerges a broader set of interrelated, self-consistent propositions. However, a set of self-consistent propositions may be false, so the theory, as we shall call the set of propositions, must be tested against empirical reality. If it fails the tests, then the theory must be scrapped, or, more usually, modified. If it passes the tests, it can be provisionally accepted as 'true', in that it explains the facts. The more tests the theory passes, the greater is the confidence with which it can be held. No theory is 'proved' true in the sense that its truth is and will always be incontestable no matter what further empirical and theoretical developments may occur, though in the case of some physical theories, such as that the planets revolve round the sun, the doubt is rather philosophical.

Theories which evolve from the hypothetico-deductive method rarely appear as immediately testable theories. There is a period of incubation which precedes this, as theories are often derived from extremely simple frameworks which describe either nothing which appears in the real world, or something which could appear only under very artificial experimental circumstances. The logical implications of such simple preliminary theories or 'models' are often explored in detail, as in the case of many economic models. Sometimes the deductive structure is of great complexity, and certainly the deductions are not self-evident without analysis, as in the Richardson model of the arms race described in chapter 9. In other cases the model is just a picture of a process without a significant deductive element, as in the model of the governmental decision-making process on pp. 52f. Such models are simplified visual pictures of a process for the purpose of making the basic structure comprehensible. This discussion of theory construction is itself a model of the process where the model is of the picture type.

The function of such simple models is as a prerequisite of a full-scale theory in cases where the theory concerns very complex structures. Sometimes the purpose of the models is to lay bare the logical nature of the situation under examination, when this would be impossible in the more complex real-life situation. Models of this sort are involved in the examination of rational conduct in part II below. However, the simple model is often the basis on which a more complex model is built. Once the operations of the simple structure are understood, it is easier to add the complications which bring it nearer to reality and thus to being a genuinely testable theory.

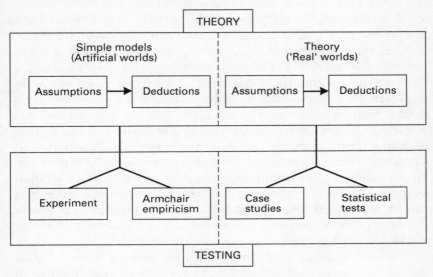

Figure 2.1

This is illustrated in a stylised way in figure 2.1. The top half of the diagram labelled 'theory' illustrates the processes of theory development. On the left-hand side we have the hypothetico-deductive method as used to construct 'models' or theories of artificial worlds, normally simplifications of the real world. The models start with the assumptions and work to the deductions which can be made from these assumptions, and the combined set of the two sorts of propositions is the model. On the right-hand side is a similar framework for the theory proper. In structure it is the same as for the model. There are a set of assumptions and a set of implications deduced from these assumptions. Together these form the body of the theory. The difference is that the propositions describe what goes on in the real world, and not a simplified version of it. A theory can be tested against evidence; if it cannot, it does not qualify as a theory, as understood scientifically.[2] Models which concern a simplified world are not

---

[2] Not every proposition in a theory is necessarily testable, even in principle. However, the non-testable propositions must be a part of a theory from which the testable ones

testable in the same way. As they are not intended as explanations of the real world, direct testing is an irrelevant activity.

Models are not independent of reality. They are steps in the development of a theory. The aim is to isolate the basic structure of a problem so that more insight can be gained into the behaviour of the real world even before a theory in any strict sense has been formulated. Formal criteria for assessing whether a model is likely to lead to a fruitful theory are hard to establish. We can only make subjective judgements about whether the model appears to make sense or not in terms of the real world. I have called this 'armchair empiricism', a term which is neither rigorously defined nor widely used as a technical term. If a model appears to have some use as the basis for a theory, then, apart from exploring its implications in detail, there is sometimes the possibility of experimenting to see how people behave in the circumstances in question (for example, Rapoport and Chammah 1965). These experiments, the province of the experimental psychologist, give information about behaviour only in artificial situations, but, if the judgement that the model will lead to a theory is correct, then there is the possibility that these experimental results will be capable of extension or interpretation into the more complex world described by the theory itself.

There are a variety of different ways of testing a theory. I shall discuss two forms. First, a theory, as I have stated earlier, applies not just to a single event but to a class of events. There is a natural division between, on the one hand, testing the class as a whole and on the other hand examining the individual elements within the class. When both the behaviour and the environment are complex, it is unlikely that all of the elements in the class to which the theory applies will behave in exactly the way predicted. As far as the class is concerned, the propositions are statistical, and single counter-instances do not refute them. This form of testing is discussed further in chapter 8.

The second form of observation is to look at the individual items and try to interpret their behaviour in terms of the available theory. This is a 'case-study' method. The case in question may have many attributes which can be described statistically, so there is no clear-cut division between case study and statistical methods. Statistics alone do not distinguish the two forms of activity from each other. The real

are derived in the way that a non-observable 'centre of gravity' plays a crucial role in a theory from which we derive perfectly testable propositions about the behaviour of physical objects. These unobservables are known as 'theoretical concepts' and form a crucial role in any empirical science. See Braithwaite (1953) and Nicholson (1983).

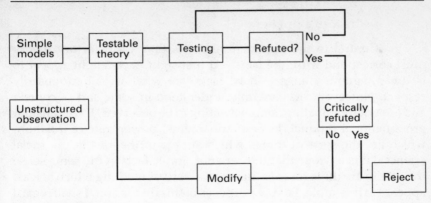

Figure 2.2

distinction is between tests done on a group of the phenomena under discussion and those done on an individual element.

The relationship between theory and testing can also be represented in a stylised way, as demonstrated in figure 2.2. The process starts in the box labelled 'unstructured observation'. This is the informal process of perceiving that there is some situation for which a theory is appropriate. It represents no formal step. A simple model is then formulated which is not yet explanatory of the real world. This is elaborated until it is at the level of testable theory. It is then tested and, if refuted, would normally be modified to go the rounds again in the feed-back loop illustrated. In principle, it might be 'critically refuted' in the sense of being totally rejected by the evidence. This is rare in science as a whole, and certainly so in the social sciences. There is usually some enthusiastic supporter of a theory who will try to modify it repeatedly in the hope that some version of it will become empirically acceptable. Even hopeless cases fade away as their adherents die or lose interest rather than meet an obstacle which forces them to be universally rejected.

If the theory passes the initial tests, it is then subjected to further tests which either put it back on the refutation path or send it round again on the testing cycle. Each time it survives the cycle, it acquires a greater degree of credence. However, it never comes out of this cycle, as no theory is completely proved. The theory spends the rest of its days circling around the retesting cycle unless at some point it is refuted and has to be modified. Even theories of the highest standing seem to come out into the modification cycle from time to time in the light of some new evidence or theoretical advance.

33

4 FACTS AND EVIDENCE

Central to the argument above is that a satisfactory theory must correspond with 'the facts'. At first sight, facts might appear to be unambiguous things – 'hard facts' are what we all supposedly respect. However, facts are only understood in some sort of context and are not free-floating, simply waiting to be observed. If we consider gross national product, level of armaments, power, rate of inflation, which are the sorts of things which appear in theories in the social sciences, it is obvious that they are not simple facts in the same sense that 'there are three roses in this vase' asserts something which at least appears to be simple. For the purposes of this discussion, I shall regard such simple statements as unproblematic and consider the more complex problems.

Consider the apparently straightforward example of the telephone. If a modern telephone were to be wafted back in time to the sixteenth century, no one would have any idea what it was. They would have no sets of concepts to recognise it by and relate it to: in other words there would be no *conceptual framework* into which it fitted. It is only when one gets to the point of being able to say that one sees the object 'as a telephone' that it makes sense and that a 'fact' such as 'X per cent of households in Britain have a telephone' becomes meaningful. It is seeing something 'as a telephone', or whatever it might be, that relates it to a conceptual framework. It is normally unnecessary to stress this, as we operate in a world where there are many conceptual frameworks in common – such as in the case of the telephone. Thus, my argument is that facts become facts only in terms of a conceptual framework and do not exist in some sort of free-floating isolation. This might make it seem that science, dependent on facts, is a lot less secure than it might have seemed at first.[3]

However, there are three significant points to note. First, given a conceptual framework, which can be very broad (I come back to this in section 5), facts can be facts in their old reassuring way. Secondly, the degree to which facts depend on disputed conceptual frameworks for their meaning varies in such a way that there is a whole domain which is relatively unproblematic. Thus, the meaning of the sentence 'The dog walked down the street at seven o'clock this morning' does not depend on a disputed conceptual framework. It depends on knowing the meaning of the various words involved, such as 'dog' and 'street'.

---

[3] It is this type of problem which leads people to refer to facts as being 'theory laden', that is, they have meaning only in the context of some theory, though I think it better to refer to this as a conceptual framework.

These are not known in isolation, but in a general context of understanding or language. All that this means is that we partition our perceptions and are able to name different things and communicate about them. The level of interpretation can be low and the sentence would be understood equivalently in the sixteenth and twentieth centuries, and indeed in all societies which had languages into which the sentence could be translated. Further, there are many practical concepts like this which appear in almost all conceptual frameworks in international relations which today are fully understood all round. 'Aircraft', 'television' and 'submarine' are routine concepts in the discipline and are not problematic.

Admittedly there are many issues in the social sciences where the interpretative element is more significant and the problems therefore more acute. Thus, to see something 'as a government', 'as armaments' or 'as an alliance' implies a complex conceptual framework. However, my third point is that, even in these cases, the frameworks are widely understood and, as far as communication is concerned, there is not a serious conceptual problem in that a problem can be worked through in terms of commonly understood words. A large number of people either accept a common definition or at least understand other people's definitions, which is what is crucial for communication. Thus, five people – a Jewish, Muslim and Christian fundamentalist, a liberal Christian and an atheist – would disagree with each other on many issues and gravely misunderstand each other over many more; but they should still reach a high level of understanding on the terms used above even when they disagreed on the 'best' definition of them, something which might or might not be affected by ideology. If they differ as to whether an item of equipment is defensive or offensive, this is not due to a different conceptual framework so much as a disagreement *within* a conceptual framework, as occurs widely in all sorts of conflict. However, a study showing the negative relationship between the level of armaments and the rate of economic growth could be understood in similar terms by all of them. Similarly, there is commonly widespread disagreement about whether some military action is aggressive or defensive, but rarely any that a military act has taken place, or about its consequences in terms of actual control of territory. In the case of people from very different cultures such issues are serious; anthropologists do have some serious problems, but it is possible to exaggerate the problems as far as most matters are concerned.[4]

4 Concepts such as 'democracy', 'freedom' and 'legitimacy' present harder problems. However, the relevant questions are not ones such as 'What is a democratic

The problems of the social scientist get more acute when we make statements such as 'The level of armaments of country A is 25 per cent higher than the level of armaments of country B.' To find the level of armaments we have to add up a whole range of very different things such as submarines, trained soldiers, tanks and so forth, which we can do only by arbitrary methods. A common one is to do so in terms of their cost in terms of money, but this is open to a number of objections. Thus, a very effective weapon might be very cheap; weapons suitable for the Arctic might be inappropriate in the desert; the skill and morale of troops are hard to evaluate. Hence we are forced into arbitrary methods for measuring our armaments levels, which means that the choice of an equally justifiable method would give a different result. Our 'facts', then, are very much at the mercy of the way in which we decide to calculate them, and different, perfectly justifiable calculations might give us rather different facts even within the same conceptual framework. However, the rules by which we do these 'additions' are laid out clearly, even though they are arbitrary, and those items which go into the calculations are all interpreted in terms of common conceptual frameworks. Clearly, this is a difficulty in the social sciences, though not one which invalidates the whole exercise. Though different measurement procedures give different results, we would expect them to be qualitatively similar. Thus, while we might not take the 25 per cent very seriously and concede that another justifiable measure would give us 23 per cent, we would be more concerned if on one set of measures the gap between the two countries systematically increased whereas on the other it decreased.

5   COMPETITIVE THEORIES: SCIENTIFIC RESEARCH PROGRAMMES AND PARADIGMS

The account of scientific investigation given in section 3 above was a description of an 'ideal type' of scientific investigation in a relatively stable intellectual context, that is, in the context of an agreed set of conceptual frameworks. It was overly clinical and bears little relationship to the actual practice of scientists, as the entertaining account of one such investigation by Watson (1968) shows. It underestimates the competitive and even combative nature of much scientific endeavour.

government?' but 'What do *I* understand *you* to mean by a democratic government?' and 'What do *you* understand *me* to mean by a democratic government?' They are questions of understanding, not agreement. Many concepts of this sort are muddied by their explicit exploitation by politicians who are interested only in their persuasive value, not their meaning.

The true scientist is sometimes represented as someone who is inhumanly committed to the truth (Popper 1959). The demise of the theory in the testing and comparison process is watched, we gather, with the pleasure of one who sees error confounded, even one's own. Such accounts are farcical. Physicists, who always have the reputation of being that little bit purer than the rest of us, battle as viciously as the rest for their theories and for the right to assert precedence where the truth of the theory is reasonably established. Newton, one of the greatest scientific geniuses of all times, was nasty and petty in his claims for precedence over Leibniz. Even Einstein, perhaps the nicest human being to have practised physics, stuck with irrational tenacity to his views on the uncertainty principle ('God does not play dice'), and was not in the slightest bit pleased with counter-evidence (Snow 1967).

In the social sciences, a large amount of theory is developed with some political ideology in view, and it is arguable that it is in the service of political ideologies rather than truth that the most important developments have been made. This does not mean that the theories are harmed by the motives from which they originated; it does mean that the testing process must be rigorously carried out according to principles everyone accepts, irrespective of their ideological position.

The view of the development of theory as normally involving a conflict between rival theories has been the source of a great deal of analysis and argument. The two classical contributions are those of Imre Lakatos, who wrote an extensively quoted essay on the 'Methodology of Scientific Research Programmes' (Lakatos 1970) and Thomas Kuhn (Kuhn 1970), who introduced the concept of a *scientific revolution*.[5] In Lakatos's interpretation, a scientific research programme is a developing set of theories all derived from the same base or 'hard core' which the theorist is not going to call into question. The hard core could be the 'realist' view of international relations that the dominant actor is the state and the states aim to maximise power. Such a theory is not static but developing, and new theories emerge out of the old where the new theories are judged superior if they explain more than

[5] This is a very brief and necessarily over-simplified account of these ideas. Even in the originals the definitions of the concepts are not always precise, which is perhaps inevitable but makes for confusion. Margaret Masterman counted twenty-one different senses of 'paradigm' in Kuhn's work (Masterman 1970). One could set up a set of definitions whereby paradigm and scientific research programme were identical. However, I do not think this is particularly helpful. I favour the definition in which a shift in a paradigm requires a shift in the conceptual framework whereas two different scientific research programmes can operate within the same conceptual framework. I discuss the issues in greater detail in Nicholson (1983). See also Kuhn (1970) and the essays in Lakatos and Musgrave (1970).

their predecessors. Within the research programme there are a whole range of sub-theories dealing with aspects of the problem – for example, a theory of imperialism. There is often more than one research programme – another one is the Marxist research programme, which comes up with rather a different theory of imperialism. Such competing programmes occur in the natural as well as the social sciences. In Lakatos's framework, research programmes are in conflict with each other. Each programme has its protagonists, who are often deeply committed to it and work hard to justify it. However, there is often not a strict comparison between the two (or more), and a research programme becomes favoured if it is *progressive* in the sense of being able to explain more and more in the context of its conceptual framework. Even within the scientific research programme there are conflicts. Alternative theories can be consistent with the hard core. A test is a comparison between the alternatives to see which provides the better explanation of the behaviour of things.[6] It is possible that one easily surpasses the other, but it is more likely that neither does the job perfectly. Both go back for modification and recomparison by their supporters, and the cycle described in section 3 repeats itself. The result of the process might be the elimination of one theory, the moving together of the theories, or, indeed, the formation of a new theory which is not a compromise between the two but something genuinely novel. None of this is the smooth process which it may appear to have been with hindsight. At any given point in time research programmes appear messy and unclear, and it is often very difficult to tell whether it is progressive or degenerate (another of Lakatos's terms).

On occasion, the conceptual frameworks involved in the analysis of some issues are totally different. A classic example in the natural sciences, already alluded to, was the debate over whether the sun went round the earth or the earth went round the sun. This concerned an issue which was fundamental to astronomy (and much else besides), and further there was no compromise – no restating of the theories could encompass both. Such totally different perspectives on the phenomena in question were called *paradigms* by Kuhn – a name which has caught on and been used and abused ever since its introduction. Paradigms are not just competing theories where, at least in principle, the dispute between the protagonists can be

---

[6] Lakatos argues that theories are tested only in comparison with other theories and never against 'absence of belief', which my presentation implies. I think this is misleading. A statistical test for an association between two variables can be premised on the notion that there is no relationship or that the relationship is of a complex sort. Lakatos seems to think that we have to have a particular hypothesis in mind.

resolved by an appeal to evidence. The very concept of what is evidence is in dispute. Thus, while it was agreed by the supporters of both theories that the movement of the planets was to be explained, the concept of a planet was different in each. The switch between paradigms is called a *scientific revolution* in that we are shifting into a whole new framework in which to pose and answer questions. There are some problems about how or why we switch paradigms, and it is argued that it is not really a rational process at all. On this view, we choose our basic, underlying paradigm for extra-rational reasons. This has led some writers, notably Feyerabend (1975), to argue that the basic choices between theories are fundamentally value choices. However, the implications of the previous section are that even apparently different traditions use a common conceptual framework and, inasmuch as they are using a commonly understood language, this point need not become an issue.

Scientific revolutions are rare. The competition between theories is usually more lowly and can be settled by appeals to facts and evidence in a common conceptual framework as generally understood by the disputants. Unfortunately conceptual inflation has set in, and the word 'paradigm' is often used to mean almost any sort of difference between scholars. Social scientists have been willing to use it far too readily, so that its original and important (if admittedly loose) meaning has been almost lost.[7]

6 THEORIES OF HUMAN BEINGS

One fundamental difference between human beings and anything else we might theorise about is that the human beings can understand the theories of which they are the subject. Thus, the knowledge of these theories of which they are a part can influence their actions. This sharply distinguishes humans from, say, stars, which continue doing whatever they were doing before and after any theory describing their behaviour. The knowledge of theories by humans might make them act so as to conform more closely to the theory or, on the contrary, to act so as to disconfirm it. This is sometimes regarded as a fatal objection to the social sciences, vitiating any possibility of prediction. This is true only under certain circumstances in that, in principle, it is possible to incorporate the knowledge of the theory into any prediction which might be made; that is,

[7] John Vasquez, in an important book with which I have otherwise much sympathy, *The Power of Power Politics* (1983), is guilty of this sort of abuse. His example has encouraged others (Banks 1985).

knowledge of the theory can be an element in the theory – in general this does not produce an infinite regress (Nicholson 1983). Often the point of the theory is to generate the conditions which will make it cease to apply. For example, the epigraph to Richardson's book on the arms race, *Arms and Insecurity* (1960a), in which he expounds the theory we shall examine later, says that the contents represent what will happen 'if people do not stop and think'. It is clearly implied that, if people did stop and think, the alternatives would be preferable to the predictions of the theory of the non-thinking actors. Further, the very act of learning the results of the theory might have the effect of altering the behaviour in such a way as to falsify it. This is very clear in much of the work on ecology, again described later. If theories predict a rather bleak future for the planet, the point is not simply to accept it but to alter the theories – something possible where human beings are the subject. An analogy (though only an analogy) is to think of a theory as being like a map. Suppose some people without a map are struggling through some difficult countryside where it is impossible to see far ahead. We watch them from a helicopter and make predictions of the track they will take. However, if we now drop them a map, they will use it to work out a more efficient route than the one they will devise on the basis of inadequate information, and by showing them our theory or map, we will have invalidated our earlier hypothesis about their behaviour.

Another version of the problem arises when people become aware of the theories about themselves. They may begin explicitly to adopt the concepts of the theory and make their behaviour self-fulfilling. Many actors in the international system have become aware of the realist theory of international relations and then adopt the principles of power politics as in some sense sanctioned by the theory.[8] I am not talking about precise predictions here, but the general approaches and conceptual frameworks which people adopt are affected by the way people have written about them earlier. Unfortunately a conceptual framework excludes various sorts of questions – the realist theory deals clumsily and inadequately with questions such as integration, for example, simply because it totally lacks any theory of how any group forms in the first place.[9] Thus actors influenced by this tradition

[8] Prominent, of course, is Henry Kissinger, who wrote some of it. Denis Healey in his autobiography (Healey 1989) writes that in the 1950s he was influenced by the writings of realists such as Morgenthau and Niebuhr.

[9] Even in the context of power behaviour it fails to explain the existence of the Mafia or the Colombian drug barons because of its obsession with the state as a primary actor. Revolutions likewise get short shrift (Halliday 1990).

tend to ignore variables which others perceive as significant, but then reinforce their perceptions by their behaviour.

Another way in which knowledge and belief in a theory affect behaviour and bring about a self-confirmation of beliefs might be the case in economics (Hargreaves-Heap 1989). Keynesian and monetarist theories of the economy make different predictions about, say, the effect of an increase in the money supply in an economy with significant unemployment. If the businessmen believe in the Keynesian version of the economy, they will act in the Keynesian way, thus providing support for the theory, whereas if they believe in the monetarist version, they will act according to monetarist principles.

This factor blurs the distinction we made above between 'scientific' and 'engineering' disciplines. All social science disciplines are to a degree engineering disciplines in that knowledge of them can influence conduct. Marx wrote that 'The philosophers have only *interpreted* the world in various ways; the point, however, is to *change* it' (Marx 1950). The problem is that interpretation results in change, and it is part of the theorist's job to be aware of the possible effects of the interpretation. However, I think I am right to stress the emphasis of some forms of study on altering things and others on explaining things, even when their boundaries are blurred.

PART II
RATIONAL
BEHAVIOUR

At first sight the concept of rational behaviour does not seem too problematic, at least when looked at as primarily involving the effective pursuit of goals. Amongst the problems of this viewpoint are two which are of particular concern in this study. First, problems quickly appear as one tries to extend conceptually simple procedures, which work well enough in an impersonal world, to conflict between strategic human beings. The theory of games has been put forward as a basis in which the concept of rational behaviour can be applied to conflict behaviour. There are limitations even here, and the 'solutions', beloved of the true-believing games theorist, are either non-existent or highly contrived even in some simple and applicable cases. Problems and paradoxes are quickly reached in trying to apply simple concepts of rationality to conflict behaviour. Nevertheless, stylised conflicts can be related to the 'real' conflicts which pervade the international system, and the conceptual underpinnings of issues such as deterrence can be examined.

Secondly, rational choice theory often proceeds as if the goals people pursue were unproblematic. While we like to think of ourselves as rational, the issues become more complex as we delve deeper and emotions cease to become an optional extra but are a central issue. Where do attitudes come from? Under pressure, such as in crises, pressures mount which affect choice behaviour. This is just a special case of 'normal' behaviour. Much of our behaviour looks odd unless we bring in some broader issues to try to explain it.

In this part, we start from a theory of rational choice and work through some of its limitations. I argue that it is an invaluable basis for a research programme in the more general theory of decision making which can embody the criticisms in a broader framework.

3 RATIONALITY AND CONFLICT

1   RATIONALITY AND INTERNATIONAL RELATIONS

The subject of 'international relations' is often regarded as an account of rational actors interacting with each other. In some views of the discipline, states are held to be the primary rational actors, and their interaction is all that is of significance, certainly when it comes to the issue of peace and war. Even if we extend the number of actors to include multinational corporations, religious organisations and other actors on the scene, the basic principle is still there – for the most part an account of international relations is an account of actors rationally pursuing goals. State decision makers are particularly concerned to insist that they are rational. While wielding their vast weaponry, nuclear and otherwise, they are eager to reassure us of their rationality, a reassurance that, for our peace of mind, we are only too anxious to credit. States ruled by apparently deranged rulers cause us particular concern.

In such circumstances it seems appropriate to investigate the concept of rationality in decision taking with some care. The next five chapters are devoted to it. It will appear that, from both logical and psychological points of view, rationality and rational decision are much more complex and ambiguous concepts than might appear from the heartier expressions of both scholars and practitioners. This chapter, and the next two, concentrate on the logical points, while the final two consider the psychological factors.

Initially I shall look briefly at the issues involved in making rational decisions about nuclear deterrence. It has been claimed that, in one form or another, it has preserved the peace between the two super-powers during the period of the Cold War – no mean achievement if the claim can be substantiated. Its failure could mean the end of the world. Thus the stakes are high. It is essentially a problem in decision taking in conflict situations. Simplified, but with the essentials of the problem intact, the argument about nuclear deterrence runs like this. I

45

shall state it in terms of two countries called A and B to avoid annoying the patriots. If A offends B in some serious way, then B can attack A with nuclear weapons and devastate its society. In the period of the Cold War such an offence might have been the invasion of West Berlin by the Warsaw Pact. However, in today's and the probable near future's technological environment, it is not possible to destroy all its nuclear weapons, and A can respond and likewise devastate B's society. The capacity to retaliate despite having been devastatingly attacked is known as the *second strike capacity*. Thus the initial offence results in the destruction of both societies. Hence, the argument runs, the initial offence will not be given, because of the horrendous consequences which it will set in train.

A weakness in this argument comes at the second stage after the initial offence has been given by A. This has harmed B. However, B's response is supposed to be to bring upon itself even more disastrous harm, which would scarcely seem a rational thing to do. A, in pondering the initial offence, might reasonably think that B will not in fact bring this down upon itself and that it can therefore get away with the original offence. After all the principle which was to restrain A in the first place has to go into abeyance when it comes to B responding. Clearly this is a problem. For this to work, B has to convince A that at least there is a significant likelihood of it acting in a way which appears irrational in the appropriate set of circumstances. For the deterrence to be mutual, both have to convey this to the other. It is widely accepted, at least by scholars of deterrence theory, that there are some difficulties in this argument. Attempts to mitigate the difficulties involve adding in steps in the process so that small offences can be met with small, and hence more credible, responses which might curtail the process. Even here we still have the same problem, though on a smaller scale (there are others too, which we shall consider in chapter 4). Ultimately, however, underlying this, the actors have to demonstrate a willingness to destroy the world, including themselves in certain circumstances.

Nuclear deterrence is much in vogue amongst the tough-minded, who pride themselves on a clear-headed view of reality, and who view themselves as having the potential to act rationally no matter how distasteful this reality might be. Detractors are thought of as sentimental idealists who will not face the reality of human wickedness. However, the theory has its difficulties as a theory of rational conduct. It therefore beomes prudent for the tough-minded as well as the tender-hearted to examine more carefully the concept of rationality implied in this and other conflict situations, and find out just what its peculiarities are. Its oddities are not restricted to nuclear deterrence; conflict in many of its manifestations produces a plethora of paradoxes. However, this is the most important of the cases where the oddities come to light. While I shall proceed by analysing trivial conflicts between simplified people, the basic topic includes the most significant dilemmas facing the human race.

As we shall show, rational decision making under conflict, where the actions of other calculating actors affect the outcome, is very different from decision-making where the outcome depends on some inanimate feature of the situation, such as the weather. Decision taking in conflict involves 'strategic decision making' where what I do affects someone else whose actions likewise affect me. Thus in deciding what to do, I must not only take into account what my rival will do, but analyse what they will do in terms of what they think I will do. They likewise are wondering what I will do in formulating their own actions. Nothing similar occurs in non-strategic decision making – also called 'parametric decision making', as the parameters are fixed and not affected by any thoughts about my own actions. Thus it will rain or not rain independently of whether I take out my umbrella or not – the weather is not trying to trick me (though there are times when it feels as if it does). This distinction is fundamental. One's initial assumption is that a rational actor, a fugitive from justice and lost in a jungle, uses the same sort of principles in trying to work out how to avoid the (non-strategic) mosquitoes or the (strategic) police. One might suppose that one form of decision making would be merely a modification of another. One would suppose this wrongly. I shall show that the two forms of decision making involve very different principles, and that the one is a poor guide to the other.

No doubt people have been intuitively aware of this since they have tried to reason about conflict or indeed any form of human behaviour. However, it has been clearly formulated only with the advent of the 'theory of games', which is a theory of rational behaviour in conflict situations. Much of the analysis which follows stems in one way or another from this theory.

First, we shall discuss the nature of rational belief and rational behaviour. Initially this is discussed in terms of the rational behaviour of individuals, often in trivial circumstances. There are a number of problems involved in transferring the results of an analysis of individual rationality to groups, such as governments, though I shall leave these on one side for the moment. In this way we can get to the core of the problems more easily.

2 SIMPLE RATIONALITY

'Rationality' and its grammatical relatives are used in a narrow sense by the body of theorists who work in the area known as 'rational choice theory'. It often involves little more than an assertion that rational conduct is efficient conduct in the sense of the actors most effectively pursuing their wants. This minimalist view of rationality is, effectively, that people choose that which they want the most, supposing only that their preferences are consistent – a view which seems extremely trivial and scarcely worthy of such a grandiose description as 'rational choice'. However, there are some complications.

There are two aspects to rationality in this narrow sense. First, there is the question of analysing an individual's preferences and ensuring their consistency. This is not always as easy as it seems at first sight. Secondly there is the question of 'rational belief'. An individual must have some rational belief concerning the possible consequences of any act. As decisions are typically taken in uncertain environments, this involves being aware of a number of possibilities.

First consider the question of preferences. A rational individual is supposed to consider the consequences of all the possible options from which a choice could be made, and rank these outcomes in order of preference from the most preferred down to the least preferred. This ranking of preferences – called a 'preference ordering' – must be consistent in the sense that if A is preferred to B and B is preferred to C then A must also be preferred to C. This characteristic is known as 'transitivity'. This does not seem an unduly onerous condition. The analysis of preferences is not as trivial as it sounds in that the decision maker can make different collections of things in mixtures as complex as it is possible to make. The problems are compounded when risk and uncertainty are introduced. Thus, though conceptually simple, the problems can be practically complex. Take a relatively straightforward problem such as how to travel from London to Glasgow. I can fly (from one of two airports); I can go by car, by train, or by bus. In making a choice I balance the different attributes of the various alternatives such as price, length of journey, comfort of journey, safety and so on. The trade-offs can become complex unless one attribute overrides all others such as expense (which must be minimised) or time (which must likewise be minimised). Thus the question might involve some difficult computational problems, but they are normally solvable: there is a *solution* in the sense of an alternative which is in some sense the 'best alternative', determined by my preferences and the available options.

This concept of a solution is central to decision theory, but it is one which causes some problems when we come to consider conflict problems. The crucial issue in the non-conflict situation described above is that the world is not plotting either against me or for me, and that the solution exists in a world which is neutral towards me and is uninterested in my choice.[1]

The next problem is that of rational belief. Rational belief is also construed rather narrowly. We want to know what the chances or 'probability' are of both the pleasurable and the unpleasurable consequences of the various options. If we are planning an excursion to the country and are concerned about the weather, the problem is at least in principle relatively easy. From any given state of the weather today we can assess the probabilities of rain tomorrow where this probability is based on the observed frequency with which rain has followed similar weather conditions in the past. We have a large number of near-identical situations as observations. However, not all cases are as simple. If I am thinking of going to a particular country and want to know the probability of a coup d'état during my stay, there is no way in which I can meaningfully get an objective probability in the same sense as with a weather forecast, as I do not have a group of past events which are near-identical. How one analyses this situation is controversial. Some scholars such as Savage (1972) – with whom I am sympathetic – argue that one does in fact formulate a subjective probability, whereas others, such as Elster (1983), argue not. We certainly have some notions of 'high-risk' and 'low-risk' countries. Perhaps more importantly we can have notions of what will increase and what will decrease the risk. We derive these from a notion of what the relevant factors are in the determination of a coup d'état and whether they have become stronger or weaker. A worsening of a severe inflation in a country where the army has a tradition of interference in politics would be widely accepted as giving grounds for believing that a coup d'état is more likely. It will not give us a numerical probability, though, in the sense that one can be given about the weather or about the likelihood of a male, aged sixty, weighing 75 kilograms, having a heart attack. Thus people can rationally disagree about the risks involved, and we cannot lay down hard and fast rules for formulating rational belief on this matter. However, we can exclude a number of principles. For example, astrology would

[1] Solutions are not necessarily unique. There can be a set of alternatives all consistent with the rules of choice. In this case we can either regard the solution as indeterminate amongst these options or assume that it is determined by convention or some other not obviously rational rule. For convenience, and because it does not affect any subsequent argument, I shall regard solutions as unique.

not be regarded as a procedure for establishing rational belief on the likelihood of a coup d'état, and decisions based on astrological forecasts would not be regarded as rational,[2] despite the current vogue for such forms of mysticism.

Thus, in many cases, we cannot lay down procedures for establishing objective degrees of rational belief, though we can exclude others. We require people to be consistent in formulating their probabilities and to follow the rules of the probability calculus. Unfortunately this requirement is often ignored in real-life decision making (Cohen 1972).

The issue of rational belief raises a further problem. In an uncertain situation it is generally the case that more information enables one to get a more reliable judgement about the probabilities of the relevant outcomes. How much information should a decision taker collect? Are there any rules? There is limited time to search for information and limited capacity for coping with the information even if it is available. If for some reason the time for decision taking is constrained, as it often is in emergency situations, the limitations on the capacity for information processing are even more acutely felt. There are procedures for tackling such problems in ways which can be regarded as rational. However, the word 'ways' remains stubbornly plural, and we cannot define unique procedures which can be regarded as the only rational way for tackling such problems.

The apparently trivial statement that rational conduct means choosing what is most preferred obscures the non-trivial problem of finding out what options are available and which one of the complex set of options is in fact preferred. There is a rich body of theory, originating particularly from economics, which enables us to tackle a whole range of interesting problems.

What the rational choice theorist does not do is enquire into the nature of the preferences themselves. To return to our London–Glasgow, example: if a person prefers speed to safety on a journey to Glasgow, this does not interest the choice theorist, who merely takes it as a piece of data in the choice decision. The theorist would certainly not enquire into why the chooser wanted to go to Glasgow in the first place. It is argued that, providing these minimum rules of consistency are met, it is no business of the rational choice theorist to judge the rationality of preferences themselves. Thus, if I prefer speed to safety, that is my privilege.

[2] Except in the indirect sense that if a potential instigator of a coup were known to consult astrologers, we would be rational also to consult them in order that we should know what sorts of strategies were likely to be pursued.

What is sometimes found disturbing is that this makes no judgement on moral grounds either. A person may have flagrantly immoral sets of preferences, but these are not thereby irrational. There are serious problems in this use of the word 'rational', but as such usage is widespread, we shall retain it. The problems arise because we think of the word 'rational' as a judgement implying approval (as indeed in a limited sense it is). Thus, to describe conduct which is outrageously immoral such as the Holocaust as 'rational' appears offensive, for we are effectively talking of the rational pursuit of evil. However, we would not normally object to speaking of the *efficient* pursuit of evil, which, with this present restricted usage, is more or less what is meant by the use of 'rational'. That the word 'rational' might also have some other half-formed and barely remembered connotations is unfortunate, but need not lead us into inconsistency. In particular it need not lead us into the inconsistency of being diffident about passing moral judgement on a rational act. This usage of 'rational' has the merit of separating judgements of rationality from judgements of morality and therefore adds, not detracts, from our moral precision and effectiveness.

This use of 'rational' is referred to by Elster as the 'thin theory of rationality' (1983). Its value is not denied, but the need for a 'broad theory of rationality' is also suggested. A broad theory of rationality goes beyond mere consistency and also considers the rationality of the broad set of beliefs in which the preference judgements are embedded. Thus, Voltaire tells of a religious group who believed that, once a child was baptised, it went straight to paradise. They therefore baptised all their children and killed them (Ayer 1986). On this viewpoint, such behaviour is entirely rational. However, this is taking liberalism too far. A broad theory of rationality rescues us from the dilemma of regarding the Holocaust as rational (providing it was efficiently carried out) by arguing that the belief structure on which it was based was irrational. However, while it might rescue us from this dilemma, it does so only in this particular case, unless one is always going to argue that immoral ends are always based on irrational belief systems, which is a view hard to defend. However, how we define a rational belief structure is a delicate issue which I shall avoid at this point as going beyond the goals of this book, beyond suggesting that a broad theory of rationality must also include the requirements that the general rules of logic must be followed in judgements both of values and of probabilities. We should not adopt belief structures involving contradictions. Similarly, in formulating beliefs, rational decision takers should follow the laws of probability (not necessarily know-

51

ingly). Likewise they should obey the rules of arithmetic, unlike the character in Dostoevsky's *Notes from the Underground* who held that this would inhibit his personal freedom.

However, why should we be rational? Rationality is sometimes held to be a cold and arid characteristic, and a 'rational person' something of a cold fish. 'Rational people' are juxtaposed with 'feeling people' – to the disadvantage of the former. If we build a society with rational people, are we not in danger of building a soulless society? There are two answers, one of defence and one of positive advocacy. The defence is that 'feeling' and 'rationality' are not contradictory. While it might seem rather arid to refer to being in love with someone as merely reflecting a preference, even a passionate preference, the inadequacy of the formulation is not owing to its being wrong, but to its missing out important things. The rational view of preferences does not claim to be a comprehensive account of preferences, but merely a partial account and useful within its context. I advocate rationality by arguing that, if we take decisions rationally, in general they are more likely to be effective. This might sound rather prosaic, but even the most passionate lovers who live in different towns will find their love more effectively consummated if they make effective plans for meeting and first study the road map or appropriate time-tables before seeking each other's company. If I want to be an effective decision maker, then I shall also be a rational decision maker. If I am affected by a decision, and my interests and preferences coincide with a decision maker, then I shall hope for someone who is rational in their decision making. This is of particular importance for political decisions. Inasmuch as I approve of my rulers' goals, I should also want them to be rational. (If I think they are wrong, I might want them to make mistakes, though only of certain sorts. Many mistakes are harmful to everyone.)

3   DECISION TAKING AS A GROUP PROCESS

So far, I have discussed decision taking as if it were the act of individuals. However, most decisions of significance are taken by groups of people acting together. The members of a group will normally not have exactly the same view of the situation – they will differ in what they want and they will differ in their perceptions of the world. Further, decision making is a process which takes place over time. It is often a convenient analytical tool to assume that decision makers are 'unitary actors' and act as if they were single individuals. It is a justifiable simplification for the purpose of demonstrating many issues, and I shall continue to use it when convenient. However, it is inadequate for the discussion of broader sets of issues. It is perfectly possible for each individual member of a group to act rationally but for the group as a whole not to. A related issue is that decision-making environments are very complex and hard to understand. There are typically many possible courses of action and vast amounts of information to consider on which to base a decision. To find the 'best' course of action is therefore difficult. These issues, which involve the complexities involved in viewing decision making as a process, are the subject of this section.

First I shall outline a simple model of the process of decision making which, in a general sense, applies to all forms of decision making, including decision making by individuals and decision making by groups whether in business, government or elsewhere. Foreign-policy decision making is just one of these.

The process of taking a decision can be broken down conveniently into four stages. Firstly, information is received in the form of raw data; secondly, this information is processed and evaluated, i.e. the important is sifted from the unimportant and the implications of various pieces of information are assessed; thirdly, the actual decision is made and a course of action (which may be to do nothing) is selected. Finally, the action is carried out. We can apply this schema to deciding to go to the cinema. People search for information by looking to see what films are available; they evaluate this information by reading the film criticisms, checking the prices and locations of cinemas and so on; they decide in the light of quality of film, convenience of cinema, price of cinema seats and so on which film to go to; finally they go to the chosen film. The processes will not normally be quite as clear-cut as this, or so neatly ordered through time, but this is essentially what happens.

In the case of a foreign-policy decision, much the same thing happens, though on a grander scale and with the critical added factor that there are many people involved who form a variety of sub-groups with loyalties to different organisations and views of the world. This is shown in figure 3.1, where the four stages are laid out. The more formal the decision-making process, the more clearly are the stages likely to be separated. While different political systems and states have different procedures, the processes take place in some form or other, so it is not surprising that the administrative structures which have evolved in states to cope with these problems have marked similarities.

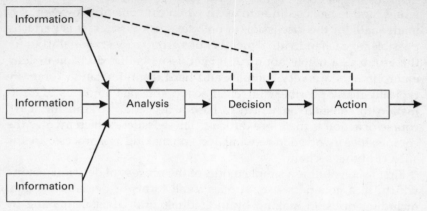

Figure 3.1

Information is received by the government from a variety of different sources. The information might be about the actions of some other state or non-state actor. Information comes in a whole variety of forms from official diplomatic messages, communications from the embassy in the other country, intelligence reports, newspapers (whether these are officially primed with information or unofficial organs), official statements not directly expressed in the form of communications, and so on. Information from the various sources is not always consistent – intelligence reports and ambassadors' evaluations can, and frequently do, contradict each other.

The raw data are then passed for evaluation and analysis by the Foreign Office, Ministry of Defence, intelligence agencies or whatever is the appropriate department and by whatever names it works under in different countries. They can then be passed on in a suitable form for decision making by the minister, Cabinet or whatever is the relevant political decision-making group. Although in principle the stage where they pass through the bureaucracy is one of processing and evaluation, it is difficult to separate it from decision making, as smaller decisions effectively have to be taken there to avoid overwhelming the necessarily small group of top decision makers. They sift and condense information so that it is possible to comprehend the issues in a short time. But the selection of information necessarily involves some distortion, no matter how conscientious and impartial the official might be.

The decision itself may be taken by a variety of people. Important aspects of policy are decided on by the head of government along with the Foreign Secretary. The relative importance of the two can vary widely according both to the state and the individuals occupying the posts.

A decision involves the selection of a course of action. It may also be to send a message of some sort; most Foreign Office actions are of this character. In this case the activity remains within 'the government', but when physical action, such as some military move, is being taken, the appropriate people must be informed and instructed. The distinction between decision and action beomes significant. What the government finally does or says becomes the input for another government, and becomes information for it to respond to by working through it in a similar manner.

If a decision is very simple, as with the decision which film to see, the picture will be adequate and the simple linear process might be appropriate. However, foreign-policy decisions are normally complex and the linear process breaks down. Thus, in the evaluating of information, more information may be required, and there will be a feed-back loop, represented by the dotted lines turning backwards. Similarly, a decision taker may require further elucidation of the problem or further facts. In problems of any complexity the flows of information and analysis will circulate round the loops several times before emerging as an actual decision and accompanying action.

Though the decision about the film and foreign policy share these steps, they differ in almost everything else including the characteristics we are interested in, namely complexity and group decisions. In foreign-policy decisions, potential information is boundless and the possible alternative courses of action are numerous, while almost any situation is open to several interpretations.

Decision making takes time, which is a scarce resource for the decision takers. This will put a constraint on the number of loops the decision can go through. If the decision has to be made by a particular time, this likewise imposes a limit on the degree to which it can be refined. Decision taking in very complex environments where it is implausible to think of choosing some 'best' course of action has been widely studied. H. A. Simon introduced the terms 'satisficing' and 'bounded rationality' to describe the process of search until one devises a 'satisfactory' rather than a 'best' solution (Simon 1976 and 1982; March and Simon 1958). The decision maker (or group) searches through the alternatives until such a satisfactory solution is found and then adopts it. Unlike the 'global maximiser', the 'satisficer' does not look at every possible alternative, which in many cases would be an impossible task. This is plausibly the rational thing to do in a complex environment.

How does the group of people involved in the decision-making process relate to the idealised unitary actor? The individuals in a group will have different views on any question which have to be integrated in some way. The military are paid to be paranoid and see enemies behind every bush; the Treasury is deeply concerned about not spending too much money; the Department of Trade is concerned about inhibitions to trade. Different people's perceptions and values about a situation are deeply influenced by the role they play in the government, and they will look at any particular problem from their own perspective. We can break things down further and ultimately look at organisations as collections of at least partially self-interested people. In principle the whole process peaks at the decision-making step and can be reduced to the single minister or very small group actually making the decision. In practice, this clearly does not happen, as the process prior to this can steer the decision in a desired direction and provide the decision taker with information which suggests one particular course of action. Even when a decision is taken, the actors who are supposed to implement it may or may not carry out the instructions of the executive, or they may interpret them in their own particular way. For example, in 1914, the German Chief of Staff mobilised a day before he was told to do so. In 1962, Kennedy's orders to withdraw missiles from Turkey were ignored – twice (Allison 1971). The problems of 'command and control', which are essentially the problems of ensuring that orders are carried out, are not confined to military organisations, though they are particularly acute there. There is particular concern expressed about the relationship between decision and action in the case of nuclear weapons (Bracken 1983; Blair 1985). In the case of many decisions it would seem that, even under favourable circumstances, a decision can be seen more as the consequence of a bargain conducted by groups with very different perceptions and interests than as some approximation to the choices of some single rational actor.

Does this, then, suggest that we should abandon the rational actor model (or at least the unitary actor model)? Clearly this is a complex debate, which I shall only outline here (Allison 1971). It can be taken as common ground that there are discrepancies from rationality, and to attempt to interpret the actions of governments, whether internally or externally, as the behaviour of coherent unitary rational actors is doomed to failure. However, governmental decisions are normally by intention rational. Further, they are justified at the time and in retrospect as being rational – at least in intention. Deviations from rationality might occur and inconsistencies loom up because of the bargaining within the decision-making apparatus but, it can be argued, the broad sweep is rational and the deviations are deviations from a broadly rational norm. Thus, while in the Cuban Missile Crisis there were many features on both sides which conflicted with a rational attempt to pursue the presumed goals, the broad analysis on both sides can be interpreted as rational. This is not true in all cases – the Suez Crisis is a good case in point – but it is in some, and therefore, as a theoretical basis for some behaviour, its development is worth while. Moreover, as actors normally see themselves as rational, the discrepancies between the actual and desired behaviour, even when these are large, are important to comment on.

From a normative or prescriptive point of view the argument is more powerful. Decision making should be rational in so far as this is possible. The problems are analysed with a view to overcoming them, not submitting to them. If groups do not develop procedures which lead to rational decisions, then it is desirable to design them so that they do. A decision-making structure is – or ought to be – designed so that it can cope with the decisions it normally has to deal with and where a reasonably high percentage of successful decisions are made. This is untrue in many cases. Many decision-making structures are manifestly unable to fulfil their ostensible aims. This is an argument to adjust them so that they do, but in order to do this we have to have some concept of rationality against which to judge it.

4 THE THEORY OF GAMES

The major step in the development of a theory of rational behaviour in situations of conflict came with the development of the *theory of games*. The theory of games (or game theory) is the unfortunate name of a body of theory which prescribes how 'rational people' should make choices in some rather stylised conflict situations. A 'game' in everyday speech means some activity which is carried out for the entertainment of the participants or, with professional sports, of the spectators. A game in the theory of games is much more broadly defined to mean any strategic situation. By a strategic situation I mean one in which my pay-off depends not just on my choice but on those of the other players, which are made where all the actors are aware of this and all make the assumption that the other players, like themselves, are in some sense rational. The theory of games is mainly concerned with conflict situations, though not completely. As I illustrate below, there are games both of conflict and coordination and, perhaps most interesting of all, games which are a mixture of the two. The theory is not as concerned with entertainment as its name suggests. Far from being for fun, many of its applications, such as those to military strategy, chill the heart and appal the imagination. Its names belies the deadly seriousness of its applications.

The seminal work on the subject is *The Theory of Games and Economic Behavior* by John Von Neumann and Oskar Morgenstern, which was published in 1944. The discussion, as its title suggests, was in terms of economics, when not in terms of games such as poker. In 1944 its putative readership was otherwise occupied, and this, coupled with the difficulty of reading several hundred pages of mathematical argument, meant that it took two or three years for its significance to be recognised. From then on, however, its influence has been profound, not just in economics but in all the social sciences where intentional conduct is analysed. It has even spread to biology, where some behaviour can be analysed *as if* it were intentional, even in situations where it would be absurd to suppose it was (Axelrod 1984; Maynard Smith 1982).

The following examples illustrate the nature of strategic situations. Suppose the police are hunting a robber in the mountains. The goal of the police is to catch the robber and that of the robber to evade capture, so it is a simple case of conflict. The police, in planning where to look, will try to work out where the robber will be, knowing that the robber will be working through similar calculations and working out where the police might look. Both parties are very conscious of the other's attempts to guess how they are thinking (the first part of *Butch Cassidy and the Sundance Kid* illustrates this process from the robbers' point of view). This is a straightforward, strategic conflict where the participants have opposing goals. However, suppose the police are looking for someone who has got lost in the mountains. In that case the goals of the police and the quarry are the same, since the quarry wants to be found. The quarry will try to work out what the police would see as a good place to go, such as a refuge, or leave a message on a conspicuous hill. Similarly the police will try to work out what the quarry will do given that they are carrying out a search. The reasoning is still strategic, but it is a game of collaboration, not conflict. The theory of games has usually been applied to conflict situations, and this is also the emphasis of this book. However, the more general applications should be remembered.

In its pure form the theory of games is simply a branch of pure mathematics. From a particular set of mathematical postulates, a rich, interesting, and sometimes surprising set of mathematical conclusions is derived. It is this mathematical structure which is, strictly speaking, the theory of games. To be useful to the social scientist these conclusions have to be interpreted in terms of the real world, which has not always proved easy.

In its original form the theory is prescriptive and not descriptive. That is, it recommends a course of action, defined as rational, and then goes on to describe the consequences of such conduct. It is open to dispute whether the recommendations are rational, as there are several possible definitions of rationality. However, the theory tells us what would happen if the particular behaviour rules recommended are followed. A descriptive theory, on the other hand, describes what people actually do, whether the action is wise or foolish. It is possible for a prescriptive theory to turn out also to be a descriptive theory. A useful first attack on many problems of the actual behaviour of human beings is to assume some form of rationality, but to be prepared to abandon it if it becomes untenable as a description of their behaviour.

There is no doubt that the formal statement of conflict problems has clarified the nature of conflict, though some of the clarifications reveal inherent problems rather than provide solutions. Further, there is a great deal of work which has been inspired by the theory of games, even if occasionally purists refuse to acknowledge it as such because it does not fit into the framework of a deductive, axiomatic theory. Game theory has stimulated much experimental work on how people behave in various gaming situations, and it has also suggested the description of conflict situations in game-theory form. While an analysis of conflict according to the strict precepts of game theory leaves us little wiser about how people really behave, the formulation of the problems in broader game-theory terms is of great help both as descriptive of conduct and as a prescriptive tool. Indeed, if the theory of games is considered to include the formalisation of gaming problems, then this, the child of pure theory of games which is its more austere but less worldly parent, has added considerably to our understanding of the problem of conflict. This falls far short of a solution to the problem of conflict by the simple application of a neat mathematical theory, but such a hope was entertained only by the optimists.

In analysing conflict, Von Neumann and Morgenstern picked on two particular features which seemed to have potent theoretical implications. First was the classification of games according to how many players were involved. In two-person games we have a straightforward conflict, but when there are more players, as with the n-person game (where n is more than two), alliances can form. This raises a number of questions, many of which are still open and which people had been aware of before the theory of games (see chapter 11).

The second, rather less obvious feature was the classification into *zero-sum* and *non-zero-sum* games. A *zero-sum game*, a name and a concept which have now crept into use in ordinary language, is one in which whatever one player wins, the other loses. Thus, the total benefit of the two players is zero – hence the name. Of two people playing cards, if one wins £10, the other necessarily loses £10. It is a case therefore of total conflict, for if one benefits, the other necessarily loses. Zero-sum games are often called *constant-sum games* to emphasise that they include such problems as the division of a cake, where everyone benefits but where the total benefit is a fixed constant sum; so, if I get a larger piece of cake, you get a smaller. There is no way of combining together to produce a larger cake. Clearly, in such games, negotiation is irrelevant. There would be no point in trying to negotiate a poker game. The weaker players would be enthusiastic, but the stronger players would refuse as they could do better by playing. Even in principle there cannot be a mediated solution to the zero-sum games.

As its name suggests, in the non-zero-sum game the gains of one are not necessarily the losses of another. Take a simple example. Suppose two musicians live in neighbouring flats which are not well sound-proofed.[3] One likes to play the piano in the evening, the other to practise the drums. If both play together, they neither get a great deal of satisfaction. However, if they can agree to play on alternate nights, they both might feel better off. Quite what is the best possible arrangement, and whether there should be nights when neither plays, depends on how much they like or dislike each other's playing. There are various different distributions of playing and not-playing which will give different degrees of satisfaction, and some distributions are preferred by *both* parties to others. If the parties are on speaking terms, it is clear that they could reach some sort of agreement. In non-zero-sum games it is common for negotiations and agreements to be formed by which both parties benefit. However, agreements are often difficult to reach or enforce. These cases, common in our study of international conflict, raise some difficult and intriguing problems, which are discussed in the next chapter.

In the theory of games, the aim is to find a 'solution' to various forms of game. That is, we prescribe rules of play and enquire whether they imply a unique course of action for the players, who will win, and what the winning prizes will be. If such rules can be specified, then this is what we mean by a solution to the game. Clearly not any rule will do. We could always find some set of rules which would give a

[3] R. B. Braithwaite discusses a similar example in Braithwaite (1955), p. 78.

solution in this sense, but, if the rules were totally arbitrary, there would be little point. We want to find some set of rules which can in some sense be regarded as 'rational' and bear some relation to the rules of rationality one would use in non-strategic situations.

However, the solution may be problematic. The world in which player A is trying to find the best solution is in part determined by the actions of player B, whose world is also in part determined by the actions of player A. If player A chooses the best strategy in the light of certain actions by player B, it is by no means clear that player B will want to continue acting in the same way. If A made the assumption of a static player B, it would be rather like the players in one football team playing as if the members of the rival team stayed in the same position all the time. If B adjusts to get the best out of the revised situation it will alter the situation again, so A might adjust in its turn and so on. There is only going to be a solution when the best strategy for A in the general conditions created by B is that when B is also playing its best strategy. Thus, A acts in the best possible way against a strategy of B, and B has no incentive to move. Unfortunately there is no particular reason why such a pair of solution strategies should exist, though of course they might. It would seem unlikely that in general they should. However, if there is no solution in this sense, then in what sense can we argue that there is in general a rational way of playing a game? It is certainly not the same as a rational recommendation for parametric situations, nor is it clear that it would be some recognisable extension of such principles.

Von Neumann and Morgenstern showed, remarkably, that in the case of the two-person zero-sum game, it was possible to define a concept of solution using principles which were a natural extension of ordinary maximising assumptions. I give an account of their theory in chapter 5. Thus they were able to extend the concept of rationality to a certain class of strategic situations while still retaining its essential characteristics. Solving the two-person zero-sum game becomes in principle a computational problem and, providing one accepts the extension of rationality to be described, poses no conceptual difficulties. It produces a vast array of practical ones. Because of the many possibilities, the practical problems of computation in a game like chess are enormous, and we are shielded from any practical solution to the game by the computational complexity of the problem.

The problem is that the extension of rationality which applies so nearly to the zero-sum game does not apply in general to the non-zero-game. Nor is there any obvious modification which does. Though people have struggled heroically to provide rational rules which would enable the non-zero-sum game to be solved – and have succeeded in some classes of cases (N. Howard 1971) – there are many cases which stubbornly resist such treatment and continue to provide problems and paradoxes. Nor, unfortunately, are these curiosities with little practical application. In the next chapter I shall show that many of the central problems in the analysis of international conflict can be represented as games to which there are no obvious solutions.

4 CONFLICT AND THE PARADOXES OF RATIONALITY

1 THE 'PRISONERS' DILEMMA' AND THE 'SURE-THING PRINCIPLE'

The following rule appears trivially self-evident as a rule of rational conduct. It is known as the 'sure-thing principle'.

Suppose that I am going for a walk and wondering whether or not to take my dog with me. I am unsure whether it will rain or not, which will clearly affect my enjoyment. If it does not rain and I have my dog I am happiest, because I can throw sticks for it on the beach. I am still happy, but not quite as happy, if it does not rain and I do not take my dog, for I can still sit and admire the sea. I am less happy if it rains. However, if I have my dog, I can still play with it, but I know I will have to clean it up when I get home, which detracts from my pleasure. I prefer this to the fourth possibility of walking along the beach in the rain alone and without my dog. My problem is whether to take the dog with me on my walk when I do not know whether it will rain or not. For clarity let us suppose that I am willing to put numbers to my degrees of contentment (though the core of the argument does not require this). Such numbers are known as *pay-offs*. We can then lay the problem out as follows in what is known as a *pay-off matrix*:

Matrix 4.1

	Event	
	No rain	Rain
Not take dog	3	1
Act		
Take dog	4	2

As I will be happier by taking my dog whether it rains or not, it appears a trivial recommendation that I should do so (the dog's interests are ignored in all this). It is a 'sure thing' that I will be better off taking the dog, and so there is no point in going to any trouble to find out what the weather predicts. The reader can be forgiven for thinking that, if the best decision theory can do for us is to provide recommendations like this, it is a waste of time.

Now consider the following extension to the problem. On this walk I am hoping to meet a lady towards whom I am romantically inclined but for whom I am not so overwhelmed by passion that all I want is her happiness in every detail. She also has a dog which is (in my view) bad-tempered and walks slowly, so a joint expedition with my (vigorous) dog has serious drawbacks. The situation I would most prefer is to take my dog but for my friend's to be left behind. My next preference is for neither of us to take our dogs. Next down the list is for both of us to take our dogs, while my least favoured position is for my friend to bring her dog but for mine to be left behind. In this case, we walk slowly, my friend's attention is distracted, and I do not even have the pleasure of my own dog's company. My pay-off matrix is the same as it was when the rain was a factor affecting my pleasure. That is:

Matrix 4.2

| | Event (that is, my friend's choice) | |
	Not take dog	Take dog
Not take dog	3	1
My choice		
Take dog	4	2

Again it would seem obvious what I should do: I should take my dog. However, suppose my friend's preferences are similar to my own in reverse. Ideally she would prefer to bring her dog but for me to leave my (in her view) restless and quarrelsome dog at home. Like mine, her next preference would be for neither of us to take our dogs. Third she would rank both of us taking our dogs, and finally the position most disliked by her is when I take my dog but hers is left at home. Her pay-off matrix is then as follows:

Matrix 4.3

| | Friend's choice | |
	Not take dog	Take dog
Not take dog	3	4
My choice		
Take dog	1	2

Applying the self-evident sure-thing principle, she will bring her dog. It would appear foolish to do otherwise. If we both follow this principle we will both bring our dogs and both end up getting two utility units each. However, if we had disobeyed this rather basic, and apparently indisputable rational principle, we should *both* have been happier, with three utility units each. This is paradoxical and appears absurd, but it is true. It stands out even more clearly when it is represented in the joint pay-off matrix.

Matrix 4.4

	Friend's choice	
	Not take dog	Take dog
No dog	(3, 3)	(1, 4)
My move		
Dog	(4, 1)	(2, 2)

This illustrates that, when we get into conflicts with other people, rules that serve us so well that it is scarcely worth while identifying them when confronting 'nature' (which does not have preferences of its own) give us poor results when confronting people, who *do* have preferences. Perhaps these rules are the best we have – we must explore this – but they are clearly not very good.

The issue demonstrated here is known as the *prisoners' dilemma*, a classic problem in this field of study. It derives its name from the following story.[1] Two men in possession of guns are picked up by the police. Though they are committing no crime other than possessing offensive weapons, the police have a strong suspicion that they were earlier involved in an armed robbery, though they cannot prove it. The two prisoners are therefore taken into separate rooms and each is made the following offer, in the knowledge that the other is being made the same offer: if you confess to the armed robbery and your partner does not, then we will speak up for you in court and you will get only one year in prison. If you confess, and your rival also confesses, our plea for leniency will carry less weight and you will get five years. However, if you do not confess and your partner also does not confess, you will not be convicted for the robbery – but you will both get two years for carrying arms. If you do not confess but your partner does, you will bear the brunt of the punishment and get ten years. The prisoners are not allowed to communicate with each other before pleading in court.

We can arrange the alternatives and their consequences offered to each prisoner in the pay-off matrix below.

[1] This procedure is not allowed in many countries, at least officially. The example does not pretend to be very realistic, either legally or practically.

Matrix 4.5

	Prisoner A	
	Not confess	Confess
Not confess	(2, 2)	(10, 1)
Prisoner B		
Confess	(1, 10)	(5, 5)

Remembering that in this case a high number, meaning years in prison, is disliked more than a low number, we can see that the dilemma is the same as that involved in meeting my friend with or without the dog. It would seem clear that both of the participants should confess as, no matter what the other one does, each individually will do better. However, this results in both of them getting five years in prison, whereas, by refraining from confessing, they could both get only two years and be better off. They end up with a mutually undesirable solution which could have been bettered for both of them. So much for the apparently impeccable 'sure-thing principle' when we move into strategic situations.

The reason for regarding this as a dilemma, or even a paradox, is obvious. Both players act in a rational manner, but they end up in a position which could be improved on for both of them. Both would have been better off if they had selected the other strategy. Individual rationality in this case does not lead to social rationality, which is a disturbing conclusion and violates many intuitive preconceptions of the consequences of individual rational conduct. Intuitively one feels that, if everyone is motivated only by his individual self-interest and acts according to some precepts of rational conduct, then at least some of the actors, the 'winners', should be better off. However, this case shows that this is not true. Two people acting according to rules of individual self-interest *both* fail to achieve as much according to this criterion as if they had violated such rules.

2   AVOIDING THE PARADOX: SOME TENTATIVE APPROACHES

If the prisoners' dilemma takes place once only, then the above reasoning is impeccable, though disturbing. However, such interactions are relatively rare. In the prisoners' dilemma itself, the years in prison are sufficiently long for us to assume that decisions taken after the prisoners come out will be unaffected by their attitudes to each other at the trial (though even this is by no means sure.– the long-term act of revenge is a well-known motif in the cinema – see, for example, *High Noon*). However, in the case of my friend and me with the dogs, it might be presumed that the situation would repeat itself.

We could talk about the situation and, it is hoped, resolve it. Even if we were unable to talk – since it is an area within some emotional prohibition zone – we would still regard a single day as just one in a sequence and assume that how we behave today will affect how we behave towards each other in the future. In general we hope to persuade other people to behave favourably towards us by a mixture of rewards and punishments. Suppose we have slipped into a pattern where neither of us brings our dogs. If I now cheat and bring mine, I shall no doubt suffer the following day when my friend brings hers. The knowledge that this might happen therefore deters me, so we remain at the cooperative point. My friend is similarly deterred from bringing her dog by my implicit counter-threat to bring mine. We have a strong form of deterrence here. If I bring my dog, but she does not bring hers, her pay-off is only 1. As she can increase it to 2 by bringing her dog, the threat to do so is very credible and I will believe it.

When a situation essentially repeats itself as in this case, it is called the *iterated* or *supergame* version of the prisoners' dilemma. The attempt to find the conditions for cooperative play has been the focus of a vast amount of academic investigation.[2] Sometimes these are referred to as 'solutions' to the prisoners' dilemma, but this is misleading. The 'pure' prisoners' dilemma reveals a significant conceptual problem in conflict decision making which must be considered even if it does not arise very often. A strong and at least superficially surprising result was shown by Howard (1971), which is that a sure-thing principle is *never* an appropriate strategy in a strategic situation and that thus the prisoners' dilemma is not just some strange peculiarity. Once a situation is strategic, so that a person chooses against a planning opponent instead of an unthinking nature, disinterested in the result, the whole situation is altered and the one does not simply involve some simple modification of the other. The supergame presents different problems altogether. It is a game suggested by the prisoners' dilemma rather than a version of the prisoners' dilemma itself. We want to know when people will defect and when they will collaborate. Despite the amount of work done, there is still a good deal of controversy. However, it does not involve a conceptual problem except inasmuch as it merges into a 'pure'

---

[2] A particularly interesting development is due to Axelrod, who simulated various plausible rules of conduct in a computer 'tournament' to see which one did the best. 'Tit-for-tat', the strategy of playing cooperatively providing one's rival does but defecting if the rival initiates a defection, came out remarkably well. See Axelrod (1984).

prisoners' dilemma at some stage. We can argue that the prisoners' dilemma supergame provides us with a rather strong form of deterrence in that, if one partner defects, it is in the direct and immediate self-interest of the other to counter-defect.

Another version of the supergame, which I shall call the 'limited supergame' of the prisoners' dilemma, is one of the most useful as far as the application to international relations problems is concerned. The 'rules of the game' are as follows. As long as actors use their collaborate strategy in one play of the game, they can continue to use it in the next or to switch to the defect strategy. However, on playing the defect strategy they are committed to playing that for the rest of the game. Thus, a shift to defect is not a reversible process. I shall illustrate this with two examples taken from international relations which can be appropriately modelled in this way.

Suppose we have two hostile countries wondering whether to develop some expensive new form of defence system – 'Star Wars' (the 'Strategic Defense Initiative – SDI) is a good example. The situation is such that, if neither has such an anti-missile system, then there is a stalemate. If both have a system, then there is still a stalemate, so neither has a strategic advantage. However, the acquisition of an anti-missile system is very expensive, so that the stalemate with such systems is worse for both parties than it would be without, because of the high costs involved. If one country has the system but the other has not, then the strategic advantage is substantially weighted in its favour, and we assume that this advantage is worth the cost of acquiring it.

For the sake of clarity, I shall put some numerical values to the advantages and disadvantages of various courses of action, emphasising that these numbers are for illustration and commit us only to very weak forms of measurement. Suppose that the strategic gain to a country due to having an anti-ballistic-missile missile system when the other does not have one is 250 national interest units. However, if the position is reversed and it is the other side that has the system, the strategic loss is seen as -250 national interest units. However, the cost in terms of economic resources of acquiring the system is 100 national interest units, so the net gain of being in the strategic lead is 150 units. If both obtain the system, the strategic balance is arrived at, but both are paying a cost of 100 units. Thus we can build a pay-off matrix as below which can be seen to be essentially the same as the prisoners' dilemma. The *status quo* is regarded as zero.

Matrix 4.6

		Country B	
		Not carry out programme	Carry out programme
Country A	Not carry out programme	(0, 0)	(−250, +150)
	Carry out programme	(+150, −250)	(−100, −100)

Assume that the two countries are currently at the *status quo* point. Both are working out what to do. Suppose that country A decides to go in for building anti-missile missiles. At some time this will become known to B, which will recognise that, if it does not initiate a similar programme, it will be at a strategic disadvantage. There is therefore an unambiguous gain in responding by also carrying out a programme – from the threatened −250 to the somewhat less serious −100. This is worse than the original position, but, at least, is better than being in the strategically disadvantageous situation. The end result will be −100 for both parties; both will have made themselves worse off. The analysis does not end at this point. The far-sighted initiator will have seen this possibility and recognise that attempting to start the programme will end by making both sides worse off. This may deter a potential initiator who can see the mutually damaging result. This is appropriately modelled by the limited supergame. As long as actors stay in the collaborate position, they can at any point in the future continue with the collaborate strategy or move to the defect strategy. However, once defection has taken place, the reverse is not possible.[3] States do not back down very rapidly from major programmes, though they may slow them down (as seems to be the case with the US 'Star Wars' programme). Thus it seems reasonable to model this situation with a game, based on the prisoners' dilemma, in which the players can move downwards or to the right, but not reverse this process. If shifts can be made from collaborate to defect quickly, then this form of deterrence would appear to be very effective in that any short-term gains would be quickly cancelled out by the long-term losses. Unfortunately this is less likely when delays in reacting to an opponent's move are long, as would be likely in the example given. The period of gain before the rival has replied might seem worth the ultimate loss. Further, a state might be afraid that the rival state would introduce the

[3] This type of analysis has been elaborated by Brams (e.g. Brams 1985) and called the 'theory of moves'. In essence it suggests that the actors consider the long-term consequences of their moves rather than the immediate ones. See also Zagare (1987).

anti-missile missile system so as not to be caught out in the losing situation. To study these questions requires an elaboration of the model which would make it more complicated (though still suscepti- ble to analysis). If the simple model were the whole of the story, the anti-ballistic system should not be built – but the complications cannot be ignored. The merit of the simple model is that it clarifies the nature of the problem and suggests directions for the complications and modifications of the model to take.

So far the games have been presented as symmetric games between two parties – even when, as in the first example, the actual acts available to the two participants were different. However, a common enough situation in life in general, and international relations in particular, is for one party, to be called A, to be able to make a move which will benefit it at the expense of another, to be called B, where B is able to respond to this move of A but does not have the ability to initiate a similar move against A. I shall call this game 'truncated prisoners' dilemma', in that only one of the parties is able to initiate any action. Suppose we have the following case. There is a territorial dispute between two countries where one country occupies the land but the other covets it. The owner has no reason to initiate any action, and indeed it is not clear what such action would consist of. However, the coveter can initiate an action, say an invasion. Now the owner has a choice – to resist or not to resist. We can represent this in the form of a *game tree* or 'Extensive form of the game', as shown in figure 4.1.

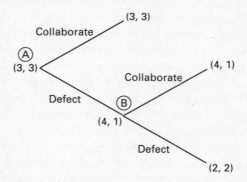

Figure 4.1

If A plays the collaborate strategy, the game goes to (3, 3) and carries on from there. If A plays the defect strategy, the game moves to (4, 1). At this point B has the option of collaborating and remaining indefi- nitely at (4, 1) or defecting to (2, 2). Thus B has a powerful deterrent over A, in that it is very credible that if it is the victim of a defection by A, it can, and presumably will, play the defect strategy in consequence. Thus, the maintenance of the mutually collaborate strategy would seem likely and the deterrence successful as long as the game remains in its present form. The argument has followed the limited prisoners' dilemma analysis except for making it asymmetric. The symmetrical case is one of mutual deterrence. However, in this case we have a one-way deterrent structure. This is a common form of deterrence in international affairs. Something of the sort exists, for example, between Spain and Britain over Gibraltar. Because nothing very much happens – it is not one of the spectacular events in international affairs – we tend not to notice it. It is the spectacular, not the prosaic, which commands attention.

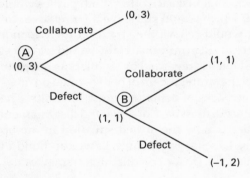

Figure 4.2

I have presented the numbers symmetrically despite the asymmetry of the situation, which makes it look as though the actor who covets the defender's assets is in a better position than the defender. In fact, the reverse is more likely to be true, for the defender actually has the benefits whereas the coveter only wants them, but, by the nature of the problem, has not got them. The coveter may see the *status quo* as manifestly unjust so that the problem appears as in figure 4.2. Unless justice itself is a goal of the coveter, separate from the primary outcomes, this is still a truncated prisoners' dilemma with asymmetric pay-offs. In this case it is hard to maintain that A is the privileged actor. The examples discussed have been so simple as to be implausible. The paradox of the one-shot prisoners' dilemma could be just a curiosity which makes us ponder a little more carefully on the nature of rational conduct but has little practical significance. However, it is more than that. Structures based on the prisoners' dilemma model provide a simple picture of some types of international conflict. It is not suggested that any (or at least many) real-life conflicts have such simple structures as these games. They do, however, form a basis for classification: by looking at these simple games, we can gain some insight into the nature of more complex conflicts.

3 GAMES OF DISARMAMENT

Just as we can look at the problems of rearmament in the prisoners' dilemma framework, so we can look at the problems of disarmament. Becoming more cooperative in a prisoners' dilemma supergame is also possible.

Suppose that two countries which perceive each other as hostile have a high level of arms directed against each other. Both parties would like to move to a lower level, which would still leave their relative strategic positions the same but would relieve the strain on their economies. However, for either party to cut arms unilaterally would leave it strategically weak to a degree which is regarded by its rulers as not justifying the economic saving. Let the strategic gain of being armed on one's own be 100 units and the drawbacks of being unarmed 100 units. The cost savings are 50 units, so the net drawback of unilateral disarmament is 50 units. The *status quo* base is now the armed situation in the bottom right-hand cell of matrix 4.7. Starting from this, we can build up the following situation, which is a prisoners' dilemma framework:

Matrix 4.7

	State B	
	Arms reduction	Arms *status quo*
State A — Arms reduction	(50, 50)	(−50, 100)
State A — Arms *status quo*	(100, −50)	(0,0)

Posing the problem in this form exposes the bare bones of the logic of the situation. If A decides to reduce its arms it would lose, not gain, in national interest unless B did likewise. B, however, would have no particular incentive to follow by reducing its arms as it would also lower its national interest from the bonus figure given by A's reduction. More pessimistically, then, we conclude that the non-cooperative position also has some strong elements of stability, in that neither side is likely to make the move necessary to get the system to the stable cooperative position.

This highlights, but no more, the reason why unilateral disarmament moves are very rare. Disarmament and arms control negotiations are normally concerned to try to get over this hump by making all parties reduce arms together. This means that they move directly from the bottom right to the top left-hand box without a transition through the other corner boxes, which neither party is ready to accept.

As is becoming clear, our procedure when faced with a problem is to reformulate it in a simpler form. We then see if such a restatement is a legitimate description of the reality we are ultimately trying to describe. If we are concerned about altering the reality, we aim to devise a scheme which overcomes the difficulties and facilitates benign moves in the system. Clearly disarmament is one such policy area, and I briefly describe two schemes for overcoming the difficulties.

The first was suggested by Osgood (1962) and is known as the Graduated Reduction in Tension (GRIT) approach. Briefly, there are many situations, such as during the Cold War, where big jumps in the reduction of tension by a negotiated process are not feasible. It is more realistic to assume that any reductions in armaments or tension in general will come about by a sequence of small moves.[4] This is illustrated by expanding matrix 4.7 by putting in a host of intermediate strategies as represented below in matrix 4.8.

Matrix 4.8

		State B			
	B_1	....			B_n
A_1 (50, 50)		....			(−50, 100)
	.				
	.				
	.				
	.				
State A	.				
	.				
	.				
	.				
	.				
	.				
A_{m-2}			(2, 2)	(0, 3)	(−2, 4)
A_{m-1}			(3, 0)	(1, 1)	(−1, 2)
A_m (100, −50)			(4, −2)	(2, −1)	(0, 0)

[4] This is not the case when there are major shifts in the international system such as after a war. Here, as after 1918 and 1945, there are big jumps. The current situation between the super-powers, in terms of which GRIT was originally conceived, also involves a major readjustment of perceptions because of the revolutionary change in attitudes of the Soviet leadership, resulting in large reductions in arms levels. The GRIT policy becomes unnecessary in such circumstances, though it may still be useful to reassure the cautious. However, it is primarily relevant to situations of stable tension.

In the bottom right-hand corner we see what is in effect a cluster of little prisoners' dilemmas which are encompassed in the larger disarmament game. The argument is simply that an agreement is more likely in such a small game because even if the agreement is dishonoured by one of the parties, the other does not lose very much. By a similar argument, either party can signal a willingness to reduce tension by making a unilateral move upwards because, if it is not followed, the cost of failure is not very severe. Instead of being played all at once, the game is played incrementally. In effect this has transformed the game into a sort of supergame.

Another related and very ingenious way of considering the problem of disarmament was devised by Salter (1984). It is based on the same principle as that which guarantees equality in dividing a piece of cheese amongst several people. The person who cuts the cheese chooses their own piece last. The cutter then struggles to cut equal-sized pieces, as otherwise they will be left with the smallest piece.

Moving to larger human conflicts, let us suppose we are dealing with two antagonists in a potential disarmament situation. Each agrees to divide its arms up into a large number (say one hundred) of segments. Both are then able to choose which of the rival's segments the rival will have to do away with. Consider this from the point of view of the decision makers of A. They will choose that segment of B's arms which is perceived as most threatening. However, the decision makers of B will have split their arms into segments such that the loss of any segment would result in an equal loss in security. The reasoning behind this is that, if they were unequal, A might take advantage of this and choose a segment which reduced B's security disproportionately. Similarly A will have split its arms up into segments which will result in an equal loss of security if they are chosen and when B chooses will lose one-hundredth of its security, though its gain by getting rid of the most feared hundredth of B's security will be more than proportionate. Both sides are gaining in this deal, but again incrementally. This can best be illustrated in figure 4.3. The straight line OM represents the aggregate loss in security to A as segments of armaments are abandoned. The line would be the same irrespective of the order in which the particular segments were arranged. However, the gain in security which A gets through being able to get rid of successive segments of B's arms is greater than this and represented by the curved line. The procedure will benefit A until the point at P where the distance between the two lines has reached a maximum: beyond this point it will find itself losing security at a faster rate than it is gaining it. A similar sort of analysis applies to B, and it would be presumed that this process comes to a halt at the point where the first of either A or B begins to feel that the marginal security reductions outweigh the marginal security gains.

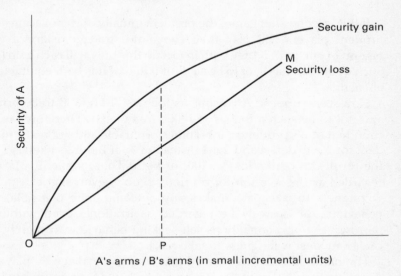

Figure 4.3

This analysis of disarmament is not intended to provide blueprints for disarmers. The idea is to provide a conceptual underpinning to the analysis such that the underlying structure of the situation is made clear. Blueprints based on faulty conceptual foundations are likely to founder. The purpose of this sort of analysis is to make them clear.

4   THE GAME OF 'CHICKEN'

The prisoners' dilemma does not exhaust the paradoxes of rationality. Another game known as 'chicken' raises what are possibly even more acute problems. The generalised pay-off matrix consists of two acts, cooperate and defect, as in the prisoners' dilemma, but the pay-off matrix, given below, differs in the significant respect that the bottom right-hand entry is lower for both parties than any other. I have made these negative pay-offs high to emphasise the point.

Matrix 4.9

	State B Cooperate	Defect
State A Cooperate	(3, 3)	(1, 4)
Defect	(4, 1)	(−100, −100)

If this is a one-shot game, the problem initially does not seem acute. Prudent players will play their cooperate strategy risking a worst pay-off of one unit. If they both in fact do this they will each gain (3, 3). Such a solution has a lot to be said for it in that it is both equitable and efficient.

However, suppose A reasons as follows: 'I know B to be prudent and not to be such a fool as to risk a loss of 100. Therefore, as I am confident of B's prudence, it becomes profitable and not really imprudent for me to defect and get 4 instead of 3.' If B thinks likewise, then the result can be the loss of 100 for both. Thus, while (3, 3) can be regarded as the solution for cautious people, even slight degrees of willingness to take risks makes any outcome quite plausible. Such behaviour can scarcely be regarded as irrational even within our narrow view of rationality as self-seeking behaviour. It merely indicates a modest willingness to take risks.

The name 'chicken' is derived from the game allegedly played by American youths in the 1950s and which was communicated to a wider public by the film with James Dean, *Rebel Without a Cause*. Two teenagers drive their cars towards each other. The first one to veer to the left is 'chicken' and loses (presumably in terms of face). If both swerve they both lose face, but not relatively, whereas if neither swerves they are both dead. These consequences can be laid out as follows:

Matrix 4.10

	B Swerve	Continue
A Swerve	Draw	A is 'chicken', B wins
Continue	A wins, B is 'chicken'	Both dead

The ordering of the consequences in matrix 4.10 can plausibly be assumed to be that of matrix 4.9. If A really wants to win, he must convince his opponent that there are no circumstances in which he will swerve (such as by locking the steering wheel). If face means a lot to the players, then there is a serious dilemma for them.

Many situations we wish to model, such as deterrence, are better represented by the supergame of chicken (that is, the chicken game played many times over), where some more problems are raised. Consider the game as follows. At the mutual cooperate point of matrix 4.9, we assume that only A is contemplating initiating a move; B is assumed passive for reasons of expository convenience. If A continues collaborating, both parties still get 3 each. If A defects, the pay-off will be 4 and the rival's 1. Will B now continue to cooperate and remain at (1, 4) or defect, bringing about the (−100, −100) solution? This position is a strong one for A, for the act of dislodging A from it is costly for B. Unless motivated by revenge, B would do best to be philosophical and accept the reduction in this pay-off. If we now assume that both A and B are equally alert, then A's desire for gain is intensified by a dislike of loss, for, if B makes the non-cooperative move first, A will similarly find himself in a loss position and can do little about it. Both parties are then aware that it would be highly beneficial to them to 'pre-empt' the other, that is, to act first in an aggressive manner. If they both act together, they will end up in the mutually harmful bottom right-hand cell.

How, then, should rational players in this awkward situation behave, assuming that they start from the cooperative position? To deter credibly, one has to threaten credibly to act severely against one's own interests, which is not the normal interpretation of rationality. To maintain one's position one must be conditionally irrational – or at least give a convincing pretence to the other side that one is. But this, from many points of view, is a difficult psychological position to adopt.

To give a provisional answer to this question, it is convenient to divide chicken games up into 'mild chicken', 'severe chicken' and 'extreme chicken', depending on the severity of the defect–defect outcome. 'Mild chicken' is a game where, because the loss is small, it can readily be recouped in the supergame; a defect response can reasonably be expected to be profitable in the long run. Matrix 4.11 represents such a game:

Matrix 4.11

	Player B	
	Cooperate	Defect
Cooperate	(3, 3)	(1, 4)
Player B		
Defect	(4, 1)	(−1, −1)

'Severe chicken' is one in which the defect response to a defection cannot be recouped in any plausible set of iterations, and a responder must lose. Matrix 4.9 above is an example. 'Extreme chicken' occurs when the response involves the destruction of the responding party, such as is the case in nuclear deterrence. While clear demarcations of these categories are not possible, their general nature is clear.

The supergame of mild chicken creates no great problems in principle. While it is not as stable as the prisoners' dilemma super-game (nor has it been so thoroughly investigated) in that the costs of punishment are more severe to the punisher, nevertheless, actors looking into the future will see the possibility that short-term losses of punishment may be worthwhile to secure the long-term compliance of the opponent in the cooperative solution. Hence, the system should not break down in the first place (that is, the deterrence should work), as both parties see that any defection will bring only short-term gains.

Severe chicken is not so easy, however, and it is here that we come up against one of the most difficult problems of analysing rationality in conflict situations. How can a player deter the rival from defecting? The problem is to make it clear to the would-be attacker that the deterrent will be activated (though in fact 'may be' will do), despite the fact that it would appear to be more self-interestedly rational not to do so. The point of deterrence is to prevent an act taking place by making clear the risk of adverse consequences, so the best solution is that nothing happens, which, in this case, means that the cooperate–cooperate strategy continues. The personalities most likely to produce a mutual cooperate solution are those who are unaggressive in the sense of initiating anything but, if roused, are known to respond vigorously. If both parties are of this temperament, then the situation will be very stable. If only one is, then it will still be stable as the rival will know that an attempt at defection will result in punishment. However, by bringing in 'personalities', we may have helped in a descriptive analysis of the situation, but done nothing for an analysis of rational conduct. We have still to face the problem of how the rational actor deters in the severe chicken situation.

There are four ways out of this problem. They apply directly to the simple 'ideal-type' games of chicken described above, but they also have their interpretation in real-world situations. The first is to try to convince the rival that the pay-offs are not what they seem. It can be done in two ways. Either the costs of punishment can be presented as less severe, or the value of the benefit can be exaggerated. In a limiting case, the game can be transformed into a prisoners' dilemma. Short of that, the game can be presented as a game of mild chicken, and as an element in a supergame and for which the punishment would nor-mally be activated.

The second way out is to argue that it is an issue of morality which compels the punisher to punish. The deterrent must be activated not because it will benefit the deterrer, as it will not, but because there are some higher goals which the deterrer must pursue. 'The aggressor must not go unpunished' is often uttered as a moral truth even if the utterance might have more pragmatic motives.

The third way out is to pretend to be irrational (or indeed to be irrational), though there are problems as to what we really mean by this (Elster 1983). We can regard it as the apparent willingness to accept great losses, and indeed, perhaps, not quite to understand what these losses entail. It would be rational to pretend not really to understand the problem. The important thing is to be convincing.

The fourth is to make it clear that 'revenge is sweet'. By adding the pleasures of revenge to the primary pay-offs, the game is transformed into a prisoners' dilemma.

In one form or another, these arguments all appear in international contexts. Severe chicken occurs frequently in situations where a mutual defect solution can be interpreted as war.

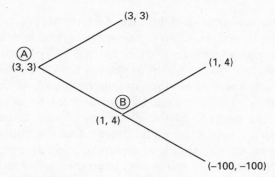

Figure 4.4

While two-party symmetrical chicken represents many cases in international relations, other situations are more appropriately modelled in terms of limited, truncated chicken, as shown in figure 4.4. The underlying rule of this game is that either party can move from cooperate to defect, but not vice versa. If both play the defect strategy, this ends the game. This model represents, admittedly crudely, situations where one party can initiate an attack on the other, whereas the other cannot. Thus, in a territorial dispute where one side holds some territory which the other side claims, such as over the Falklands, the holder cannot initiate anything, and it is entirely up to the claimant. However, if military action is initiated, the holder can either accept it or counter-attack, resulting in significant losses for both sides. If we are discussing a war, then it is useful to think of the game as terminating with the war. After a war, it is usual for the whole structure of the situation and the potential pay-offs to be fundamentally altered.

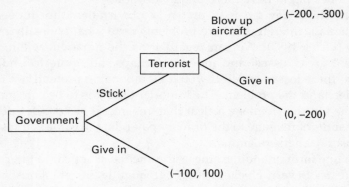

Figure 4.5

The truncated game also models the case of a terrorist hi-jack of an aircraft, which also illustrates some of the ways in which deterrers make deterrent strategies seem credible (see figure 4.5). I put in a set of speculative pay-offs in terms of which to discuss the issues: the first pay-off in each bracket represents the government's pay-off and the second, the terrorists'. The terrorists, by initiating the hi-jack, have started the game represented by the game tree. Some demand is made, usually with a deadline for its fulfilment, and the initiative is then given to whichever unfortunate government finds the aircraft at one of its airports (typically not one of the governments central to the dispute). Clearly the government's favoured outcome in this case is that it will 'stick' and hope the terrorists will not blow up the plane. The terrorists want the government to give in, and they think they are most likely to achieve this by convincing the government that they will in fact blow the plane up. I have made the game chicken as far as the terrorists are concerned. Their tactic is to pretend that it is prisoners' dilemma and that the pay-offs of −200 and −300 are reversed. They have to do this by trying to persuade the world that they have goals which are more important than their instinctive wish to live. They can appeal to the traditional military virtue that death with honour is better than life with dishonour. The disgrace of surrender would be too much to bear. This has inspired many people in the past and can readily sound convincing. Added to a belief in a cause which tran-

80

scends the individual, this can be a strong motive for being ready to die. This is further reinforced if the cause for which the terrorists are fighting is religious and they believe that after death they will go straight to heaven. In such circumstances it seems surprising that people are not readier than they are to plunge into paradise, though it is fortunate for the rest of us that they are not. This brings us up against the ambiguities of belief, for we do sometimes doubt even the fanatic's eagerness for sacrifice in such circumstances, and with good reason. Nevertheless it is in the interests of the terrorists to convince everyone else of their fanaticism.

A typical government attitude is to regard any particular incident as part of a supergame. They do not deny the pay-offs, but argue that by conceding, one is encouraging a repetition of the incident. However much they may regret the immediate disaster, concession would merely incite a repetition of the game. Some governments have made this an explicit policy in advance. Thus, it is Israeli policy not to negotiate for kidnapped diplomats. It is announced in advance that the strategy will be Non-Concede and so, clearly, it would be impossible for the Israeli government to back-track on this in any actual situation. The argument that the incident is a supergame is often reinforced by moral arguments – 'It is wrong to give in to blackmail' – where this is uttered as a moral precept rather than a practical rule of self-interest.

It is clear that we are on some delicate conceptual ground. If the pay-offs stated are the primary pay-offs, then in all these options we are doing one of two things. Either, as in the first, we are trying to pretend that our primary preferences are not what they seem; or alternatively, we bring in some underlying preferences (such as 'honour' and the importance of 'the cause') and pretend that the game becomes different because of them. We might pretend to believe in these underlying preferences or we might really believe in them. A danger is that we might start by pretending and end up by convincing ourselves. I return to these issues below.

The aim of using these games, at least as presented here, is to clarify ideas. Behaviour in the prisoners' dilemma is likely to be very different from that in the chicken game, and so, by analysing conflicts in terms of these and other simplified cases, we can gain some insight into their basic structure.

In this discussion I have assumed that in war there are no winners. This need not always be true; states have often benefited by the fighting of wars. However, today most people hold that wars without winners – at best only relative winners – do exist and perhaps are common, though this, according to Calvocoressi (1987), is a relatively modern idea and would have been regarded as absurd prior to the nineteenth century.

5 ANOTHER LOOK AT NUCLEAR DETERRENCE

At this point it is convenient to draw on various aspects of the discussion of rationality to look again at the concept of deterrence.

Let us briefly recapitulate. Deterrence involves a threat. The deterrer makes it clear to the opponent that, if certain harmful acts are undertaken, then the deterree will be punished so that the overall consequences of the act become too expensive to be attractive. Mutual deterrence occurs when both parties threaten each other with 'Don't do it or else . . . '. Given that a hostile move has taken place, the act of punishment may itself benefit or harm the deterrer. The first of these positions is illustrated by the prisoners' dilemma, while the second is illustrated by chicken. Clearly, the prisoners' dilemma form of deterrent is much more credible than chicken deterrence. In the case of chicken, both players would do well to *pretend* that it is prisoners' dilemma, whatever their private beliefs may be.

Now consider a crude version of nuclear deterrence in matrix form.

Matrix 4.12

		B	
		Attack	Not attack
	Not attack	(0, 0)	(−1,000,000, +100,000)
A			
	Attack	(+100,000, −1,000,000)	(−900,000, −900,000)/
			(−1,200,000, −1,200,000)

The figures are deliberately extreme. Both sides believe it would be to their advantage to destroy the other side totally providing there was no counter-attack. Such a view would require an extraordinarily casual attitude to human life, but one which nevertheless can be found. The nuclear dilemma has been discussed in these terms where at least such an evaluation of advantages by at least some participants (on both sides) is regarded as a possibility. What is left ambiguous in this example is represented by the two pairs of figures in the bottom right-hand box: a counter-attack by the victim may or may not be preferable to doing nothing. (As it does not affect the basic argument, the consequences of a second strike attack are assumed to be the same as for a first strike.) If the top entry in the bottom right-hand box is the one which is seen as appropriate, then the game is one of prisoners' dilemma. It implies that an attacked country derives benefit (if only in the satisfaction of revenge) by carrying out a counter-attack. If this is thought to be the case, then the credibility of deterrence as a means of avoiding nuclear attack is high. If the bottom entry represents the valuations of the decision-makers, a counter-attack makes things even worse for the victim as well as the attacker. Such a configuration of values is not implausible. A country which has just suffered nuclear attack might be helped by its attacker, if only out of a desire to exploit it. Also, the extra fall-out in a world already heavily contaminated would harm the second attacker as well as its victim. Further, the only benefit is the satisfaction of revenge. Thus, a chicken picture is as plausible as a prisoners' dilemma picture. Another factor must now be included in the debate on deterrence. The use of nuclear weapons on any large scale would have severe ecological effects which would almost certainly be adverse. There would be a 'nuclear winter', in which the temperature of the world would be significantly lowered, probably for a period of years. How serious this would be is a matter of scientific debate laced with politics. If nuclear winter is severe, this means that the use of nuclear weapons will harm the initiator even if there is no response from the adversary. Hence, a plausible matrix involving nuclear winter is depicted in matrix 4.13:

Matrix 4.13

		B	
		Not attack	Attack
	Not attack	(0, 0)	(−1,500,000, −500,000)
A			
	Attack	(−500,000, −1,500,000)	(−1,400,000, −1,400,000)
			(−1,600,000, −1,600,000)

If this is the case then we should have a very stable situation, as there would be little sense in anyone initiating an all-out nuclear attack. This game is known as 'assurance'. Putting a as the best outcome, b the next best and so on, it can be represented by matrix 4.14:

Matrix 4.14

	B	
	Cooperate	Defect
	(a, a)	(d, b)
A		
	(b, d)	(c, c)

or in numbers:

83

Matrix 4.15

	B	
	Cooperate	Defect
	(4, 4)	(1, 3)
A		
	(3, 1)	(2, 2)

The ordering of the three cells involving the playing of a defect strategy are the same as in prisoners' dilemma, but the exception is the top left-hand cell, which is the best for everyone. Providing each player is 'assured' that the rival will play the cooperate strategy, then the obvious thing to do is follow suit. In a simple game with full information, such as this, the assurance is provided if we assume self-interest. However, in games where there is not full information, either because of doubts about the rival's pay-offs or because of the complexity of a more realistic case, there may be no assurance provided, and defect strategies might be played.[5]

It is arguable that the superpower conflict was always perceived by decision makers as assurance even before the possibility of nuclear winter was recognised. Whether for moral reasons or even for purely self-interested ones, it was always unclear whether the elimination of a superpower would benefit its rival.

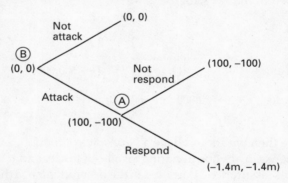

Figure 4.6

However, this is not the only issue. A central problem is whether a small aggression by B would be responded to by an all-out nuclear punishment. This is shown in the extensive form of the game (see figure 4.6). From A's point of view this is chicken, and B might legitimately wonder whether a counter-attack would be made. The

[5] I discuss assurance and the situations when there is doubt about whether a situation is assurance or prisoners' dilemma in Nicholson (1989).

deterrent looks unsure. The implausibility of setting off a nuclear war in order to check some modest set-back initiated by a lunatic led to some further development of deterrence theory. Herman Kahn (1965) developed a notion of a ladder of escalation where responses to an attack were made at the same level. In the same spirit it led to 'flexible response', which effectively means that if A grabs some advantage from B, B will respond but at the same level. This can be illustrated conveniently by extending the truncated game depicted in figure 4.6 into one involving several stages as in figure 4.7.

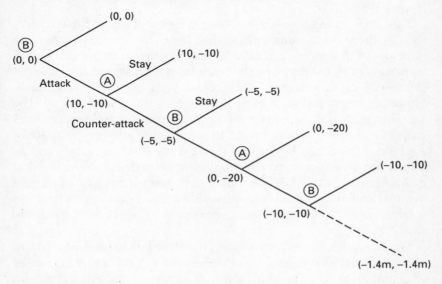

Figure 4.7

For simplicity I again assume asymmetry with B as the possible aggressor. At stage 1, B has the choice of doing nothing or attacking A where the attack is far short of a nuclear attack. As in the earlier examples, if there is no attack the *status quo* continues indefinitely. If the attack takes place, then A has the option of doing nothing or counter-attacking at the same sort of level as the initial attack. I assume the pay-offs to be of the prisoners' dilemma form, so this will benefit A as compared with doing nothing, though both will be worse off than if they had stayed at the *status quo* level. Again B can stay or attack. An attack will improve its position at the expense of A, though there will now be a substantial loss as against the original position. This can continue until at the nth stage we have reached all-out nuclear war. Though the game is a long one, we can reasonably assume that its

85

general properties are known to both parties. The situation would seem to be reasonably stable. If B did attack, A would counter-attack. However, both would see the slippery slope they were on and that it would be mutually disastrous for them to slide too far down it. Thus, this game has the dual benefit that, because the nature of the game is clear before it ever occurs, the initiation of the attack is unlikely to take place. Further, even if by some chance it should, then there is reason to assume that it would not go very far as both parties can see the consequences of its getting out of hand – namely all-out nuclear war (Brams 1985).

This appears to solve some of the problems of nuclear deterrence, though there are a number of difficulties. The first is whether the structure of this game adequately represents the structure as it would be perceived by the participants. It has been represented as a clear-cut sequential game where equality comes after each alternate move. However, neither side is likely to see it as quite so clear-cut. The initiator may well see itself as righting some long-standing and patiently endured wrong rather than initiating some cynical act of aggression, which is how its rival might see it. Hence, the equality which tacitly appears may not be seen as such by the real-world counterparts of A and B, who may both see themselves as relative victims. Rationally, of course, one would rather be a small victim than a large victim, but it still makes some point of agreement harder to find.

Secondly, the theory presupposes the clear-headedness and rationality of the decision takers. This is where the subject matter of chapter 7 becomes relevant. The initial move in such a sequence would mean a crisis and the general pattern of crisis decision making, discussed in chapter 7, comes into play with all its attendant dangers. We could not rely on calm rational procedures taking place, and panic may well ensue; the slide down the slippery slope might come extremely quickly. If the rival was not perceived to be cautious (and the perceived lack of caution might be a misperception), there could also be the temptation to leap-frog a few stages, thus accelerating the move to mutual destruction. The study of crisis decision making induces caution in accepting the view that the process will stop at some reasonably early stage.

Thirdly, there is the possible slip between decision and action. In its abstract form, deterrence theory presumes a decision taker who issues orders which are obeyed and, very crucially, are not anticipated. However, if there is a severe crisis and actual warfare, albeit on a small scale, there will be a great deal of confusion, and the control which the decision taker exerts over his agents may be weak. They may not receive orders, they may anticipate orders, they may panic, and a whole host of other things. The problem is recognised, but the escalatory tendencies of a crisis-ridden military organisation are still there (Bracken 1983; Blair 1985).

These points undoubtedly weaken the rescue attempt which has been made on the rationality of nuclear deterrence. There is, however, a perverse way in which these weaknesses can add to the credibility of the basic deterrence structure. The weakness of the original deterrence structure, where there was a jump straight to total nuclear war, was that it was hard to imagine that anyone would regard certain mutual destruction as an appropriate response even to a significant attack on its interests. However, a moderate response to a moderate attack is very plausible. Military systems are geared to perform such believable acts even if the plunge down to nuclear war is seen as a likely consequence once the process gets started. Thus the dangers of situations getting out of control can paradoxically increase the effectiveness of the state of deterrence. The fear that the process of activating the deterrent might get out of hand induces caution in the actors, who fear that their own rationality and that of their rivals might collapse under the pressure of a large-scale crisis.

The presentation of deterrence so far has obscured one significant factor – the distinction between a general state of deterrence and a particular act of deterrence. Suppose, in a territorial dispute, riots take place in the disputed territory which tempt B to intervene to pursue its interests. In this particular situation A might utter a deterrent threat specific to the conditions which apply. B will then take the threat into consideration when deciding whether or not to intervene. A decision-making process takes place in B where the actors are explicitly considering and deciding on the choices which are available. However, there are also the situations where deterrence operates all the time, that is, where there is an underlying state of deterrence. The actors involved in the territorial dispute wanted the territory all the time, but they recognised the continuous deterrent threat and hence did not think about the problem very often. It is not part of an active decision-making process. This is the general assumption about nuclear deterrence. Decision-makers in the Soviet Union and the United States have not considered daily whether they could attack the other country and then suddenly felt a sense of deterrence as they remembered their rival's weaponry. It is presumed that they did not reflect very often on the underlying possibilities of launching a first strike. Normally no active decision processes were under way.

However, there might be specific times when the actors wonder if they can get away with something. At such times a decision-making process is going on. At least a possible interpretation of the Cuban Missile Crisis is that the Soviet government thought it could get away with its policy of installing missiles in Cuba – that is, that the *deterrent state* initially failed. However, once the United States began to take various sets of decisions, and make the escalation to nuclear war seem possible if not probable, then the Soviet Union backed down and was satisfied with only minor improvements to its position. In this sense the *deterrent act* succeeded. There is clearly an ambiguity about whether one says in this case that deterrence did or did not work. The state failed, the act worked, and it is necessary to distinguish between the two as the distinction, to a degree, avoids the ambiguity which has played a part in various controversies about deterrence (Achen 1989; Lebow and Stein 1989).

A final problem is how one knows whether deterrence has worked. We can tell if it has failed when a particular act occurs which it was intended to deter. However, successful deterrence means that nothing has happened – but how does one tell what 'caused' this 'non-event'? Deterrence concerns what goes into a decision-making process and therefore depends on knowing people's states of mind – a notoriously difficult problem. In the case of a deterrent act, it is possible in principle to determine whether it has worked providing one has sufficient access to the decisions of the deterred party. Even if this is not explicit, there are plausible guesses one can make, as with the Soviet Union over Cuba. In the case of a state of deterrence it is less clear. We can say that it has failed if that which it was intended to deter takes place (Cuba again). However, if the act never takes place how do we determine whether it was because the actor did not want to commit it or because it was deterred? A very detailed examination of the decision-making processes over the years might reveal discussions about some act being considered but dismissed because of the risks of deterrent action by a rival. This would be evidence in favour of successful deterrence. The problem is not in principle insoluble – that is, it is an empirical statement. However, in the case of the relationship between the super-powers, we simply do not have the evidence at this stage. Though widely made, confident statements about the success of deterrence in preserving the peace (or, of course, its irrelevance) are unsubstantiated and unsubstantiatable without the examination of a mass of data which are currently unavailable.

5 THE ZERO-SUM GAME: SOLUTIONS AND INTERPRETATIONS

1 THE SOLUTION OF THE ZERO-SUM GAME

The zero-sum game is the case of pure conflict where interests are totally opposed. Such purity, even such a sinister purity, is a rarity in social life, but it is useful as a basis against which concepts of conflict can be compared.

A game such as the one-shot prisoners' dilemma (a non-zero-sum game) has a solution in the sense that there is a pair of strategies resulting in specified pay-offs which cannot be improved upon by either acting alone. We might feel uneasy with such a solution, as it is manifestly inefficient for the two players, but it seems a likely consequence if two people are caught in such a trap. There is more hope, however, in both the limited-play case of prisoners' dilemma and the supergame version. The one-shot game of chicken has two solutions, so at least in the symmetric case there is nothing to choose between them. Indeed if both actors pursue their favoured position, the end point may favour neither of them. In the limited-game version of chicken the situation is wholly ambiguous in the sense that no set of rules which can be plausibly interpreted as rational gives an unambiguous solution point. Indeed with non-zero-sum games we are often presented with situations where there is either no solution or several solutions. There is nothing in the solution concept as discussed so far which guarantees that if there is a solution, it will be unique.

Unsurprisingly the solutions of the zero-sum game, in a sense we come to in the next section, are rather clearer than that of the non-zero-sum game. There are ways which lead to a solution to the two person zero-sum game which are neat and clever while the non-zero-sum game seems to present us with more paradoxes than solutions, though the paradoxes are often fruitful, as the last chapter showed. However, most social situations are more appropriately represented by non-zero-sum games, which might make it seem that the theory of games offers us nice solutions to rare situations, but nothing much for the main part of reality. This is only partly true. Zero-sum situations do exist. For example, voting situations in legislatures have been fruitfully represented as zero-sum in that there is a win–lose situation which at least roughly approximates to it, an approximation which is sufficiently good for many purposes (Riker 1962). Further, in situations of strong hostility, where the discomfort of the other side is the prime motive, the game can approach a zero-sum game. Thus zero-sum games are not without application in the world outside the gaming room. They also have their pedagogic role. Some of the issues in game and conflict theory can be easily seen in the context of the zero-sum game, so we now turn to a simple instance of it. The reader should not be put off by the simplicity of this game, or by its remoteness from international conflict situations. The interest of the analysis is more in showing a 'pure' form of conflict against which we can compare the less extreme but more complex forms which are found in reality than in the direct value of its applications. It clarifies various concepts of rationality in conflict situations and is of great conceptual interest and importance. Its practical interpretations exist but are limited, however, and readers who are more interested in application can move on to the next section.

I shall describe the essentials of the zero-sum game in terms of an extremely simple game – one of such simplicity that no one would be likely to play it. Practical games players should resist the temptation to look for hidden subtleties: it really is a very simple game.

Suppose Albert and Billy are the contestants in playing a game in which each is given three coloured cards. Albert has a green, a purple and an orange card, while Billy has a red, a blue and a yellow card. The game involves choosing a card to lay out simultaneously with the rival's card so that each is in ignorance of the other's move and a payment is made from one player to the other depending on which cards are laid out. Suppose that Albert puts out the green and Billy the red; then the rule of the game specifies that Billy pays Albert £3. As in the earlier games discussed in the last chapter, this sum is known as the pay-off. A positive number 3 indicates that £3 is paid by Billy to Albert and is Albert's pay-off. A negative number means the sum is paid by Albert to Billy and is Billy's pay-off. Suppose, however, that Albert had played the orange and Billy still the red. The rules now specify that Albert pays Billy £5. We specify who pays whom, and how much, for each of the pairs by means of the matrix below, that is, the pay-off matrix of the game. A positive number indicates that Billy makes the payment to Albert, and a negative number indicates that Albert pays Billy.

Matrix 5.1

		Billy (pays out positive numbers)			
		Red	Blue	Yellow	
Albert	Green	3	2	4	Numbers
(pays out	Purple	4	−1	−2	represent
negative	Orange	−5	−2	5	£ units
numbers)					

The question is: 'How "should" Albert and Billy, as two rational people, play this game?' At first sight, there may seem to be little to be said. It is not the same for both parties, and intuitively might be said to favour Albert slightly, as there are five cells with payments from Billy to Albert and only four with payments the other way round. However, this advantage is not very clear-cut. Suppose Billy plays the yellow: Albert would do well to play the orange and get £5, instead of only £4, which would result if the green were played. However, if Billy plays the red, Albert would be better off playing the purple. What should Albert do?

Let us assume a particular rule of choice, and then I shall show that the particular rule chosen has a great deal to be said for it. The rule which we advocate to Albert is: examine each of the three available choices, and see what would be the outcome if Billy were to counter this in the way which is worst for you. (This is, of course, the outcome which is best for him.) Then choose the card which corresponds to the best of these worst outcomes. In other words, find the lowest number in each row of the pay-off matrix and then select the row which has the highest of these lowest numbers. This is known as the 'maximin' rule, that is, the rule of maximising the minimum. This rule plays a fundamental role in the theory of games.[1]

A parallel rule is given to Billy. We can clarify the situation by putting in a further column in which is given the worst pay-off in each row for Albert, and another row in which the worst pay-off for Billy is given (matrix 5.2). (Remember that a high positive number is bad for Billy, as it represents his payments out.)

If Albert operates the rule suggested, he will play green, which will mean that the worst which can happen to him is a gain of £2; Billy, using the same rule, will play the blue, so that the worst result for him is to pay out £2. We see, however, that this 'worst result' is exactly what occurs. The green and the red are played and Billy plays Albert £2.

---

[1] It also appears as the 'minimax rule' when looked at from the point of view of B, who is trying to minimise the maximum loss. Maximin seems to be the more general way of expressing it.

Matrix 5.2

		Red	Billy's move Blue	Yellow	Albert's lowest gain (the row minimum)
Albert's	Green	3	2	4	2
move	Purple	4	−1	−2	−2
	Orange	−5	−2	5	−5
Billy's lowest gain (the column maximum)		4	2	5	

This might seem an unenterprising rule of conduct, but what are the alternatives? Suppose that Albert and Billy play the game a number of times. Suppose also that each decides that the best method of play is to assume that his opponent's last move will be the same as his next one, and to make the best response to that. Both start off by being naïve optimists: Albert plays his orange in the hopes of getting £5, while Billy plays the red in the hopes of getting £5. Billy is delighted as his hopes are fulfilled; he gets £5 at the expense of Albert. Albert is disappointed and on the next move shifts to playing his purple, making Billy pay out £4. Billy therefore shifts to the yellow and gets £2. Albert responds by going from the purple to the orange and receives £5, and so Billy moves back to the red and gets £5, after which we can repeat the process. We shall thus get a cycle of four different results with payments to Albert of −£5, +£4, −£2 and £5, giving an average per time of 50 pence. Now Albert can see that, no matter what Billy does, by playing the green consistently he can always get at least £2 and perhaps more. However, Billy can also carry out this mental exercise and realise that it is in Albert's best interest to play the green. If he assumes that Albert is 'rational', then he will choose the best strategy against the green, which is, of course, the blue. So we end up with the strategy originally prescribed. If Albert continues to play the green over a number of trials, there is nothing Billy can do to improve his position. A shift to the yellow will increase his losses to £4, and a shift to the red will increase his losses to £3. Similarly, Albert cannot improve his position by a unilateral move. Thus, the position seems to be an extremely stable one.

The essence of this scheme is that it assumes that the rival is prudent. If he is not, then the maximin policy might not be the best. The maximin policy can be described as a 'prudential policy'. Whether 'rational' or not, it is undoubtedly a rule of prudence; and, in this case, it is the only discernible prudent way to act.

The value given by the selection of the green and the blue is the minimum value in its row in the matrix and the maximum value in its column. It is this which makes it a prudent goal to aim for, since neither party can make a unilateral move which will benefit him. As this is a zero-sum game, it follows that such a move can only benefit his opponent. This is the only point in the matrix with these properties. A point such that neither side can profitably move away from it is regarded as an *equilibrium point* and the strategies which give it as *equilibrium strategies*. The equilibrium strategies are also known as the *solution* of the game.[2] The general notion behind such a concept of a solution is that, if one player uses the appropriate strategy, then the other can do no better than also using his solution strategy. Much of game theory is directed towards finding solutions and equilibria of this sort.

However, in many matrices the minimum row value and the maximum column value will not coincide. This is shown in the following (absurdly) simple two-choice game.

Matrix 5.3

		Billy's move		
		Blue	Yellow	Row minimum
Albert's	Green	−1	2	−1
move	Purple	1	0	0
	Column maximum	+1	+2	

Suppose they now play the maximin strategy. Albert will play the purple, and Billy will play the blue, and the pay-off will involve Billy paying Albert £1. However, Billy will then move to playing the yellow and no payment will be made. Albert responds by moving to green and so on. There is no saddle point in the way there was with the earlier matrix, which means there is no stable point and hence no obvious solution. Unfortunately this is not a curiosity, and indeed might be supposed to be the norm.

However, this difficulty can be overcome. Suppose the players are playing a sequence of identical games[3] using this particular pay-off matrix. In the previous analysis the players both used the same strategy on each occasion. By using different strategies on different

---

2 When a solution exists in a zero-sum game which has the characteristics of being the maximum of its column and the minimum of the row, it is known as a *saddle point*. The pay-off to A is known as the *value of the game to A*, and analogously for B. In the zero-sum two-person game the value of the game to A must be the opposite of the value of the game to B. The one which is positive is known generally as *the value of the game*. In the non-zero-sum game this condition clearly does not apply.

3 In strict theory of games terminology a 'game' is the set of rules defining a game and a 'play' is an instance of the game being played. Hence one plays a 'play' of the 'game' of chess. I use the word 'game' in the text informally rather than technically.

occasions, called 'mixed strategies', a broader game can be developed which does have a saddle point. This is explained in the appendix to this chapter.

The result obtained by Von Neumann and Morgenstern which really makes the theory of the zero-sum game interesting is that, by using a mixed strategy, any zero-sum between two players, no matter what the form of the pay-off matrix, has some pair of strategies which will yield a saddle point. That is, there is always a 'safe' way of playing a game, where 'safe' is defined in this particular sense. This means that, in all two-person zero-sum games, there is a rational rule, which is a relatively modest extension of the rules of rationality applicable to non-strategic situations, which results in a solution. For these sorts of games, therefore, there seems a natural development from strategic to non-strategic rationality.

If Billy is bound to lose such a game, why should he be willing to play it? He may, of course, be forced to play, but a theory which applies only to games which one of the players is forced to play does not seem entirely satisfactory. There are two relevant replies. First of all, exactly the same theory applies to a game in which the pay-offs to the two players are equal to some constant positive sum, so that both can win. Consider the following game, where each of the entries in the pay-off matrix is represented by a pair of numbers in brackets. The first number represents the pay-off to Albert, and the second that to Billy. The sum of the numbers in any of the brackets comes to 20, and the game is thus constant-sum.

Matrix 5.4

		Billy's move		
		Red	Blue	Yellow
Albert's	Green	(13, 7)	(12, 8)	(14, 6)
move	Purple	(14, 6)	(9, 11)	(8, 12)
	Orange	(5, 15)	(8, 12)	(15, 5)

By applying the same maximin rule of choice in this case as we did in the first game we analysed, we find that the solution is for Albert to play the green and for Billy to play the blue, with the result that they get 12 and 8 respectively. While the game clearly favours Albert, it is still worth Billy's playing it, as he gets 8 units out of doing so. For the purposes of analysis, however, the two games are identical, the zero-sum game being merely a special case of the constant-sum game in which the pay-off to Albert plus the pay-off to Billy equal zero. It is clear that it is in the interests of both players to participate in any positive constant-sum game, in which the saddle point involves gains for both. The critical characteristics of the constant-sum game (whether zero-sum or not) is that the sum of the pay-offs to the two parties should be equal irrespective of which pair of strategies is played.

The second response is that we can look at this not just as a procedure for recommending Albert and Billy how to play, but as a method for either Albert or Billy to determine whether to play at all. If Billy is asked 'Would you like to play this game?', he would be wise to look at the prospects of winning by analysing them in this manner. In the zero-sum examples, he would decline the offer, as he would be bound to lose, though for the positive-sum game described above he would obviously accept. He could not have come to this decision without having some sort of theory with which to analyse the game, and the theory suggested here seems to be a good one for the purpose. It is not useless simply because it is not actually put to use in play.

One might also ask why two rational people should trouble to play games which are so absurdly trivial. Only the very young, the very bored, or those researching into the theory of games are likely to play such simple games as noughts and crosses. The theory is of practical use only if it can be extended to cover more complex situations. In principle this can be done, but in practice it is extremely difficult because of the enormous number of options which have to be considered. However, this is not the main defence. For the most part we are not in the business of recommending strategies of play in non-trivial zero-sum games (they would become trivial if we did in fact solve them). The basic purpose of this analysis is to develop a set of concepts with which we can understand more about the nature of conflict. These become conceptually more complex as we proceed. What is important is that the concept of rationality in some maximising sense has not suffered any severe set-backs in its first confrontation with a strategic situation. We have merely extended some common-sense notions.

2 HOSTILITY AND THE STRUCTURE OF GAMES

The applications of the zero-sum game are fewer than superficially might be supposed. However, there are some interesting applications, particularly if we broaden the sense in which we use utility to include not just the satisfaction from the outcomes alone but also attitudes to other players and to the way in which a game is solved.

Let us suppose that we have a game which has pay-offs ranked by the actors according to the non-zero-sum game of assurance, which, it will be remembered, had the matrix with the same rankings as matrix 5.5.

Matrix 5.5

		II	
		C	D
I	C	(4, 4)	(1, 3)
	D	(3, 1)	(2, 2)

These rankings are the inherent values of the outcomes of the two players, who are each indifferent to the outcomes of the other partner. They are prescribed by the game. I shall call them 'autonomous pay-offs'. If we use the convention again that the earlier a letter appears in the alphabet, the higher up in the scale of preferences the outcome is for the particular actor, we can represent the autonomous game more generally than before as:

Matrix 5.6

		II	
		C	D
I	C	(a_1, a_2)	(d_1, b_2)
	D	(b_1, d_2)	(c_1, c_2)

However, if the actors also feel hostility towards each other, then the autonomous pay-offs are not the only source of satisfaction or dissatisfaction. Gaining a higher value than a rival is in itself of value, in addition to the autonomous pay-off coming from the recipients of the prizes in the game itself. I shall call the pay-offs which result from a comparison with other players' pay-offs 'relational pay-offs'.[4] In the limiting case, all each player would be interested in would be gaining an advantage, so that whether they had an advantage or not over their rival would dominate all other considerations, that is, the values in the autonomous pay-off matrix. In such a case, the pay-off matrix would consist of the differences between the basic pay-off of the player and the rival's pay-off. If we take matrix 5.5 as the basic pay-off matrix of autonomous pay-offs, this will result in the following zero-sum game:

---

[4] This argument might seem to imply that there is some objective reality in which we can compare the gains and losses of the various actors. Indeed, this is the basis of the coveter's regarding the situation as unjust. This violates the principle known as the 'non-interpersonal comparability of utilities' of the different actors. However, the argument in the text involves the perceptions of the actors and not the 'true' utilities, whatever they may be.

Matrix 5.7

$$
\begin{array}{ccc}
 & \text{II} & \\
 & \text{C} & \text{D} \\
\text{C} & (0, 0) & (-2, +2) \\
\text{I} \quad \text{D} & (+2, -2) & (0, 0)
\end{array}
$$

This is, by definition, a zero-sum game, in which both players use the defect strategy, with the result or solution of (0, 0). We notice that now the interpretation of C and D as 'cooperate' and 'defect' begins to look rather odd, but it will be convenient to keep the letters as labels.

This is a rather extreme assumption. It assumes that the only goal each actor has is the discomfiture of their opponent. A common situation is more likely to be in between these two extremes, where the inherent value of an outcome and the advantage achieved over the rival are both relevant. We can represent these for A alone in the general matrix as follows. In this, λ is the 'hostility factor' for A.

Matrix 5.8

$$
\begin{array}{ccc}
 & & \text{II} \\
 & \text{C} & \text{D} \\
\text{I} \quad \text{C} & (a_1 + \lambda[a_1 - a_2]), & (d_1 + \lambda[d_1 - b_2]) \\
\text{D} & (b_1 + \lambda[b_1 - d_2]), & (c_1 + \lambda[c_1 - c_2])
\end{array}
$$

If λ is sufficiently large, it is possible for the game to be changed from a game of assurance to a game of prisoners' dilemma, and if λ is large enough for the difference term to dominate the basic outcome, it approaches a zero-sum game. This can be illustrated in terms of the basic assurance game illustrated in matrix 5.5, with the added factor for hostility. For convenience of exposition, I assume the game is symmetrical not only in basic pay-offs but also in the degree of hostility.

Matrix 5.9

$$
\begin{array}{ccc}
 & & \text{II} \\
 & \text{C} & \text{D} \\
\text{I} \quad \text{C} & (4 + 0\lambda, 4 - 0\lambda) & (1 - 2\lambda, 3 + 2\lambda) \\
\text{D} & (3 + 2\lambda, 1 - 2\lambda) & (2 + 0\lambda, 2 - 0\lambda)
\end{array}
$$

If λ is zero, then this is the basic assurance game from which we started. However, suppose $\lambda = 1$. In this case we have the pay-off matrix of:

Matrix 5.10

		II	
		C	D
I	C	(4, 4)	(−1, 5)
	D	(5, −1)	(2, 2)

Clearly this is a prisoners' dilemma game.

If we go yet further and assume that hostility is intense with $\lambda = 100$, then the matrix would become:

Matrix 5.11

		II	
		C	D
I	C	(4, 4)	(−199, 203)
	D	(203, −199)	(2, 2)

This is clearly approaching zero sum, and gets closer to it the greater we make λ.

Thus it is clear that by some appropriate choice of a value of λ we can transform the game which in its autonomous pay-offs is the cooperative assurance game into other games of varying degrees of competitiveness right up to the totally competitive zero-sum game. To know which game we are playing we need to know the value of the λ parameter, which I have called, I think plausibly, the hostility parameter. If it is made negative, it of course becomes a friendliness parameter. It is interesting to note, however, that there is no choice of λ possible which will transform the assurance game into a chicken game.

This sort of problem has been discussed in the hypergame literature (Bennett 1977 and Bennett and Dando 1979), though the particular feature in which assurance changes to prisoners' dilemma and thence to a zero-sum game has not, to my knowledge, been noted. It is perhaps surprising that it has not received greater attention in the literature. It gives some clue about how some classes of game which are nearly zero-sum can be approached. One splits the preferences involved into two constituent parts, the preferences over 'autonomous' factors and the preferences due to a relationship with the opponent.

The reverse process is relevant to conflict resolution. In order to alter a game to a non-zero game in which there are mutually advantageous agreements, one has first to reduce the emotional hostility elements, after which one can get at the substantive preferences underneath. This does not apply to all zero-sum games, of course. Many players have preferences which are simply opposed. However, by bringing in issues of attitudes, we can show how they affect the underlying structure of the game and make them more (or less) amenable to solution. It gives us some clues as to how we might achieve some forms of conflict resolution. If we hypothesise that autonomous preferences are more stable than relational preferences, then, over the course of a conflict, these will change and the role of conflict resolution is to manipulate them so that they decrease. This is the object of 'cooling-off periods' in the resolution of industrial disputes. A very optimistic process of conflict resolution would be to convert hostility parameters into friendliness parameters; but I would surmise that this is a longer-term process, through one which does take place even in international relations, for example, between former 'traditional enemies' such as France and Germany.

3   GAMES OF DISTRIBUTION

Superficially games of distribution would seem to be an obvious area of application for the zero-sum game. In the case of a territorial dispute, for example, there is a constant amount of land which has to be divided. In an industrial dispute there is a constant amount of surplus which has likewise to be divided, while in a legal dispute over a will there is a constant inheritance to be divided. Unfortunately, in many of these cases, though the object in dispute involves the division of a constant sum, the methods of arriving at the division involve a cost. Thus, with the inheritance a dispute will involve lawyers' fees and the size of the inheritance net of the legal costs, no matter how it is distributed, will vary according to how lengthy the proceedings are, which in its turn will normally depend on how acrimonious the whole business is. Thus it becomes a non-zero-sum game, where the size of the total outcome to all parties depends on the strategies they adopt. This is common: the apparently zero-sum game involves costs in the settlement which are not trivial in relation to the whole and which then render it a non-zero-sum game.

In some forms of social activity where the distribution is not brought about by some power struggle but by appeals to fairness and justice, it might appear that the zero-sum game is relevant. Even here, though, we must raise some doubts. Suppose two people divide a cake. They might fight about it, and the winner take all, thus incurring costs and hence making the situation non-zero-sum. However, they will more probably split the cake equally, arguing that this is in some sense fair. It would appear to be a zero-sum situation. However, by having a fair division we have added something to the total welfare in that we have now had an instance of justice or fairness which would have been absent if we had divided the cake in any other way. We have added to the satisfaction of the cake itself the satisfaction of fairness, which would have been absent if we had divided it in some unfair way. This is similar to the way in which we have added to the autonomous pay-offs of the last section the satisfactions of winning.

APPENDIX: MIXED STRATEGIES

As shown above, not all pay-off matrices have saddle points and hence solutions. However, by broadening the game with mixed strategies, it is possible to derive a game which has. I shall now explain the techniques by which this is done.

Consider the following simple game:

Matrix 5.12

		Billy's move	
		Blue	Yellow
Albert's	Green	1	0
move	Purple	0	1

There is no saddle point, and the two players can see nothing to choose between the two alternative strategies.

Now suppose the players are playing a sequence of identical plays using this particular pay-off matrix. Previously the players used the same strategy on each occasion. Now consider the possibility of their using different strategies on different occasions.

Let Albert play the green half the time and the purple half the time. If he were to do this according to some fixed rule, such as alternating the two, then Billy would soon realise this and be able to play consistently so as not to lose anything. However, if Albert were to play the two cards an equal number of times but in a haphazard manner, then Billy would have no basis for making a choice between his two strategies. If he played the blue consistently (assuming for the moment that Albert does not take advantage of this), then half the time he would lose one, half the time he would lose nothing, and the average loss would be ½. The same would be true if he played the yellow all the time. We have thus invented a new strategy for Albert which consists of playing the green and the purple an equal number of times in a random manner, giving an average pay-off of ½ against any action of his opponent. We can represent the pay-off matrix of this new derived game as below:

Matrix 5.13

| | | Billy's move | |
		Blue	Yellow
	Green	1	0
Albert's move	50% green 50% purple	½	½
	Purple	0	1

By playing this new strategy, Albert can ensure for himself an average payment of ½. This randomised strategy is the *mixed strategy* as opposed to the *pure strategy* of playing just a single strategy on all occasions.

However, if Billy still sticks to a pure strategy of playing the blue on every occasion, Albert will abandon the maximin strategy and play the green, gaining a payment of 1. To guard himself against this, Billy must also play the mixed strategy of the blue and the yellow on a half-and-half basis in a random manner. When both play the mixed strategies, the four possible combinations of green–blue, green–yellow, purple–blue and purple–yellow will occur on a quarter of the occasions, and the average payment made by Billy to Albert will be ½. The resulting pay-off matrix will be:

Matrix 5.14

| | | Billy's move | | |
| | | | 50% blue | |
		Blue	50% yellow	Yellow
	Green	1	½	0
Albert's move	50% green 50% purple	½	½	½
	Purple	0	½	1

The middle point of this matrix is a saddle point and hence an equilibrium. Any deviation of either from this mixed strategy can be taken advantage of by the other, so this is the prudent strategy which we would recommend to both players. By a modest extension it is also the rational strategy.

Now let us apply this to the example in the text and apply the 50–50 mixed strategy to this case, where the entries at the four corners represent the original matrix.

Matrix 5.15

		Blue	Billy's move 50% blue 50% yellow	Yellow
	Green	−1	½	2
Albert's move	50% green 50% purple	0	½	1
	Purple	1	½	0

If they both started by playing the 50–50 strategies, then Billy would pay Albert ½. However, he would soon see that by playing the 'pure' strategy of blue alone, he would push Albert down to 0 and not have to make a payment at all. This would then lead Albert to switch strategy and we would be back to the beginning. Albert's 50–50 strategy has failed. However, what Albert has to do now to guarantee himself a payment is to alter the proportions in which he plays his strategies. If he uses a strategy of 75 per cent purple and 25 per cent green, the matrix will look like this:

Matrix 5.16

		Blue	Billy's move 50% blue 50% yellow	Yellow
	Green	−1	½	2
Albert's move	25% green 75% purple	½	½	½
	Purple	1	½	0

The middle point of this matrix is now a saddle point. The fundamental theorem of the theory of games shows that for all two-person zero-sum games there is some mixed strategy for the players which gives a saddle point, and thus, at least in principle, such games can be solved on the basis of the maximin principle.

The concept of the mixed strategy has been explained in terms of a series of games in which the players employ different strategies on different occasions, but it can be applied even if the game is to be played on only one occasion. The pay-off resulting from a mixed strategy is really an average of the possible pay-offs. Even if the game is to be played only once, this average can be taken to represent the 'rational hope' of playing such a mixed strategy, although the final result will be either 1 or 0. This 'rational hope' (more properly referred to as the 'mathematical expectation') can be interpreted as the price an insurance company would be prepared to pay Albert for the right to play the game once. In this case, the insurance company would be willing to pay him half of whatever units were in question – minus a little allowance for profit.

As described, the games are unrealistic. However, we can give an interpretation of the concept of a mixed strategy in the single-play game. Billy wants to conceal from Albert which of the two strategies he is going to use while also wanting Albert to think he is equally likely to use either. The best way of concealing one's intentions from a rival is to conceal them from oneself. This is perfect security. It is what happens if a choice is determined by a random device such as tossing a coin. However, the crucial issue is not that Albert chooses his strategies according to some random device, but that, as far as Billy is concerned, he might as well do. The impression which Billy would wish to convey is of being equally likely to make either choice. If the probabilities had been one in ten, then the impression should not be one of complete uncertainty, but rather one of 'probably going to use one strategy, but not quite for sure'. Precisely how the selection is made is not very important. A mixed strategy is a formalisation of creating uncertainty about one's strategy in a rival's mind, but also shows how it is sensible in different situations to create different degrees of uncertainty.

6 EMOTION AND RATIONALITY

1 RATIONALITY AND VIOLENCE

In much of the analysis of international conflict, particularly that which looks at it as the rational pursuit of goals, violence is viewed as a means to achieve particular ends: it is regarded purely instrumentally. Proponents of *Realpolitik* argue that international politics is (and in some versions, should be) the pursuit of power by states where the final arbiter of power is physical violence. Perhaps the clearest statement of this point of view is Clausewitz's *On War*,[1] written with the experience of the Napoleonic Wars in mind (in which Clausewitz fought both with the Russian and the Prussian armies, though himself a Prussian). This is still much read and admired, particularly in military academies. The use of violence is considered a cost, but one which might reasonably be borne in order to attain particular ends. In working out policies where violence might be relevant, politicians weigh up the benefits and costs (including violence) of a particular action and perform those actions for which the benefits outweigh the costs, in much the same manner as one might when planning the route of a new railway. Much of the classical theory of international relations is implicitly or explicitly based on this view. There are qualifications to it. There are moral issues involved in violence, though hard-liners consider these exaggerated. The moral issues are discussed in the final chapter of this book.

Such views fit into a rational choice framework without difficulty, though it is a mistake to suppose that a rational choice analysis of international relations implies this particular version of the 'realist' theory of international behaviour. Other sets of goals, and for that

---

[1] It seems generally agreed that the most satisfactory translation into English of Clausewitz's *On War* (first published in 1832) is that by Michael Howard and Peter Paret (Princeton: Princeton University Press, 1976). Howard's *Clausewitz* (Oxford: Oxford University Press, 1983) is a useful summary of Clausewitz's life and thought, while the lengthy introduction by Anatol Rapoport to the Penguin edition in 1968 is good, and highly critical of the effects of Clausewitz's thought on current ideas.

matter actors, can quite properly be posited and the analysis consider the effective pursuit of those goals.

The cool Clausewitzian view of human motivation is a useful first approximation for the analysis of international behaviour, somewhat akin to the economists' assumption of profit maximisation as a device for explaining business behaviour. However, as a more general approach to human motivation, in particular when violence is relevant, it is seriously flawed. People's attitudes to the use of violence are often ambiguous, ambivalent and complex, and one cannot treat violence simply as an unambiguous cost. In this chapter, I shall explore some of the over-simplifications involved in assuming that costs, benefits and preferences are simply givens in our analysis and, in particular, I shall consider our ambiguous attitudes to violence in greater detail.

2   THE USES AND ABUSES OF AGGRESSION

Before analysing the problem of violence in the context of a rational choice framework, I shall discuss some of the broader issues of human violence. This is the purpose of this section.

One need not be a committed Freudian, or indeed the follower of any other school of analytical psychology, to accept that the instinctual drives which served a useful purpose in preserving and developing the human species in a primitive form of society still function. However, they manifest themselves in greatly modified forms to permit the effective development of highly complex modern human societies. That such drives emerge at times dysfunctionally in modern society is not too surprising.

The study of the basic roots of human conflict has proceeded along two tracks. Biologists have studied animal conflict, partly as a means of analogy, and partly because some knowledge of the animal elements in human behaviour might yield insights which would enable it to be more reliably controlled. The other path is that of the analytical psychologists, both the Freudian psychoanalysts and the other, often competing, schools, which draw attention to the fact that the rational processes of decision are heavily determined by unconscious motives. Psychoanalysis has a bad name in many circles, but this is only partly justified, as I shall argue.

Human beings are mammals and have much in common with other mammals, and indeed with all other sorts of animals. Physiologically, there is a great deal that can be learnt about the human body from the examination of animals. Perhaps to a more limited extent, there are things to be learnt about psychological behaviour from animal conduct. Certainly a large number of psychologist-hours have been devoted to the study of the psychology of the rat in the hope of finding out about such branches of knowledge as the learning processes of humans (and rats); so it is not outrageous to suggest that some clues to human social behaviour might be gleaned from the social behaviour of animals.

This sort of study, however, should be approached with extreme caution. People in human society are very different from animals in animal society. Humans differ from the other animals in being highly intelligent and, partly as a consequence of this, have developed extremely sophisticated languages in order to communicate very complex and subtle ideas to other members of their species. As far as we know, no other animal has a means of communication as effective as human language. Because of their high intelligence and elaborate language, it has been possible for people to develop societies of extreme complexity. The overriding difference between human society and animal society is that humans can, in some rather vague way, design the society they wish to live in. Even if 'design' appears too strong a word, human society certainly alters at what, by evolutionary standards, is a phenomenal rate. Human society today is radically different from that of a thousand years ago, whereas, to the best of our knowledge (for no one is known to have studied them at the time) colonies of rats or herds of gorillas behave in much the same way now as they did then. Animals alter their social behaviour only when the environment changes in such a manner as to force adaptation. Humans can alter their social structure autonomously and without the impetus of environmental change.

If we look at animal societies, aggressive instincts do have some clear purpose, particularly as fighting between members of the same species rarely involves the death of the losers. In the case of foraging animals, the more evenly spaced they are over territory in which there is food, the better they will be able to prosper as a group. So, if animals attack each other when they trespass on each other's territory, this even spreading-about is achieved. The fighting here serves a useful purpose providing it is not lethal or over-damaging to the combatants. Similarly, a species is likely to be best preserved if those members who are physically stronger breed the most, as they are more likely to produce strong offspring. One way of deciding physical strength is to fight, as stags do: the winner (who is normally the stronger) mates with the doe, with the greater likelihood of producing healthy, strong offspring. This is good from a species preservation point of view, particularly as the losing stag is not killed. At an earlier stage of the development of society, the human aggressive instincts of man served a purpose clearly analogous to that which the same sort of instincts serve in other primates. The establishment of leadership patterns, the need to develop good hunters, and the usefulness of keeping different tribes of people apart to spread out the supply of potential food all combined to make aggressive attributes useful. Unfortunately, the invention of weapons has made human violence much more lethal than other animal violence, making death a common consequence of human fighting, but a rare one for other species. While we need procedures for establishing such things as leadership patterns in human societies, it is less obvious that a capacity for physical violence is the best way of doing this. Fortunately we have invented many other ways of determining leadership patterns, such as elections, but the impulse to violence remains and is all too often used. It is conceivable that the partially suppressed manifestations of the urge to violence are at the root of the readiness of people, when organised into groups such as states or nations, to seek recourse to violence to solve their disagreements.

In particular, it is hard to see what species-preservation function is served by human warfare. This is not to say that aggression diverted into appropriate channels is not vital to modern society. It is possible that creative activity of any kind, artistic or scientific, comes from the channelling of aggressive instincts in appropriate directions. However, if this channelling does not occur, the aggression turns into violence, which seems to serve no useful function to the human species.

There are, of course, many other drives besides aggression which do not serve their original animal functions or do so only in a limited form. Expressions of the sexual drive in sexual activity very rarely serve their basic, biological purpose of procreation. Human sexual intercourse is normally done for love or pleasure (not mutually exclusive conditions). Only occasionally is the prime motive the production of children. Fortunately, this has no dysfunctional effects on human society – in fact the reverse – in marked contrast with the urges to violence.

It is sometimes argued that warfare does bring some benefits to society, and is thus not necessarily dysfunctional. There are suggestions that war weeds out the weak from the strong and that this, in some sense, purifies the race. These views now seem obscene and inappropriate to modern society. There are still people who hold a mystical view of the moral virtues of war, and of the nobility of death in action. If there were no opportunity to display such virtues, then the human race would be the poorer and become effete. Such opinions are now rather démodé, at least in their overt political expression, and they have few intellectual supporters. However, it is only in relatively recent years that Nazis and Fascists made no secret of a cult of violence, arguing that violence and war were in themselves noble acts quite irrespective of the instrumental purposes they served. While today such an explicit approval of violence is out of fashion, and our fascination for violence appears clothed in multi-faceted sophistry, it still exists, implicit in many of the 'macho' attitudes which are to be found in most societies. Because of the powerful and indeed frightening nature of the violent impulses in people it requires especially strong excuses to allow its uninhibited expression. Thus patriotism is raised to be the highest moral principle in time of war, while the defence or promulgation of religion is a common motive for committing atrocities. These justifications are not necessarily cynical and exploitative (though sometimes they may be), but are normally believed by leader and follower alike. While there seems little doubt, for example, that Hitler worked carefully on his speeches to induce the hypnotic effects they are widely reported to have had, there is also little doubt that he genuinely believed in his appalling doctrines (Stern 1975).

3   AMBIVALENCE AND VIOLENCE

The view that human beings may have some underlying proclivity to violence would present no conceptual difficulties in relating it to the general theme of instrumental decision making if this proclivity were consistent. International conflict and war often concern the use of violence, ostensibly for instrumental purposes. If people took a simple pleasure in violence, or if it were a simple cost, there would be no problem, as we have eschewed the making of moral judgements in the analysis. It would simply be included in the analysis as a preference like any other. It is people's ambivalent attitudes concerning violence and the sharp changes in opinion and behaviour when confronted with it which create the problems. In this section I shall consider some cases where these ambiguities are manifested and obscure an instrumental view of the uses of violence. Later I show how the apparent paradoxes can be made coherent.

Choices are sometimes exercised in conditions of deep emotion and lead to 'war moods' in which a sudden passion for war seems to sweep the population (Richardson 1948). Thus, the feelings of neither statesmen nor people in Europe in 1914 were those of carefully calculating people working out what was best for the national interest of their own particular land. People were excited, angry, exhilarated and full of patriotic urges; they were not plotting rational responses. Individuals, particularly young males, were eager to rush off to war in a manner which suggests neither individual nor group rationality. In the United Kingdom, from a mild pro-Germanism, opinion became rabidly anti-German and practically everyone was eager for the war – including those who would actually have to fight it. Parallel sentiments were to be found in the other belligerent countries at the time. It appears that this 'war mood' grew over about a week, and it is worth noting that it was already in full swing *before* the German atrocities in Belgium in the August of 1914, which merely added a final touch to the existing violent sentiments. These atrocities, though modest by later twentieth-century standards, were genuine, but were reported in an exaggerated and emotive form, but more as a consequence than as a cause of the war mood.

Though the First World War provides us, in this as in so many other things, with a classic example of this phenomenon, it is by no means unique. Indeed it appears to be widespread at the beginning of a war. The case of both Britain and Argentina in the Falklands/Malvinas War provides a more recent example, while Britain in the Suez case represents a sort of truncated war mood in which the war mood spread vigorously through part of the population (in fact a small majority, if the opinion polls are to be believed), but an anti-war mood spread vigorously amongst a large section of the rest. A war mood is not the inevitable accompaniment of the beginning of a war. In Britain the beginning of the Second World War does not appear to have been accompanied by a war mood. Such moods can be described as sudden preference changes, which in a sense they were. However, for the student of the causes of war, it seems proper to try to find some sort of explanation for them.

Another phenomenon which is at best only partly consistent with an instrumental view of preference is that of the 'Baroque Arsenal' (Kaldor 1981). Present military technology is very exotic, and relies on developments which, to the outsider, border on the fantastic, particularly in electronics. Only advanced electronics, it is alleged, can combat advanced electronics. This results in extremely fascinating equipment being developed. However, it is far from clear that much of it is relevant to fighting a real war or even the sort of war which would have to be threatened if the theory of deterrence is to work as it is supposed to. The work of people like Kaldor effectively rebuts the notion that a genuinely instrumental analysis of modern arms would result in the sort of arms most countries have today. While rockets can be justified in instrumental strategic terms, it is unclear that the numbers developed in the super-power confrontation could. The phallic shape of the rocket has not gone unnoticed. The fascination for arms of a spectacular sort is not confined to the technologically advanced. The recommissioning of several large and impressive battleships, dating from the Second World War, under the Reagan regime can only with difficulty be explained in strategic terms. The fascination with exotic weaponry is not just a feature of the present age. Werner von Braun, the German rocket expert who was the primary force behind the development of the V2 rockets of the Second World War, was well aware of this (Ordway and Sharpe 1979). The development of the V2 rocket during 1943 and 1944 took many scarce resources from the German war economy which it could ill afford. Von Braun would stage impressive demonstrations of rocket motors and the like for both believers and sceptics which usually worked. Hitler himself became fully won over to the programme when he saw films of a test flight of the V2. Such demonstrations did not provide an instrumental argument but were aimed at the emotions and were addressed to the hidden, unconscious romanticism which, according to my argument, is so destructive of clear thinking in military matters.[2]

Another factor which is not adequately explained instrumentally is the relationship between violence and religion. All the 'advanced' monotheistic forms such as Hinduism, Islam, Christianity and Judaism (Buddhism dispenses with even a single god) emphasise in their moral doctrines the general principles of love and kindliness (Smart 1986). This appears to inspire a small number of their adherents to great acts of sacrifice in the interests of human welfare, which command universal admiration. However, it also appears to inspire great acts of cruelty. Freud, ever sceptical about the benefits of religion, remarked that 'Every religion is a religion of love for those it embraces, and each is disposed towards cruelty and intolerance against those who do not belong to it' (*Studienausgabe*, as quoted in Gay (1985)). In the interests of religion the most appalling acts of savagery have been perpetrated at various times. These are not approved of by all the adherents of those religions. In the days of the Spanish Inquisition great physical cruelty was inflicted on the victims

---

[2] Despite the extremely frightening nature of the V2 rockets for its victims – largely British and Belgian – the sceptics may have been right. The cost to the German economy of developing the V2 was probably greater than the damage it did to the British economy. The resources could certainly have been more effectively deployed.

(who were usually other Christians, holding to other forms of Christianity than the Roman Catholic), based on a doctrine that it was ultimately for the good of their souls. The view that burning, for example, was beneficial to the victim was not confined to the Catholics. Fortunately there is little support for this view now amongst modern Christians of any persuasion. However, my basic point would not be seriously contested – that religion is and has been from time to time the legitimation for violent and cruel acts.

Cruelty in the name of religion is only one case of cruelty in the pursuit of an ideology which supposedly benefits mankind. It is unusual only in the extremity of the paradox that doctrines of love are used as the excuse (or indeed reason) for violence. Nationalism and patriotism similarly provide justifications for the release of aggression where the noblest sentiments are used to justify what in normal circumstances would be regarded as appallingly wicked conduct. Revolutionary doctrines confront similar issues to religion. They legitimise present cruelty for the sake of future virtue to make people better and purer – 'The People must be forced to be free', as the French revolutionary Saint-Just put it, echoing Rousseau. Sometimes, and a little more understandably, it is for the longer-term welfare of people as a whole – a version of Benthamism. They run into fewer paradoxes than religion, though the essential principles remain the same.

Not all participation in violence is problematic. Sometimes it can be explained in terms of simple self-defence and needs no explanation out of the rational mode, once we make some minimal assumptions about what people regard as their 'territory', for which we can appropriately use the word 'defence'. Further, moral issues aside, aggression might be perfectly justifiable from the point of view of expanding the interests of the state. Eighty per cent of wars are won by the initiator (Bueno de Mesquita 1981), which does not prove they were worth the cost, but at least suggests that the leaders were pointing in the right direction.

However, there is still a problem in fighting for the state, even if we allow that it is rational for the collectivity to fight. The self-interested individual should always be a free-rider and leave the fighting to someone else. This may not always be possible: there are powerful social constraints against being a free-rider, and governments as well as individual citizens are adept at imposing costs on a putative free-rider. However, in military organisations it is normally possible to free-ride while ostensibly joining in (as *Felix Krull* and *The Good Soldier Schweik* testify, though *Catch-22* counter-testifies), but one would expect more to follow suit given that the psychic costs of contemplat-

111

ing being killed in youth would seem to be high. Yet men often go enthusiastically, or at least stoically, into battle. The genuine reasons of self-defence, coupled with the difficulties of free-riding, are inadequate to explain all the fighting which goes on, and the enthusiasm which goes into it. Nor do they explain why people identify to the point of death with certain sorts of social groups such as nations, but with others, such as cities, they are willing to take identification only up to the support of a football club.

In standard economic rational choice theory there is a concept of 'indifference'. I use the term 'ambivalence' at some points in place of this usage. I want to distinguish between those situations where someone is indifferent between two alternatives involving low psychic energy, such as in the decision between an apple and an orange, and those involving high psychic energy, such as whether to marry a woman (man) with whom one is in love or go into a monastery (nunnery). In the first case, the word 'indifference', with its connotations of lack of caring, is entirely appropriate; but it is totally inappropriate in the latter. For many purposes the conditions are usefully distinguished. A choice between 'Death with honour' and 'Life with dishonour' is really not the same thing as a choice between raspberry ripple and chocolate fudge. In particular the psychological stress of being in the second form of 'indifference' is very high and can result in some of the unfortunate consequences described in the next chapter. Situations involving violence are normally in this group and are sometimes complicated by decision makers being unclear about their own underlying attitudes. In this sort of case there is a particular pressure to seize on to doctrines which clearly indicate one choice and which can eliminate the psychological tensions.

In its simplest form, the simple rational choice model copes poorly with the phenomenon of violence. I aim to show, though by a circuitous route, that rational choice theory can be broadened to encompass these apparently perverse preferences, but only if we consider the generation of preferences in greater detail. It might also be more convenient to drop the term 'rational'.

4   A MODEL OF THE MIND

It is proper to speculate on some model of a mind which would be consistent with these phenomena. Let us assume that, as well as our normal rational, day-to-day selves, there is an unconscious mind where primitive feelings and instincts lie dormant. If these instincts were to come out, they would be very destructive, and hence we are very fearful of them becoming manifest. However, they are also very strong, so there is a tension between two strong forces – the powerful violent instincts which wish to emerge, and the equally powerful 'repressions' which keep them in check. However, these instincts can be triggered off, and when they burst out they can erupt with enormous ferocity. We all have these powerful feelings, but, because of their rather crude nature, our more civilised selves are shocked at them. This does not prevent us from being unconsciously influenced by them, perhaps very significantly, and for some purposes allowing them to come out. Because of their shocking nature we need exceptionally good reasons for letting them come out, and hence the justifications for war are often raised to the highest moral peak. Historians might argue that a particular war was fought for trade routes, empires or markets, and indeed give convincing reasons for their interpretation. However, at the time the participants thought more of duty, patriotism, honour, God and other noble causes. For many, perhaps most people, it is only such high principles which can legitimise the expression of their violent selves, of which the other parts of their psyches disapprove. Association with violence by means of uniforms and tales of heroic deeds gives social and sexual approval. If other people do something, it must be all right, and if we half want to do it anyway, this is a reinforcing notion. People in crowds, for example, notoriously behave in ways in which they would never do on their own. This argument is speculative, but I shall return to the issue of the legitimacy of such speculations in section 6, where I suggest that the extreme sceptic turns immediately, after which I hope they will return to the main argument with more sympathy.

This outline is consistent with the Freudian model of the mind. Freud (at least in his 'topological model') divides the mind into three parts, the 'superego', the 'ego' and the 'id'. Parts of the ego are in the conscious mind – that is, the person is aware of what is going on and interprets it at face value. Some is in the 'pre-conscious', which means that it can be readily brought up into consciousness. The rest of the ego, the superego and the id are all unconscious. Crudely, the ego draws the personality together and tries to mediate between the demands of the id, the superego and the 'reality' which intrudes from the outside world. The superego can be identified with an individual's conscience. It is the superego which approves or disapproves of what the mind is doing. The id is the repository of the violent and cruel aspects of human beings. It can be regarded as an evolutionary left-over from the days when these were necessary survival characteristics. If the id had its way then social life would be impossible and indeed be 'solitary, poor, nasty, brutish and short', as Hobbes believed. Hobbes viewed the Sovereign as the controller of the collective id. Freud allotted that function to the superego, at least in personal life. The superego controls the id and makes it possible for us to live together. However, these violent feelings are present all the time, though normally unconscious, and are not simply locked harmlessly away, but are powerful forces. Their 'repression' is part of the activities of the mind and is a necessary feature of mental activity. If civilised society is to be maintained, by which I mean a society in which power is not the only currency but there is also the cooperative behaviour which is necessary in all social groups from family to nation, then repression in the individual is required. The repression is not without cost, as these drives are very powerful. In Freudian and many other theories this is a part, though only a part, of possible malfunctionings of the mind which result in neuroses.

A picture such as this accounts for a number of things which a simple instrumental model does not. As far as social violence is concerned, unconscious factors may influence behaviour in two ways. First they give insight into the classic problem of why people are willing to fight in war, particularly given the appalling risks of death and disfigurement. The simplest explanation is that it satisfies some deep primal urge, whether one refers to this as the id or as something else. A significantly large number of people want to participate in war even though the sense of 'want' is much more complex than the sense in which a person 'wants' an ice-cream. Secondly, these unconscious ideas influence us not merely when fighting is imminent, but also in our general attitudes to issues which may involve violence. The urge to be thought 'tough' is probably a more potent factor in reflections and then decisions about military matters, such as the level and nature of military expenditure, than more prosaic considerations of what in fact might be appropriate forms and levels of weaponry to meet a particular and plausible threat. The fondness of many military men and their civilian admirers for exotic equipment is partly explicable in terms of the lucrative contracts these afford to certain people, but as much, I suggest, in terms of the satisfaction of more primitive associations with violence. Only lastly do strategic considerations come into play.

Similarly the cruelties associated with ideology and religion are readily explicable in terms of such a model. The aggressive impulses locked in the id are eager for an excuse to emerge. To admit to liking cruelty is difficult, but if it can be treated as a duty to save souls and follow the will of God, then this is the perfect excuse to combine indulgence in violence with a feeling of piety. Following the will of

God can hardly be wrong. It is possible to maintain these positions because, despite the high moral injunctions to be found in religions such as Christianity, there is also sufficient ambiguity to make almost any position tenable with a little ingenuity.

5 PREFERENCES: THE DEFINITION OF IDENTITY

In section 3 above, I considered the problems of ambivalence in the formulation of preferences and in particular in defining attitudes to violence. In this section I want to consider briefly the role of an individual's sense of identity in the making of choices, again in particular those which relate to violence.

Initially, consider the preferences in the context of consumer goods, where the issues are simpler. People do not consume purely out of self-determined pleasure. In part they determine their identity by the messages they give out to society by their purchases. This is particularly obvious in the case of clothing, which clearly plays a big role in determining people's identification with a group. Some preferences may be regarded by an individual as attributes of no great importance and certainly not a part of a person's inherent nature. I may feel I just happen to be a person who likes radishes, for example, and my essential nature would not alter if for some reason my tastes changed. However, other parts of my expenditure might be going to boost, in my own and others' eyes, my view of myself as a worthy citizen: so I buy a house, a car and so on just like other worthy citizens with whom I identify. It is this identification with other sorts of people which is crucial – not the details of the expenditure, which will in any case change as the messages of different things alter. Such preferences I shall call 'identity-defining', as they indicate to me and others just what sort of person I am.

People's consumption of economic goods and services is only one part, albeit an important part, of their lives and of their statements about themselves. Piety, kindness or toughness show themselves more in the behaviour of people towards others than in directly economic ways. They all underlie the basic way in which we perceive and identify ourselves. This complicates but does not invalidate the general arguments about rational choice. The question we have to be careful of, though, is what goals in fact are being sought by the actors. If a person wants to appear tough, then they may carry out acts which instrumentally appear foolish for the gain of a particular goal, whereas if the true goal is recognised as being the assertion of identity then it becomes comprehensible.

115

This raises a number of problems when we come to behaviour in conflict situations, particularly those involving violence. Negotiators often like to perceive themselves as tough and, in situations such as those modelled by chicken, can find themselves in very confusing situations in that there is a horrendous range of psychological conflicts in which they are trying to appear tough while being torn between the attractions and horrors of violence described above in our discussion of ambivalence.

6 JUSTIFICATIONS OF THIS ANALYSIS

The above analysis is speculative. From all points of the political, intellectual and moral spectrum, scepticism (and outrage) is often expressed about analyses of behaviour in terms of unconscious mental processes in general and Freudian analyses in particular. Can one reasonably consider explanations along the lines I have suggested?

There are three arguments which a critic of this approach needs to take seriously. First, it seems clear that there is a problem to be explained. I have suggested that there are two manifestations of unconscious urges to violence – the direct fascination with and a willingness to participate in violence; and the indirect effect it has on our attitudes to things associated with violence, such as armaments. The first is hard to deny. It is impossible to analyse a great deal of the violent behaviour we observe in terms of the rational pursuit of instrumental preferences. It does not follow that my explanation is the only possible one, but it is one which puts the phenomenon into a coherent framework. The extension of the argument to the indirect effect of the fascination for violence is more controversial. It is plausible, but other interpretations are also possible.

Secondly, critics, particularly Karl Popper (1963) and his followers, accuse psychoanalysis of being irrefutable and hence unscientific. The attitude of many psychoanalysts bears out this view; some of them almost wilfully disregard the most basic principles of scientific evaluation and indeed take a pride in it. While Freud himself was no paragon in this respect, some of the criticisms of him are unduly harsh. The core of his work was done before the major developments in the philosophy of science in the inter-war years; it is arguable that he was rather better than most medical doctors of his generation, and many subsequent ones. However, despite hostility amongst some supporters of psychoanalysis, there has been for many years an increasing concern with stating psychoanalytic findings in testable form and testing them (Edelson 1984; Fisher and Greenberg 1978).

This is not the place to give a detailed treatment of this issue, which I have done elsewhere (Nicholson 1983). One should distinguish between the formal structure of a theory or set of theories and the views of the more excitable members of a profession which follows them.

Thirdly, if we concede the first point, or indeed are willing to accept that any significant mental processes are unconscious, then it should be possible to construct some theory of these unconscious processes where 'theory' is to be understood in a standard, testable sense. Such a theory would be a set of propositions which made intelligible certain expressed thoughts and actions of individuals which were inexplicable by a consideration of purely conscious goal-seeking behaviour. To some extent, the various forms of psychoanalytic theory make such behaviour explicable. The existing theories are no more than provisional, and are scientific research programmes rather than theories. The Freudian model I briefly outline does make some sense of various forms of behaviour; there may well be later ones which make better sense. However, to rule out the unconscious mind as not proper material for scientific investigation seems odd (and unscientific), particularly when there seems to be a clear need for explanations of conduct in these or similar terms.

7   THE RELATION TO RATIONAL CHOICE

Superficially the considerations of this chapter might seem to be subversive of the whole notion of rational choice. In some circles they are believed to be. However, the welding of these concepts into a rational choice framework can result in a more potent tool for the analysis of human behaviour in general and international behaviour in particular. The basic discussion is clearly consistent with the idea of pursuing goals effectively: it merely goes more deeply into the origin of goals, which the classical rational choice analysis eschews. However, it leaves the way open for a broader view of choice and, at least in principle, of rational conduct. Instead of considering simple rational choice theory as narrowly construed, it is better to regard it as a scientific research programme in choice in general, without becoming involved in rationality, a tendentious enough concept in any case.

The core extensions to classical rational choice theory developed so far are two. First, that to be useful, a theory of choice must broaden the goals beyond instrumental rationality to include others. The ones I suggest are 'relational', which was discussed briefly in chapter 5, and

117

'identity defining', which was discussed in section 5 of this chapter. Second, and central to this chapter, is the significance of the complexities of choice behaviour when they involve factors of great emotional moment such as sex and violence. The emotional significance of violence often makes us very ambivalent about its use, and frequently it is central to our notions of ourselves as 'tough' or 'tender'. These complicate, but no more, the rational choice framework, but in complicating it, bring it closer to an analysis of how people really take decisions and the constraints under which they operate.

Consider again the British government's attitudes to the Falklands when the islands were invaded by the Argentinians. One can rationalise the British behaviour in terms of instrumental rationality by reference to future possible aggressions if this act by the Argentinian Junta were allowed to go unchecked; that is, one could regard it as one play in a chicken supergame in which future plays might involve pay-offs such as Gibraltar.[3] However, this is not the most natural interpretation of the rhetoric and attitudes expressed at the time in Britain. Whatever the reality, the rhetoric was certainly not that of instrumental rationality, but consisted of appeals to traditional patriotic virtues, appeals which were enthusiastically received. Nor is it the most obvious interpretation of the behaviour of the members of the government and in particular the Prime Minister, Mrs Thatcher, who seemed fully in the grip of these patriotic sentiments. The creation of an image of toughness and resolution (a favourite word with her throughout her premiership) seemed to be a more obvious interpretation of her motives than simply the reoccupation of some unimportant islands (or even to remain in power domestically), while the glamour of war was clearly to be found in the popular press and, in a confused and half-denied way, amongst members of the government themselves. The whole event seemed much more involved with the defining of identity (including self-identity) than with instrumental rationality, for which the argument was rather weak. A part of this identity was the glamour associated with patriotic violence.

The widening of the rational choice framework to examine the origins of preferences more carefully enables it to be adapted and used more fruitfully in the analyses of situations where rationality is

[3] There had been earlier plays in this supergame where other countries had not counter-defected. Thus the Argentinian government had been deeply influenced by the Indian invasion of Goa, in 1961 which had not been countered by other powers. They regarded their position vis-à-vis the Falklands (or Malvinas) as similar to that of the Indians over Goa and assumed the international community would react passively (Dillon 1989).

118

'warped', as in international crises. The rational choice model is still used as the basis for analysis, but the pressures on the decision makers induce such warping, but in systematic and hence analysable ways. This is the subject matter of the next chapter.

7 INTERNATIONAL CRISES: THE WARPING OF RATIONALITY

1 THE NATURE OF INTERNATIONAL CRISES

From time to time, there are crises in the international system – periods when the issues of war and peace appear paramount and where the prospect of war creeps out of the history books and appears a present reality. People watch each news bulletin, and snatch nervously at their newspapers to see whether an impending cataclysm has approached or receded. By its nature, an international crisis represents some deviation from the normal pattern of international behaviour. It is nevertheless a particularly important type of event. It is often these periods of international trauma that trigger off war, and from which new patterns of behaviour emerge or old ones are consolidated. They are not the norm, but they have important consequences, including war, and have therefore been the object of a great deal of study. Decisions in crises also raise further problems in the discussion of rationality.

One of the worrying things about crises is that, while on some occasions people seem to behave with commendable coolness and sense, on others they clearly do not. At precisely the moment when rational assessment and rational decision should be paramount, such procedures are particularly under threat. The crisis of 1914 is often held up with scorn as a case where apparently reckless men plunged the world into the most appalling suffering, whereas, so it would appear, a little common sense would have avoided a great deal of bother. However, a closer look at 1914 shows a different picture. The leaders of the various countries and their senior advisors were for the most part neither fools nor rogues. Lord Asquith and Sir Edward Grey, the two most influential British decision makers, were intelligent and humane men, as were their advisors. Neither the German nor the French Foreign Offices were staffed by rascals or idiots. Admittedly neither the Kaiser in Germany nor the Czar in Russia were very balanced men, and the latter, by common consent, including that

120

of his wife, was rather stupid. However, these two did not make the First World War on their own. How, then, did this group of men manage to persuade themselves that the only possible way of resolving the dilemma they were in was to go to war? Put more generally, it appears that on occasion crises get out of hand and escalate in ways in which the participants, often in general sane and sober people, feel caught in a trap from which they cannot escape. It is easy to dismiss this sort of behaviour as just another example of human folly. However, it is more useful to analyse the causes of this behaviour and see whether procedures can be devised which improve decision taking in these situations.

2 DEFINITIONS AND ATTRIBUTES

Clear cases of international crises, as the phrase is used in normal speech, are the Cuban Missile Crisis of 1962, the crisis over Berlin in 1948, the Munich Crisis of 1938, the crisis of the summer of 1914, and the multitude of crises among the various European powers in the two decades before the First World War. Many other cases could be included, but, for the moment, we shall concern ourselves with a definition which encompasses these.

A crisis involves five factors. Three I shall take as defining characteristics and two as contingent but which appear to be always present (Hermann 1972). The first defining characteristic is that the crisis concerns very important matters such as war and peace and perhaps the very existence of the society in question. The second is that there is an abnormal degree of uncertainty about the outcome of the crisis. There is a significant possibility of a really disastrous conclusion to it. The gap between the best and worst likely solutions is very great as compared to that between the best and worst solutions of any normal uncertain situation. The third characteristic of a crisis is that it takes place over a relatively short period of time. Of the contingent characteristics, the first is that there is an abnormally large flow of information in the system. The second is that the decision makers work under a much higher degree of pressure than is normal.[1]

---

[1] It is often argued that a further characteristic of a crisis is that it must be a surprise to someone (Hermann 1972). If a crisis could be planned for in advance, then the pressures on the decision makers which are the crucial characteristics of a crisis situation would be much reduced. The general events in the crisis might still have been predicted. Thus the Soviet leaders in 1962 knew that they had missiles in Cuba and that the United States would object. They may have underestimated the vigour of the United States' action, and in this sense it was a crisis for them as well. Though we know much less about the Soviet decision making at the time than we do about the American, nevertheless it seems clear that a crisis decision-making structure existed

All these characteristics must be examined in more detail. The first and second are general ones, found in contexts other than the international. A crisis in medicine (where the word originated) is a period of doubt when the patient could die – which is typically regarded as disastrous – or recover, essentially restoring the *status quo ante*. The utility interval – if the term is appropriate – between these two extreme alternatives is very wide, particularly for the patient. Similarly, in international crises there is a short period in which the chances of war breaking out become really significant (a conclusion which only a few would regard as anything but very unfortunate). The alternative, much preferred, is a peaceful resolution to the crisis, either by a compromise or a return to the *status quo ante*. In both the medical and international examples, disaster is abnormal. In both cases, the usual state is one where there is only a small probability of disaster in the near future from unexpected causes (a heart attack or a sudden invasion by a neighbour), but where there is a constant significant possibility that some situation will become a little disadvantageous (the patient or potential patient may catch a cold, or the country may suffer some diplomatic reverse). Normality involves moderate chances of small reverses. A crisis, however, involves high chances of large reverses, which is what makes it so disturbing.

To turn to the third characteristic first, international crises of the type we are considering normally last a few days or weeks. In this period, the rate at which decisions have to be made and information circulated, both within and between the various foreign decision-making organisations, is much greater than normal. This speed of operation has a number of consequences, such as that the full decision-making and consultative process cannot always be gone through properly, a more superficial and rapid selection and inspection of the documentation takes place, and the individuals involved in the decision-making process are put under severe mental and physical pressures which may distort their judgements. These, then, are added features of the crisis situation which we must examine, but notice that they are consequences of the defining features rather than the defining features themselves. There are many situations in which a decision maker is placed under abnormal stress, so it would be inappropriate to define a crisis, whether international or otherwise, in terms of such stress.

The relevance of the two contingent features is as follows. The above definitions do not in fact require that there should be a large

on the Soviet side. However, Brecher, Wilkenfeld and Moser find that the surprise element is less significant than one would intuitively suppose.

amount of information going between states and around the decision-making structures within the states. It is possible to envisage a simple crisis where the issues and relevant facts were perfectly simple. However, they do not seem to occur. All the crises which have been studied seem to exhibit a vast increase in communications.

The final characteristic is a consequence of the rest. If there is a large volume of work, not much time, and the work concerns important decisions, decision takers are under pressure. While this is simple to observe, its consequences are important.

In a monumental work, *Crises in the Twentieth Century*, Brecher, Wilkenfeld and Moser (1988) define crises more broadly. As their work is the biggest single empirical study of crises to date, I should at least relate their different definitions to mine and explain the reasons for the difference. Brecher and colleagues call the crisis as looked at from the point of view of the state and its decision-making apparatus a 'Foreign Policy Crisis', and where the crisis is looked at from the point of view of the system as a whole, an 'International Crisis'. It follows that an international crisis must be a foreign policy crisis for at least one state and commonly more. In the period studied there are 278 international crises and 627 foreign policy crises according to their definitions. The definition of 'foreign policy crisis' is rather close to the one given above, but differs in one major feature. They argue that what is important in giving a crisis its distinguishing characteristics is not a short time but a finite time. Thus of the crises they study 36 per cent took longer than ninety days, which is beginning to get to the limit of what can be referred to as a 'short time'. As to whether shortness as such is important, it depends on the questions we want to look at. As I am particularly concerned with decisions under pressure, the short-ness of time is a major feature and must be retained in the type of analysis to be considered below. The difference in definition comes from the difference in the types of questions which are to be addressed. Brecher, Wilkenfeld and Moser are looking at a broader class of questions. They also consider crises which take place in wartime. This makes no difference to the basic analysis of this chapter except that wartime crises are likely to take place in an environment where there is a greater expectation of crises than normal.

It is still appropriate to ask whether a crisis in this clear-cut sense is as sharply separated from non-crisis situations as this analysis would suggest. Is there not a continuum along a normal–crisis spectrum in which events become more and more crisis-like? Also, is the decision taking in crisis really so very different from the normal, or is it simply more of the same only done more quickly? The answers, based on a mass of empirical work, favour the view that crises are distinct phenomena and that the dichotomy normal–crisis is the relevant formulation rather than the spectrum. Decision making really is different.

The characteristics of a crisis which normally, though not invariably, come about are all interrelated, but fall conveniently under two heads, which I shall call the *structural* and the *psychological*. The structural are those which concern the structure of the decision making in the sense of who takes decisions and how they communicate amongst themselves. The psychological are those which concern the mental attitudes of the decision makers, and, in particular, how they perceive the world in these fraught circumstances. This chapter concentrates on both these features.

3   ADJUSTMENT TO OVERLOAD

The decision maker in a crisis is facing a very complex set of problems which have to be solved quickly. Complexity is an ever-present feature of the decision maker's life, though it may increase at such a time. It is the severity of the time constraint and the seriousness of the issues involved which provide the complicating factors. The central problem comes in reducing the complexity of the situation to manageable proportions. How to deal with complex situations is a classical problem in any sort of decision-making situation. We have in some ways to simplify it and hence distort it. We want to minimise the distortions and concentrate on the crucial issues in the problem, accepting that in the details there may be mistakes. There may not be an optimum way of reducing complexity, but nevertheless some ways are better than others.

Often the increased information is not really coped with – the system suffers an 'information overload'. Data are not processed; reports go unread or, when read, are not assimilated by the relevant decision maker in such a way that they feature appropriately in making the decision. However, there is normally some sort of adjustment, though whether the most appropriate one is often open to doubt.

A core issue is to reduce the information which swamps the decision maker. The problem is to decide what information shall be excluded. While the simple answer is 'the unimportant information', the dilemma is that normally we do not know what is unimportant until we know what it is. We have to make some prior judgements about what categories of information are likely to be unimportant in order to exclude them.

First, consider the structural responses. As far as structure is concerned, an apparently paradoxical feature of crisis decision making is that the group responsible for taking the central decisions in the crisis gets smaller, despite the fact that there is more do do. Brecher, Wilkenfeld and Moser find in their study that of foreign policy crises 78 per cent had decision-making groups of ten people or fewer and 51 per cent had only four people or fewer. There was some slight tendency for democratic regimes to have larger decision-making groups, but still 69 per cent consisted of ten people or fewer. There was also some rather ambiguous evidence suggesting that the more serious crises involved smaller decision-making groups rather than larger.

The paradox is more apparent than real. Information comes to the decision-making unit from different countries, from sources outside the government, and from other parts of the government machinery. While some outside information can be ruled out *a priori* as unimportant, coming from third and largely irrelevant parties, much needs to be attended to. The inside information can be reduced, however. In a non-crisis decision, various different points of view can be entertained, that is, a large amount of information can be considered and weighed up against other, perhaps contradictory, information. In a crisis this luxury must be denied. The small group, other things being equal, will generate fewer options than a large group. That is, internal information will be reduced and relieve the pressure on the decision takers.

Unfortunately, things are not equal, and there are pressures towards reducing internal dissent yet further. The group which is selected will tend to be more homogeneous than the normal group. The selection will be made from people who agree on essentials and who will not 'waste time' debating a wide range of issues, using up the precious commodity of time, quite apart from emotional energy. Further, even if deviants should appear in the group, they will start to be excluded from the group meetings as it is found that they take up too much of the group's time debating issues. This is not difficult. Such a group is informal with informal meetings, and is rarely constitutionally defined. The exclusion and inclusion of individuals involve no formal procedures. Thus the pressure is continually on the group to become small and homogeneous and in this way cope with the flood of information which is in constant danger of overwhelming it. All this leads to another dilemma. From the point of view of taking decisions quickly, the small homogeneous group is a good thing. However, it excludes the very thing which is desirable in taking an important

125

decision – the exploration of novelty and a sceptical attitude to accepted wisdom. This is going to be brought out by the deviant, and by the discussion of issues. The problem is that these two goals of speed and wide consideration of issues are opposed to each other – the more there is of one, the less there is of the other. The rational decision-taking group would acknowledge this and endeavour to obtain an appropriate balance between them. The problem was essentially recognised in the United States during the Cuban Missile Crisis. Whether decision makers normally think of the problem in this explicit way is doubtful, though the experience of Cuba has had a big influence. Further, there are pressures for a balance not to come about. The immediate problem for the decision makers is to save time and psychic effort in a manner which is immediate and clear. The search for novel alternatives is time-consuming and stressful, and its benefits distant and ambiguous. In this situation the pressure for uniformity tends to win over the search for novelty.

Secondly, we consider the psychological devices for reducing complexity. They too are ways of reducing the amount of information and the number of problems for decision with their attendant psychic strain. The simplest way of dealing with this is to consider only immediate problems and not worry about any underlying presuppositions. This can best be illustrated by an example. In 1914 the British government firmly believed that Germany was expansionary – probably correctly, as the work of Fischer (1967) now seems to indicate. Thus its behaviour was judged in that light by the British government. But in the heat of the crisis this was taken as a given. It was not argued about. Further, it would have been foolish from the decision-making point of view to argue about it. A debate about the underlying motives of an opponent is time-consuming and cannot be brought quickly to a satisfactory conclusion. Hence it is much more appropriate to take them as a given. Thus the procedure is to evaluate current evidence in the light of existing beliefs without questioning them. In 'normal times' (that is, times where the time constraint is not serious), if current evidence appears to contradict prior beliefs, then the evidence is reviewed with care and, if it is confirmed, the prior beliefs are modified (or so we would hope). In times of crisis such a procedure would take too long and the prior beliefs have to be accepted unless there is gross contradiction, where, of course, if people are to be rational, they have to be reconsidered.

Similar processes apply to any moral dilemmas which face decision makers. The easiest way of dealing with a moral dilemma is to deny it. Thus moral ambiguities are dealt with in the same way as empirical ambiguities – a choice is made early on which is relatively impervious to any future developments.

As with the structural problems, there is again the problem of trade-off, to which there is no clear-cut 'rational' answer. Some degree of hardening of pre-existing attitudes is perfectly rational if the problems have to be solved in the near future. However, if there are clear contradictions of previous attitudes, some adjustments should be made. A totally fixed set of basic attitudes is clearly dysfunctional as far as effective decision making is concerned. There is no criterion for fixing an 'optimum' balance between the two.

4 THE INDIVIDUAL'S RESPONSES TO CRISIS

Not all the apparent oddities of crisis decision-taking behaviour can be interpreted as rational responses to complexity and shortness of time. However, the behaviour is easily explicable in terms of perfectly normal psychological processes. The Myth of Leadership, which sneaks surreptitiously into some international relations decision-making literature, hints that leaders are above such pedestrian failings as 'normal psychological processes'. However, there is no reason to suppose that they are not subject to the foibles of the mind just as much as they are subject to the weaknesses of the body.

That decisions in crises are taken by a relatively small group of individuals gives us a fortunate bonus in the investigation of crisis behaviour. We can make direct use of the voluminous work of psychologists on both individual and small group behaviour. In some contexts we can also investigate decisions as taken in 'real-life' situations to confirm or question the results of behaviour in experimental situations. Many of the assertions about crisis behaviour are taken from the findings of psychologists, social and otherwise. The diffidence in doing this felt by some international relations theorists of a traditional stamp is misplaced. Decision makers, even of the highest and most distinguished sort, are human beings, and are subject to the same vagaries of the mind as the rest of us.

While groups and individuals do not always behave in the same ways, groups are made up of individuals. It is therefore useful, before looking at the group, to consider briefly the problems faced by the individual in a crisis.

For the individual, the crisis is characterised by a number of features. The first I shall call *high vulnerability*. Vulnerability is characterised by two things: the degree of unpleasantness of the immediate future and the likelihood of its occurring. Thus, both a high probability of a mildly unfortunate future and a very low probability of a very unpleasant outcome would mean that the individual was not very vulnerable. However, in a crisis, the possibilities of a really bad outcome grow unpleasantly large, so the individual becomes vulnerable as there is now a strong likelihood of their condition changing seriously for the worse.

Secondly, the context is very complex, and in consequence the environment is uncertain. Part of the complexity comes not just from the quantity of information, though this is important, but from the ambiguity of much of it. Definite yes/no answers are not possible to many important questions, while some of the evidence contradicts other bits.

Thirdly, the consequences of choices between alternatives are very different (this is what is meant by 'an important choice'). However, making the choice may be difficult in that the alternatives may have equally attractive (or repulsive) characteristics. The decision taker, in the jargon of decision theory, might be 'indifferent' between the two alternatives. However, such a situation – when the choices involved are very important – is far from being one of not caring, and is in fact very stressful.

Fourthly, this sort of situation, coupled with the other characteristics of a crisis, means that the individual has to work very hard. There is much to do at the simplest level; but in addition, because of the nature of the tasks, the job is likely to be very exhausting.

A dominant characteristic of the members of a crisis decision-making group is that they are under stress. It then becomes a core problem to see how people cope with this, first individually and then as members of the group.

While 'stress' often has a bad name, particularly in popular psychological literature, it is not always detrimental to efficient decision making. In cases where we can measure both the efficiency of decision making and degrees of stress, a common, perhaps universal, pattern appears to be as follows. Some degree of stress improves performance, but performance reaches a peak for some level of stress. If stress goes beyond this point, then performance deteriorates (Anderson 1976; Vroom 1964). This is illustrated in figure 7.1A.

It is also common for performance to decrease catastrophically after some point, as illustrated in figure 7.1B. While the general pattern might be widespread, individuals vary radically in their responses to stress. Some people react badly even to moderate stress, whereas others thrive on high levels of stress. This is illustrated in the two patterns in figure 7.1C.

128

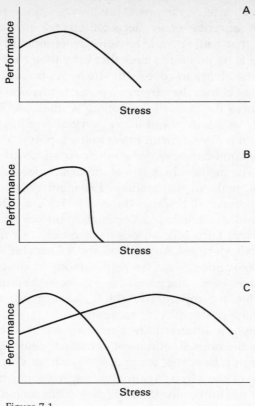

Figure 7.1

Obviously, for people likely to be involved in crises, personalities which can cope with high levels of stress are to be preferred. In many professions, 'crisis control', as broadly defined, is potentially part of the job. For example, airline pilots must be able to cope efficiently with unexpected and very dangerous situations. However, airline pilots are highly selected; one of the characteristics looked for in the selection is that they have personalities likely to be able to cope with high and sudden stress and to act effectively.

Politicians and others likely to be involved in crises are not similarly selected, at least explicitly. However, the sort of progress which politicians have to make in any political system must make them used to high degrees of stress. If they are not able to act effectively under stress, they will not get very far in the profession. All political systems appear to be very competitive (except for hereditary monarchies), and someone climbing in a political system has normally to be able to work

129

efficiently under very tense conditions. Thus there is some form of indirect selection of effective crisis decision takers. However, a common problem is that while people advance professionally whilst coping with stress, it is by no means clear that once they have got to the top they retain the ability to cope with stress. As politicians get older, like other human beings they are more prone to physical illness, which normally reduces the capacity for coping with stress (Roberts 1988; Wiegele 1976). An oddity about many, very different, political systems is that while it is very difficult to get to the top, it is also very difficult to dislodge incumbents, even when their capacities are clearly seriously impaired. The medical histories of important people, when we get hold of them, make dismal reading. President Wilson in the United States was seriously ill towards the end of his life. Churchill was senile while in office, while his earlier medical history as related by his personal doctor, Lord Moran, does not make for consoling reading for the nervous, despite his discretion about Churchill's heavy drinking (Moran 1966). Stalin, had he held a more modest office, would probably have been diagnosed as clinically paranoid. A capacity in earlier life for coping with high stress might decline without the loss of high position by its occupant.

Many people in senior positions during a crisis are relatively elderly, while many are past the normal retirement age of the countries they lead. It is rare, though it happens, for people to acquire very senior office before the age of forty-five. Age may bring wisdom (though I doubt it), but it does not bring physical resilience. Thus an individual who is high in a political decision-taking team may be rather better than the average at operating in such an environment, but there are many cases where this is not so.

The consequences of protracted stress and over-work on individuals are well known. First, of course, they bring fatigue. While this can be counteracted by the adrenalin which is the normal human response to emergency, there is a degree to which the adrenalin merely masks the underlying fatigue and begins to fail after some time. In itself and in moderation this may not be too serious. The leading politician is again typically someone who has had to work very hard, and is used to working while seriously fatigued. However, it leads to other things. If a person is prone to various illnesses, then fatigue and stress aggravate the symptoms. Eden at the time of Suez was a sick man, and it appears that the stress he was under at that time made his condition much worse. If an individual suffers from any psychosomatic disorder (and many do), then the symptoms are likely to appear. Stress-related problems such as backache or headaches are instances. Someone prone to insomnia will find periods of stress likely to bring out the problem. The response to the more painful symptoms of stress is likely to be to take some form of drug. The insomniac will take sleeping pills, the sufferer from backache will take pain-killers and perhaps also sleeping pills, various tranquillisers might be taken and, of course, alcohol is the ready, and socially acceptable, stand-by. This can all aggravate the fatigue and, while making the situation personally more bearable, is unlikely to improve the effectiveness of decision making.

The fact that decision takers are working under extreme pressure puts them in danger of producing distortions in their perceptions both at the individual and the group level. There are a number of forms of perceptual distortion which appear to be common to this sort of event and which were first clearly documented in the detailed study of the 1914 crisis made by Robert North and his colleagues (North et al. 1963), many of which have since been confirmed in later studies as occurring frequently in crises.

It is useful to distinguish between attitudes about the other parties to the crisis and about the scope and nature of the actions which are available to the participant himself. In the first category comes the tendency to see the opponent in stereotyped terms – the Militaristic Prussian, Perfidious Albion, or, at a later date, atheistic communists and war-mongering, imperialistic capitalists. One of the characteristics of extreme images is that anything can be made to conform to the image in one way or another. This leads to another common characteristic of the decision maker's perceptions in such situations, which is to see any attempt at conciliation as either weakness or a trick, rather than taking it for what it might well be, namely a genuine attempt to reach an equitable settlement. If a person has an image of some group as being completely bad, and if the enemy then acts in a manner which would normally be interpreted as good, some less charitable explanation for it has to be found. A conciliatory act is interpreted as having been forced on one's opponent, or else as a deceitful subterfuge designed to mislead one into incautious trust. Third parties to the direct crisis are viewed more and more as being either for or against the perceiving country. The concept of neutrality becomes increasingly hard for the parties to believe in – the world is viewed as being polarised into the extreme positions.

None of these tendencies is unique to crisis situations. However, in a crisis, these tendencies, which are found to some degree in any hostile international situation, are markedly strengthened. The whole process appears to be one in which normally sophisticated decision makers adopt progressively less and less sophisticated attitudes as the crisis develops. Simplistic pictures of the world replace the complex reality. Anger and fear make people resort to primitive emotions and lose their veneer of civilised sophistication. This is particularly unfortunate as it is in times of tension, when decisions might have fateful consequences, that clear, sophisticated analysis is particularly desirable.

The decision makers' views of the freedom of decision available comprise the second category of perceptions. This is a perception not so much of the other decision maker as of the decision-making environment as a whole. Perhaps the most significant characteristic of the situation is that the available alternatives appear to narrow as the situation becomes more tense. The decision makers see the situation as one in which they are almost the tools of circumstance, and the decisions they legitimately make become narrowly circumscribed, giving them little room for manoeuvre. This, of course, can easily lead to an amplification of the crisis, simply because there is no longer a search for alternatives, particularly heterodox ones. If one's own field of choice is narrowly circumscribed, then the situation can be remedied only by an action of the other side. However, if the other side feels similarly, then nothing is done to break away from what appears to be a preordained pattern – with the risk of adverse results.

With the feeling of being constrained in decision comes a reduction in the care with which the effects of potentially violent acts are evaluated. Decisions are made emotionally, without rational consideration of the potentialities of the situation from a strategic point of view. Further, the rewards of violence are seen as greater, and the dangers of delay in initiating a military programme as more serious than in times of less stress. Strategic caution dwindles, and the advocates of military vigour begin to dominate – the hawks gain influence, and the doves are ignored.

Most of the features described above can be seen as a direct consequence of the reduced tolerance for uncertainty and ambiguity. The ambiguity comes from information whose meaning is unclear, or which contradicts other information. Ambiguity is a difficult state of mind to tolerate. Many people find the notion of 'not knowing' difficult to cope with at the best of times, and are ready to jump prematurely into states of belief not justified by the available evidence. This characteristic is reinforced in episodes of stress such as at times of crisis. The strain of coping with ambiguity increases, and the easiest solution is to deny the uncertainty. From the point of view of reducing stress, an effective way is to adopt a particular picture of the situation – typically in conformity with one's pre-existing prejudices – and use information to confirm that, and exclude contradictory information. The effort of changing one's mind, or dealing with contradictory information, is then reduced. Ways of doing this are by stereotyping the images of other actors as recorded above; and by interpreting the actions and intentions of rivals and friends with much more confidence than the situation would suggest. All this is interpretable quite easily in terms of mechanisms for the reduction of stress which are a feature of coping with ambiguous situations.

Added to this, and aggravating it, are certain personal and cultural factors. Even outside tense situations, individuals vary greatly in their ability to tolerate ambiguity. While in general such toleration would be thought a desirable attribute in a decision taker, as situations are often ambiguous, it is sometimes, rather oddly, thought of as an attribute of weak people. There is a widespread confusion between being decisive and denying ambiguity. Being decisive is taking clear decisions when it is necessary, perhaps in the knowledge that it is a gamble. However, if decision takers deny the ambiguity and take the decision 'decisively' because they deny the full complexity of it, this is an undesirable attribute. It leads to decisions being taken, but often the wrong ones. Being decisive is regarded as 'tough' and 'strong' which is how many decision makers see themselves, though it often leads to horrendous results. Unfortunately the desire to appear tough and decisive in crises is strengthened, particularly by people who are afraid they may not have these attributes, and taking time to analyse complex situations is often regarded as being weak and indecisive.

5   THE GROUP'S RESPONSES TO CRISIS

So far I have concentrated on the response of the individual to stress and crisis. However, the individuals are in groups which themselves modify various forms of behaviour. Irving Janis, a social psychologist, has produced one of the most perceptive pieces of work on crisis behaviour in his book *Groupthink* (1982). Basically, Janis applies some of the findings of social psychology to investigate crisis behaviour and, in particular, to interpret some of the curiosities of behaviour in terms of a phenomenon called 'groupthink', which I shall discuss shortly. In this section I shall be discussing this phenomenon but relating it to more classical decision theories to interpret the one in terms of the other. This relates directly to the issues of rationality which we discussed earlier and which will be taken up again later on.

Briefly, 'groupthink' is as follows. Suppose a group is collectively taking a decision of importance where the situation is stressful. It need not be a crisis as defined, though crises would be one of the types of situation considered. Each individual is trying to work out the best set of decisions to take. They all try to persuade their fellows of the virtues of their own preferred solutions, while being open to persuasion of the virtues of the others. However, there are other factors at work. In particular, a powerful incentive is the approval of one's colleagues. In an ideal world, approval would be given, and seen to be given, to the person who had the most interesting ideas, and whose judgement was shrewd. However, this is not always the case. An urge to conform to the group norm is a powerful motive, as is shown both by many experiments and much casual observation. This urge to agree is a major feature of groupthink. It can lead to the group not fully evaluating the existing alternatives or searching for new ones simply because the main goal of consensus is reached – often prematurely. The risk of breaking this consensus appears to the actors (albeit unconsciously) to be greater than the risk of a faulty decision. There are many cases of individuals subsequently reporting unease with the way a discussion was going but not wanting to oppose the apparent consensus. Perhaps more powerful, however, is that people's opinions quite genuinely move towards the group mean, particularly in matters such as estimates of uncertainty, which are inherently judgements, and cannot be justified by 'objective' criteria. If the issue under review is the possibility of something harmful happening (an example discussed by Janis is the raid on Pearl Harbor), then doubters who are afraid of the dreadful event will be reassured by the others, who confidently assert that everything is safe. They allow their views to be moved in the direction which they would like to be true, and push their doubts to one side. This is, of course, a form of self-deceit – a common and often-discussed phenomenon (Elster 1986). This creates a reassuring atmosphere. The short-term goal of low psychic cost is achieved.

Of particular interest is the comparison made by Janis between the Bay of Pigs disaster and the Cuban Missile Crisis. In the two cases many of the core decision makers were the same. In the first, groupthink appears to have taken place, whereas in the second it did not (or at least, much less so). According to the descriptions of the participants (who were given to publication on a large scale, even by the standards of senior politicians), the second was much more stressful for the participants than the first. If they had allowed themselves to indulge in groupthink on the second occasion, they may have had an easier time during the crisis.

However, the consequences . . .

While groupthink is frequently found, fortunately it is by no means universal. According to Janis, groupthink is likely to be a feature of groups characterised by four factors. First, the group is insulated during the period of decision; secondly, there is a lack of tradition of impartial leadership in the sense that the leaders tend to impose their views; thirdly, there is a lack of norms requiring methodical procedures; and fourthly, there is a high level of homogeneity amongst the group members. The absence of these characteristics makes for more appropriate forms of decision making. These characteristics readily lead to a group with excessive deference to a leader. This makes a challenge to the leader by a would-be nonconformist and doubter psychologically difficult, itself leading to stress. Such a structure also imposes particularly strong feelings in favour of group approval – which, if the rest are also deferential, can mean that the pleasing of the leader is the greatest reward.

All these features lead to the warping of rational judgement. Human beings are under pressure to move away from rational forms of decision making at the very times when rationality is most needed.

6   CRISIS AND RATIONALITY

The problems stressed in this chapter have concerned other types of issues than the earlier chapters on rationality. Often the crisis situation heightens the awareness of the decision takers that they are in a 'chicken' situation, where there is no optimum within the structure for which they can aim. Thus, the best they can do is operate on 'weak rationality' principles. Further, even these might be in jeopardy in view of the serious time constraints, which means that any sort of rational decision takes the form of a rather weakened version of satisficing. There is a serious problem even under the best of situations.

The tenor of this chapter has been that even these weak rationality principles might be abandoned. The psychological pressures under which decision makers operate mean that there are strong tendencies for the decision taking to move further and further away from any principles of rationality, however weak, and result in decisions which are based on emotion and prejudice. There is a large amount of evidence to suggest that this is what has happened in many actual crises in the past.

While it would be dangerous to be over-sanguine, the story is not totally bleak. There are three reasons for some hope in a generally rather dismal tale. First, the issue of crisis decision making is one about which there is a great deal of self-consciousness in both academic and decision-making circles. While one would like to think that this was because the work of social scientists had been absorbed into decision-making circles, in fact this attention is more due to the decision making in the Cuban Missile Crisis and its perceived success.[2] Prior to the crisis, Kennedy had explicitly thought of the problems of crisis decision taking and, apparently influenced by his reading of Barbara Tuchman's *The Guns of August*, had devised a number of principles which he applied when the time came. Aware of the dangers of quick response and small decision-making groups, he devised the opposite on the American side. The decision-making group was quite deliberately enlarged in order to promote discussion, in the hope that a wider selection of alternatives would appear. Further, the group was explicitly allowed as much time as possible for discussion, to avoid the dangers of immediate emotional reactions. The technique seems to have worked as a deliberate device for provoking relatively calm responses. The trauma of the Missile Crisis, along with its handling, has led to an explicit consideration of the problems of crisis decision making, so there is at least a great deal of awareness among decision makers of the problems.[3]

The second reason is perhaps a consequence of the first. The general tendencies in crisis decision making to move away from rationality and abandon the search for novel solutions have not always been found in other cases. The Israeli decision-taking procedures in the 1967 and 1973 crises, while confirming various standard findings such as the existence and effects of stress, do not really confirm many others (Brecher 1980). There continued to be a broadened search for a wider set of alternatives. For example, Brecher's study suggests that, at least in these two cases, the procedures were as rational as the situation permitted. While the pressures are still undoubtedly present in crises, the wide consciousness of the weaknesses involved justifies at least a hope that some sort of social learning has taken place.

The third reason for a restrained optimism is, in its turn, a special case of the second. Janis points out that groupthink, though a common process, is by no means inevitable. There is some speculative evidence for suggesting which factors militate in favour, and which

---

[2] The classic study of the Cuban Missile Crisis is by Graham Allison (1971). He discusses it in terms of three models – the rational actor, the organisational processes and the bureaucratic processes models. He shows how aspects of decision taking which are paradoxical in one model are quite naturally explained in terms of the others.

[3] The January 1989 issue of *World Politics* is largely devoted to 'The Rational Deterrence Debate: A Symposium', in which the merits and drawbacks of the rational actor model are major topics.

against, the development of the groupthink phenomenon. It is something which can be guarded against by the sufficiently aware decision-making group – preferably in advance of any crisis developing.

The weakness is that, while it is relatively easy for people to understand that the decision-making structures may be inadequate for some purposes and even, at some abstract level, to be able to see the reasons for this, it is hard to accept that one's own mental processes might be subject to some sort of warping in particular circumstances. The sort of personality who achieves high political office is unlikely to be psychologically self-aware. To suggest to political leaders that they are showing signs of paranoia seems virtually impossible to do, despite the fact that the condition seems fairly common. Leaders, in fact, are more likely to be unusually offended at any suggestion that they are coping unrealistically with pressure.[4]

The analysis of crisis behaviour by social scientists is a clear case of trying to develop a theory in the hope that it will be self-refuting. Once people understand how previous crises have developed according to the theory, they will try and operate according to some different set of principles, so that its predictions do not come true. The accounts in this chapter are depressing for anyone with the future of the human race at heart. A consoling reflection is that more understanding of the problems is being achieved, and is more sympathetically viewed in decision-making circles than most other aspects of the discipline.

[4] Self-aware personalities who did achieve high office, such as Willi Brandt of the Federal Republic of Germany, found such self-awareness a serious drawback in other circumstances. There are probably others. One of the few cases of a successful and self-aware politician appears to have been Pandit Nehru of India.

RATIONAL BEHAVIOUR AND RATIONAL CHOICE: AN ASSESSMENT

In the previous chapters I have analysed the concept of decision and in particular rational decision and applied it to some problems of conflict in the international system. I shall now give a brief assessment of its usefulness in the analysis of such problems.

The simple concept of rationality applies quite well in some conflict problems, such as those which can be modelled in terms of a zero-sum game, and indeed in many non-zero-sum games, though I have not shown that here. It provides 'solutions' in the sense of demonstrating how players, defined in some sense as rational, will play the game – or at least ought to play the game if they are governed by the motives we attribute to them. A solution exists if the best strategy player A can play against a particular strategy of player B is such that player B cannot gain anything by changing strategy. The significance of the solutions are that they are a key to the rational playing of a game. If a solution exists, then each rational player should act so as to achieve that solution. If there are no solutions, then it is much less clear what rational play consists of. The formulation of such solutions is impressive, as noted in the chapter on zero-sum games, and is a triumph of the theory of games.

However, triumph though it may be in certain contexts, it leaves many problems unsolved. There are three difficulties I have pursued. First, many non-zero-sum games do not have solutions in any normal game-theory sense. These are not curious oddities of no importance but, like the game of chicken, often model situations of great importance for the substantive analysis of conflict. Secondly, even when games do have solutions, the solution is sometimes obviously inadequate, as in the game of prisoners' dilemma, where both players could gain more from moving away from the 'solution' on an agreed basis. Thirdly, the standard concept of a rational decision assumes a greater clarity of purpose than is often the case in real decision making, and for any useful theory of decision, whether descriptive or normative, there has to be a closer analysis of concepts such as 'preference', 'goal' and so on.

138

Nevertheless, it is admirable as a general basis for a scientific research programme, and it is as such that I see its basic usefulness. The general approach is of very practical use in two ways, which I shall elaborate. First, these methods are very convenient for representing the structures of various forms of conflict; secondly, it is a useful base from which to reach out and develop theories of broader conflicts involving complex human beings.

By 'the structure of a game' I refer to whether it is zero-sum or non-zero-sum, whether it is chicken or prisoners' dilemma, whether it is two-person or multi-person and so on. I also refer to whether the actors can be regarded for the relevant purposes as unitary, whether there are linkages between sub-groups within different actors – the range of categories is large but comprehensible. To find the structure is a large part of trying to analyse a conflict. While not all these structures permit a solution in the game-theory sense, a knowledge of what the structure is is an important start.

When there is no solution to a game, as in the limited game of chicken, it does not mean that reason provides no help in such situations. We should not be overawed by the solution concept, useful though it is when it exists. That real life is sometimes disagreeably indeterminate sometimes means that solutions are imposed on problems for which they are not really appropriate. However, because a situation does not have a solution, it does not mean that we have to give up in despair. Rationality in the sense of the application of reason is still relevant. We know that, if people behave in certain ways, certain results will follow, and at least we are provided with guides to action.

It is sometimes asserted that the theory of games does not allow for emotions and non-rational behaviour, but applies only to the purely rational being. The analysis of Von Neumann and Morgenstern was the analysis of people who followed particular rules to maximise the pay-offs which were given externally to the game. Indeed I think this is how they saw it – conflict between rational people who all had the same general view of the world. However, the same sort of analysis still applies, even if one player in the game follows some irrational rule. Suppose that one player in a game selects the strategy not according to the maximin principle but according to some astrological criterion. If the rival realises this, it would be irrational to follow the maximin rule, as the characteristic of the opponent could be exploited and a larger pay-off result. The game could be analysed as a game of 'astrologer' versus 'maximiser', and solutions and strategies derived. Similarly, if an opponent is known to have religious beliefs which will

139

affect their conduct in a conflict, these can be likewise exploited. The Yom Kippur War is an example of the use of such a strategy. This is an extension of the theory from the original, which is the analysis of the play of rational players, where the players are all rational, but it seems a quite proper extension to go beyond this. Whether one still wants to call this 'game theory' is merely a terminological matter. Pure or classical game theory is a very convenient base from which to move out to the study of these broader classes of problem.

There are other ways in which rationality comes into play. Through looking at the problems in simple terms (and sensibly, so as to get at their structure), we obscure the fact that real-life decision problems are complex and fraught with uncertainty. We often do not know the full facts of the situation in significant and relevant respects. In contrast to the games we have studied in chapters 3–5, we do not know the goals and preferences of the rivals with any degree of certainty. The argument of chapter 6 was that actors themselves often did not know their own preferences too clearly, never mind their opponents. Such problems are aggravated when conflicts arise between very different cultures. Again rationality in a broader sense need not fly out of the window. Problems can be approached rationally or incompetently. We have to try to assess, in a complex and ambiguous world, whether a game is chicken, prisoners' dilemma or whatever, which is itself a part of a rational analysis of a situation. In effect this means that, even if a rational criterion for action is missing, there is still the need for formulating rational beliefs about a situation. There are also efficient and inefficient ways of indicating our preferences and strategies to an opponent. If we are afraid that a chicken game may get out of hand, in that an opponent has convinced us that any defection on our part will be punished, then we have to be very careful not to mislead the opponent inadvertently into thinking that we are playing aggressively. We have not only to be unaggressive, but to be seen to be unaggressive. It is equally important to be seen as vindictive in cases of chicken where we wish to deter. In both the Falklands/Malvinas War (1982) and the Iraqi invasion of Kuwait (1990) the earlier signals given by those who in fact responded were at best ambiguous if not totally misleading. The speedy communications between the super-powers, which have been seen to be necessary since the Cuban Missile Crisis, are a more positive symptom of the awareness that any mistaken perception can and should be corrected as quickly as possible. It has been suggested (by Paul Bracken (1983)), that the dangers of crises getting out of hand are greater with present technology than was the case twenty or thirty years ago. Thus the rational thing to do is to try to avoid crises as well as to operate as effectively as possible within them. Hence, though the basic problem which is central to the chicken game leaves us without any rational principle of choice, it does not mean that rationality is totally absent from the situation in which chicken occurs. It is a part of rationality to work out when there is no principle of choice, and not to imagine that somewhere or other there is one.

The third way in which the rational choice research programme needs developing is in expanding the notion of preference. Chapters 6 and 7 moved away from the simple notion of preference, the first in a general sense and the second in relation to international crises. Classical game theory shares with economics the view that preferences are to be taken as given and neither evaluated nor explained. While this is a useful basis to start from, it is also rather narrow. If we enquire into the origin of preferences and the reasons why they change we get into more complex problems, but ones which are necessary if we are to add to the analysis of real conflicts as opposed to their mathematical abstractions. This again extends the concept of game theory, but once more in an important direction.

The further game theory goes beyond the initial rational model to incorporate a broader set of phenomena, the more useful it becomes. One of its uses is to direct attention to those situations which cannot be solved in a meaningful sense so that we do not delude ourselves into thinking we are in a comfortable equilibrium position guaranteed by the mutual self-interest of all the participants.

PART III
RATIONAL BELIEF: SOME TOPICS IN CONFLICT ANALYSIS

An aspect of rational behaviour is rational belief. Criteria for belief in generalisations as distinct from propositions about specific events are what characterise the social sciences. Central to this is statistical analysis, though of course it is not the whole story. The use and limitations of statistical methods in the analysis of war are considered. In this part, some issues of conflict on the international scene are discussed which both are substantively important and also illustrate the ways in which we try to establish propositions about social behaviour and consider their truth or otherwise.

8 THE STATISTICAL ANALYSIS OF WARLIKE PHENOMENA

One of the crucial tasks for an analysis of warlike behaviour is the formulation of theories of how human beings actually behave in relevant situations. We are trying to discover the causes of war, though this involves finding the causes of a large number of ancillary phenomena also. To analyse such things meaningfully, we make hypotheses about what factors relate to war and other relevant phenomena. These may be *ad hoc* hypotheses which seem plausible, though we aspire to groups of hypotheses bound together in a deductive framework as described in chapter 2. These hypotheses are generalisations about classes of events and are not concerned only with specific, individual events. If we want to know whether arms races precede wars or not, or how certain sorts of alliance formation relate to war, then we examine instances of these phenomena and endeavour to make appropriate generalisations. That is, we hypothesise some relationships and then test them. This is particularly critical when we come to talk of policy. If we wish to know whether a particular alliance pattern is likely to promote stability and peace or otherwise, we approach it as an instance of a generalisation about alliances and war. Choices are made in the light of expectations about the future: hence we need rational bases for these expectations. They should not be just the result of prejudice and intuition.

The generalisations we make about such international phenomena (or for that matter about virtually all social phenomena) are *statistical* or *probabilistic*. They reflect tendencies towards certain forms of behaviour which do not apply in every single case but only in some percentage of the cases. We cannot predict cause and effect in social affairs as we can with a falling stone. In what ways should we formulate rational beliefs in these generalisations? Statistical methods, based on the theory of probability, are widely considered appropriate in giving us grounds for rational belief; but are they appropriate in a

145

study of the causes of war? In this chapter I shall describe the principles and problems of statistical hypotheses and give one particular example of a statistical study of the incidence of warfare. In later chapters there will be other examples. The description is in part its own justification.

Statistics is a method of analysing groups of phenomena to see what relationships exist between the different characteristics of things. Thus, we might take a group of events such as the number of live births which take place in the United Kingdom in some particular year. If we are interested in infant mortality, then we will count the number of children born in the year who die within a year of their birth. To investigate the causes of infant mortality we look for factors which might affect it. Thus we might compare births which take place in hospital and those which take place elsewhere to see if the infant mortality rate is the same in each group. If it is different, then we enquire whether the difference can reasonably be ascribed to chance, or whether there may be some reason for it. A comparison of observed data with the 'random hypothesis' – that is, chance – is central to much statistical analysis. If the differences are unlikely to be chance variations, then we can further refine the questions and ask whether it makes any difference whether the baby is delivered by a doctor or a midwife. We can go on in this way, grouping the births of babies in various different ways, to see what factors relate consistently to high and low infant mortality. In other words, we are using an analysis of the group of events to see if we can pick out systematic factors relating to infant mortality in a situation in which we suppose that there may be many such factors.

This approach is extremely useful when we are dealing with large numbers of events such as the birth of children. When we are dealing with small groups of events, the method is much less reliable. However, wars are events which take place with great frequency in social life. We discuss just how frequently in section 2 below. The initial insights of statistical analysis into the causes of war come from examining the correlations between variables to see whether they move together and if so how. Simply finding a relationship is not the same as identifying a causal relationship, but it does give us some idea of where to start our theorising.

An objection to the statistical analysis of war is that all wars are different. However, this is true of most social events to which statistical analysis is applied, such as car accidents. A different combination of events leads to each accident, but this does not preclude us from generalising about the phenomenon. The same is

146

true of war. All wars are different, but it seems unlikely that, in the 315 wars reported by Richardson as having taken place between 1820 and 1949, some characteristics were not shared by groups of wars (Richardson 1960b). It seems more plausible to hypothesise that there are some connecting links than that there are none.

The wars that we fight or threaten to fight today are not the same as those we fought a century ago. The speed of communications and the vast change in arms ('improvement' seems hardly the word) combine to make war different in many significant respects. War, however, has still not changed completely. The human beings involved in making the decisions are much the same as they were. They still take decisions in similar small groups such as Cabinets. Thus, nuclear bombs, supersonic fighters and literate generals notwithstanding, there remain common elements in the factors pertaining to war. While it is foolish to assume that we can simply extrapolate from the past to the present, it is equally foolish to assume that there are no consistencies.

The testing of hypotheses by statistical means is possible only if the statistics exist. Fortunately there is now a large amount of data on warlike events, so that meaningful analyses can be carried out. Studies were carried out in the inter-war years by Sorokin, Wright and Richardson. Sorokin's work was part of an enormously ambitious treatise on the development of society called *Social and Cultural Dynamics*. Quincy Wright, an international lawyer, who added to this an extensive historical knowledge and a vast, intellectual imagination, headed a team at the University of Chicago to produce another large and ambitious work called *A Study of War* (1947), which involved, amongst much analysis, statistics of war from medieval times to the present. Richardson took a narrower focus – though by most criteria still broad enough – and collected data from 1816 to 1949, a period ending only shortly before his death in 1953. Richardson was elected a Fellow of the Royal Society for his work in meteorology and was also a good mathematician. His work in the study of international conflict was much the most rigorous statistically and intellectually and, for all the developments which have been made in statistical technique and the mathematical social sciences, it is still a formidable piece of social scientific work worth consulting in its own right and not just out of historical curiosity. The work of these scholars meant that by 1950 there was a large, but largely ignored, body of work. During the 1950s the neglect was remedied. Many data-collection projects were initiated (Cioffi-Revilla 1990), prominent being the Correlates of War project under the leadership of David Singer and Melvin Small. Like Richardson's work, the data collected in this project relate to the world since the Napoleonic Wars. The statistical work described both in this chapter and the rest of the book owes its origins mainly to the compilations and often the analyses of either Richardson or Singer and Small.[1]

2   THE QUANTITY OF VIOLENCE

A study of war, or of any other phenomenon, begins with classifying the data in some manner. Obvious ways of classifying wars are according to who fights them, the number of participants, the type of cause and so on. However, an initial difficulty in analysing wars is defining what a single war is. This is simply illustrated by the case of the Second World War. There was clearly a war between Germany and the Soviet Union and between Germany and the United States, but over very different things. It is not obvious to what extent these were part of the same war, except that both the USA and the USSR happened to be fighting Germany at the same time. Clearly it was not just coincidence, but the communality of interests was small. The reasons for the British quarrel with Japan were only loosely related to Britain's war against Germany, while Japan and the USSR were not at war at all except briefly and technically at the very end of the hostilities. We can extend this and ask whether the Spanish Civil War, which preceded the Second World War, should not really be included as part of it. It was certainly more closely related to the European war than the British–Japanese hostilities. Hence, while it is conventional to regard the Second World War as a single war, this depends on definitions of war which are to some extent arbitrary. Admittedly this is an extreme example, and most wars do not produce quite the complexities of either of the two world wars, which should perhaps be regarded as special phenomena. There remains a problem. Superficially separate wars are sometimes intimately related so that one seems a continuation of the other (as in the pre-1914 Balkans), while other apparently single wars are a complex interweaving of several different disputes. None of this invalidates our analyses – it merely introduces a note of caution, and we are, after all, following in the paths of historians in the classifications.

Given an acceptable definition, we want to classify wars according to some significant characteristics such as size. This is an obvious way of getting some indication of their importance and, in any case, the size itself is a matter of significance. In this section we shall discuss the way in which Richardson and most subsequent writers approached

[1] A discussion of currently available data sets is contained in Cioffi-Revilla (1990).

the problem of size, and the difficulties involved in defining the concept.

One obvious indicator of the size of a war is the number of people killed. Other possibilities are the amount of destruction or the number of people both killed and injured. The objection to the amount of destruction is that it is very difficult to measure, both because of the difficulty of getting raw data and then of evaluating them. Monetary value is, at best, a crude guide. There are a number of arbitrary steps involved in any attempt to compare the value of a peasant's hut destroyed in 1870 with a power station destroyed in 1940. However, a death occurring in 1870 and one in 1940 are more obviously comparable. The difficulty with a measure which includes casualties lies in the definition of 'wounded', which can vary widely. Furthermore, counts of wounded, particularly in earlier wars, were very rough and ready. The figures of people dead are more likely to have some semblance of accuracy – although possibly not much, as the very different estimates of deaths for the same battles testify. At least they are more dependable than those based on any other criterion.

A virtue of using size as a classification system is that it is reasonably objective and does not involve any difficulties over the legal definition of war. For the purposes of the social scientist (and often the moralist), our prime interest is in the fact that a large-scale, violent conflict involving deaths took place. Many large conflicts were not international wars. In recent times, neither the Spanish Civil War nor the Vietnam War were wars between conventionally defined states. To exclude them from the analysis of violence would, however, be foolish. The distinctions between, say, revolutions, civil wars and international wars are important, of course, even from the point of view of the social scientist, but ignoring these distinctions may also be revealing, and the size criterion effectively does this.

Superficially, the most obvious way of classifying wars would be simply according to the number of deaths: 0 to 10,000, 10,000 to 20,000 and so on. This procedure has a number of disadvantages, however. It is more natural to think of one war involving ten times as many deaths as another, or half as many, or whatever the case may be. A war with 1,500 deaths seems rather different from one involving 9,500 deaths, and should be categorised separately. However, two wars involving respectively 101,500 and 109,500 deaths appear much the same from a size point of view. Thus it is more natural to devise categories which reflect the proportions in which numbers differ from each other rather than the absolute numbers.

One easy way of doing this is to use the *logarithm*[2] of the casualties rather than the crude figures. The logarithm of the number of deaths gives us a convenient measure of the size of a war and is widely used. This statistic was called the *magnitude* of the war by Richardson, but the *severity* by Singer and Small. The difference in terminology is unfortunate, but I shall use Singer and Small's convention from now on. Thus, we shall refer to a war in which 1,000,000 people died as a war of severity 6.

Proportionate measures have added virtues in dealing with data in which there are significant errors, as in the cases of statistics of war. The estimates of war deaths are very inaccurate and involve considerable guesswork. Participants in war have both conscious and unconscious motives for misrepresenting the number of dead – usually (though not always) with a view to underestimating their own dead and exaggerating the enemy's. This leads to a range of estimates in which the highest might be two or three times the lowest. However, errors are likely to be proportional – a 50 per cent error in a war of severity 6 is probably about as likely as a 50 per cent error in a war of severity 3, though the former represents a much higher absolute number. Under our system of classification, a 50 per cent error would give the same degree of misclassification in both these two cases and be regarded as a error of equal seriousness. This seems a convenient approach.[3]

Apart from the problems raised by the inaccuracy of the data, there are others which are raised by the difficulties of definition. For example, what deaths should we include? There is a range of possibilities which can give very different results. We could include just military personnel killed in battle or who died of wounds; or all people killed as a direct result of warfare; or all those who died as a result of the war, including the indirect deaths due to disease which can be legitimately attributed to war. The inclusion of disease is by no means a trivial matter as, in earlier times, disease was much more likely to kill

[2] A logarithm is a way of representing a number as a power of 10. Thus 1,000 can be written as $10 \times 10 \times 10$ or 10^3. This is referred to as '10 to the power 3', and 3 is referred to as 'the logarithm to base 10 of 1,000'. This concept can be extended to include more than the direct multiples of 10. Thus 357 can be written as $10^{2.55267}$; 2.55267 is therefore the logarithm of 357. The number 10 is a widely used 'base' for a logarithm, though any number can be used.

[3] It is common convention to use integral values (whole numbers) of the logarithms as mid-points in the classes. As table 8.1 shows, classes run from, say, 5½ to 6½. The reason is that 5½ (or any other number and a half) is not the logarithm of a whole number, so any exact number of deaths falls unambiguously in one category or another. Given the enormous range of error in the data, this seems unnecessary pedantry. However, it would be petty as well as inconvenient not to follow the convention.

Table 8.1   *Wars, 1820–1949*

Severity (logarithm of deaths)	Number of deaths	Number of wars
0–½	0–3	
½–1½	3–32	Not readily
1½–2½	32–316	countable
2½–3½	316–3,160	209
3½–4½	3,160–31,600	71
4½–5½	31,600–316,000	26
5½–6½	316,000–3,160,000	7
6½–7½	3,160,000–31,600,000	2
TOTAL		315

Source: Richardson 1960b

a soldier than anything else. In the Boer War, five times as many soldiers died of disease (mainly typhoid) as were killed as a direct result of battle. The First World War was the first major conflict in which more than half the casualties were directly caused by the fighting.

Disease also attacks the civilian population. The influenza epidemic which ravaged Europe at the end of the First World War killed 150,000 people in Britain, compared with 750,000 killed in battle, which is not a trivial proportion (A. J. P. Taylor 1965). The severity of the epidemic may well have been due to the malnutrition and privations caused by the war.

Which grouping we take is to some extent arbitrary. What is important is that we are consistent and explicit in our selection methods throughout. Different scholars have used different characteristics. Richardson, in his definition of magnitude (Singer and Small's 'severity'), includes all military deaths, no matter from what cause and, all civilian deaths in combatant states which, as far as can be judged, are directly attributable to hostile action. He excludes deaths attributable to disease (this definition is used in table 8.1 above). Singer and Small have a narrower definition and exlude civilian deaths. They consider battle-connected deaths only, though these include deaths from disease caught in the combat area.

If we were to be as accurate as possible, then the war deaths would have to make allowance for the fact that some of the dead would in any case have died from some other cause if the war had not intervened. In the instance of military deaths this factor can be ignored, as we are dealing with relatively young and healthy men, whose death rate is insignificant compared with the other inaccuracies involved in the figures. In the case of civilian deaths, this factor cannot be dismissed so easily. Some war deaths were due to malnutrition, for example. However, the people who are most likely to succumb to this are the very young and, more particularly, the very old, whose chance of dying from some other cause is also fairly high. However, compared with the total figures for the war and the great errors involved, even this correction will not alter the whole picture very much.

The severity of wars in terms of number of people killed is not the only relevant statistical measure. Thus it fails to distinguish between a long-drawn-out war with relatively low levels of violence at any given point in time and a short, sharp but bloody war. The distinction for some purposes is significant. Singer and Small define two other measures, one of which is *magnitude* of the war (not to be confused with Richardson's measure of magnitude), which is the sum of the number of months each nation was involved. Thus, if two states fought each other for 12 months and a third had joined in for the last 6 months, the magnitude would be 30 nation-months. This measure in terms of 'nation-months' gives us an indication of how extensive or widely based a conflict was. The other is a group of two measures called *intensity*. One is the number of battle deaths (severity) per nation-month, and is a measure of the level of violence of a war per unit of time. The other is the number of battle deaths per pre-war population of the belligerent states, which reflects the degree of involvement and disruption of a war. Clearly other measures can be constructed which serve as indicators of different characteristics of wars. I shall not be using the latter measures in this book, but it is important to recognise that while data are given once our definitions are made, how we manipulate the data to devise different sorts of measures is for us to choose according to the questions we wish to ask.

3   THE ANALYSIS OF STATISTICAL HYPOTHESES

To discuss the statistical approach to war, we need to introduce some simple statistical concepts. These are fairly straightforward, however, and non-mathematical readers need have few fears.

Statistics, at least as applied to data, is the business of classifying. In the last section we classified wars according to the number of people killed: we expressed these numbers in terms of their logarithms. Such a table and resulting diagram are called a *distribution*. Distributions play a fundamental role in statistical analysis.

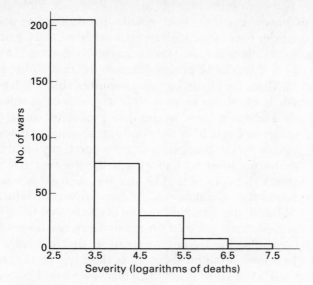

Figure 8.1

The distribution of wars according to the number of people killed is derived purely from observation; once 'a war' has been defined, there is no particular theory behind it. Let us now consider a rather different problem.

Suppose we have a bag with an equal number of red and black balls in it. If we pull out a ball, there is some sense in which we can say it is 'equally likely' that the ball will be red or black.[4] If we replace the ball (to keep the number in the bag equal) and carry out a second selection, again it will be 'equally likely' that the ball will be red or black. Suppose we pick four balls out of the bag, always replacing the ball after each selection. There are five possibilities: that all the balls will be black, that there will be three black balls and one red, that there will be two of each, that there will be one black ball and three red and that all the balls will be red. This is the total set of possibilities. Nothing else can happen. Now suppose we persuade some fanatical devotee of the experimental method to pick four balls out of the bag every day for a year in order to see how many events in each category there are – for

---

[4] These examples, where we construct idealised mind experiments to give us ideas about probability distributions, were called *fundamental probability sets* by Jerzy Newman, a leading probability theorist (Hacking 1975).

153

example, how many days there are in which only one black ball appears. At the end of the year, we can construct a diagram indicating how many times the experimenter got any given result. How do we predict roughly how many times each result will occur in the year?

Let us first consider the case of all the selections being black balls. To phrase the question differently, what is the *probability* that on 12 March all four balls will be black? The probability that the first ball selected will be black is $1/2$. Thus, on 'about' half the mornings a black will be the first ball selected. If 12 March were such a day, a second selection would take place and again there would be a probability of $1/2$ of its being black. Thus on 'about half' of the mornings on which a black ball appears first, a black ball will appear on the second; or, on about a quarter of all mornings (that is, half of a half), the first two balls selected will be black. It happens that 12 March is such a day, and the third selection takes place. On about half of the mornings on which the first two balls are black, the third will also be black, so that three black balls will be the first three selected on about $1/8$ of the days of this experiment. By repeating the argument we can see that four black balls (that is, no red balls) will occur on about $1/16$ of the days. As the chance of getting a red ball is the same as getting a black, we could have done exactly the same analysis for getting all red balls and got the same result: $1/16$ of the days.

Now let us look at the probability of getting three black balls and one red. First let us take the probability of the experimenter getting black balls on the first three draws from the bag and a red ball on the final draw. We have already demonstrated that black balls will be found on the first three draws on about $1/8$ of all days. On about half of these days the experimenter will get a red on the last draw. Thus on about $1/16$ of all days, there will be black, black, black and red in that order. However, all we are interested in is the number of black balls, not the order in which they are drawn. For example, the result black, black, red, black in that order would be regarded as equivalent to black, black, black, red. Thus there are four possibilities of just one red ball being drawn, namely when it appears in the first, second, third or fourth position. By an application of the earlier argument we can see that each of these will occur on about one day in sixteen, so one red and three black balls will be drawn on about $1/4$ of all days. The argument is identical for one black ball and three red ones, so now we have the approximate proportion of times on which four of our five categories will appear. As these four categories account for $10/16$ of the days, it follows that the final category of two red balls and two black balls will account for the remaining $1/16$ of the days. If we draw a distri-

Table 8.2   *Theoretical frequency distribution of black balls per day*

No. of black balls per day	0	1	2	3	4
No. of days	23	91	137	91	23

bution of the number of entries we predict will fall into each category, we get the picture shown in table 8.2 and figure 8.2. This type of distribution is known as the *binomial distribution*.

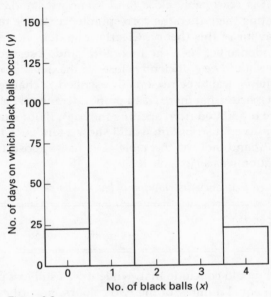

Figure 8.2

Now, it is unlikely that our dedicated experimenter will get the exact number predicted in the table. It is, after all, a chance matter and it is possible in principle, though in practice extremely unlikely, that four black balls would have been drawn on every single day of the year. This ideal distribution, which is predicted on the basis of our postulates about the selection of the balls, is known as a *theoretical distribution*, as distinct from the actual, observed distribution.

An interesting form of reasoning is based on this procedure. Let us assume that we have a theory about the nature of some chance process. In drawing a ball from the bag discussed above, the theory is that there is an equal chance (or 'probability') of the ball being red or

155

black. Furthermore, each draw is independent of the preceding draws, so, for example, it makes no difference on the fourth draw of the day whether the first three were all red, all black or any mixture of the two. The theoretical distribution was worked out on these assumptions. The theory is clear-cut in the case of drawing balls from a bag or tossing coins, but in more complicated social situations the appropriate theory is by no means so obvious, though the principle is the same. The statistician, having formulated a theory, works out the theoretical distribution which this theory would give. This can be compared with the observed distribution to see how close is the resemblance. If it is reasonably close (and there are standard techniques for evaluating this), then the correspondence can be regarded as evidence in favour of this theory. Clearly, one does not expect a perfect correspondence between the theoretical and observed distributions, but they should be sufficiently close for the deviations of the actual from the theoretical to be reasonably ascribed to chance.

Suppose we suspected that there was a preponderance of black balls in the bag (we are prohibited from opening the bag). If our suspicions were true, the observed distribution would show a tendency to move over to the right-hand side of the table. Let us suppose that the observed distribution was as in table 8.3.

Table 8.3   *Observed frequency distribution of black balls per day*

No. of black balls per day	0	1	2	3	4
No. of days	1	27	80	156	101

The statistician would conclude that, while it was still just possible that there was an equal number of the two colours, nevertheless the new hypothesis that there were more black balls than red was more likely; and also that a distribution such as the one in table 8.3 would be very unlikely to result from the systematic drawing from a bag with equal numbers of the two colours. In a rigorous investigation the probability of such a distribution resulting from draws from a bag with equal numbers of balls could be calculated, but here I have made the figures sufficiently clear for us to assume this by inspection alone.

Notice that probability has come into this reasoning in two ways. First, we generated our theoretical distribution entirely on the basis of probability. Next we compared the theoretical and observed distributions and asked whether the differences between them could reasonably be ascribed to chance or not – another, but different, argument involving the use of probability. The concept of probability is at the core of all statistical reasoning once we go beyond the most basic descriptive statistics. In the next section, we shall give an example of how this mode of reasoning has been used for the examination of the incidence of wars.

In the last example, we took almost the simplest situation we could have had, namely when the probabilities of the two events were equal. The same principle applies, however, even when the probabilities differ. Suppose the ratio of black balls to red in the bag had been only one to five. We are still interested in the number of times the black ball appears in a series of four blind selections taken once every day of the year, where, again, the selected ball is put back in the bag after each selection so that the original ratio is maintained. Here the probability of a black ball appearing on any given selection is only 1/6. If we use the same type of argument as before, the probability of getting a series of four black balls on any given day is only 1/1296. That is, picking four balls out of the bag every day, one would expect to get four black balls about once every three-and-a-half years – perhaps a surprisingly small number. If we did this exercise for one year, we would expect to get a distribution something like that shown in table 8.4 and figure 8.3.

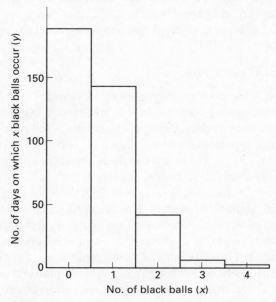

Figure 8.3

Figure 8.3 looks rather different from figure 8.2. However, in view of the very similar processes used to generate the two different

Table 8.4   *Theoretical frequency distribution of black balls per day*

No. of black balls	0	1	2	3	4
No. of days occurring	176	141	42	6	0

diagrams, it is easy to believe that they are intimately connected, mathematically. We express this intimate mathematical connection by saying they are both forms of the binomial distribution. The different shapes of the graphs indicate that different probabilities were involved.

Different ideal graphs are produced, not only by altering the probabilities involved but also by altering the underlying assumptions of the problem, which gives us a different sort of mathematical process. Thus, if when taking the balls out of the bag in the above experiment we had not replaced them, the probability of selecting a black ball would have depended on previous selections. The resulting process would not have been a binomial but a *hypergeometric distribution*. This distribution will not be of interest to us, but several others will. The basic principle is the same. We hypothesise some probabilistic process, construct the consequences of this in terms of an idealised process, and compare the reality with this to see whether it could plausibly have been generated by the same sort of process.

4   THE FREQUENCY OF WARS

Armed with the above concepts, we can examine some issues of interest to the student of warfare. In the first section we dealt with some problems of classification. Using such data we shall now look in greater detail at the types of reasoning which lie behind the formulation and justification of our belief in assertions about the international system made on the basis of statistical evidence.

One problem of obvious interest is whether there is any sort of 'periodicity' in the beginnings of wars. For example, a plausible theory of the distribution of wars is some sort of cyclic theory in which there are periods of time in which a number of wars start and others in which few wars start. Thus, it could be that the more wars are fought, the more they are likely to be fought because of some brutalising effect. However, when this goes too far, an exhaustion effect sets in, reducing the number of wars started. If this were the case, then if we arranged wars according to the date they started, there would be clusters of wars in some periods, that is, the 'brutal' periods, while there would also be years when not many wars started: the 'exhaustion'

Table 8.5   *Outbreaks of war, 1820–1929: severity 3.5 to 4.5*

No. of outbreaks of war per year (x)	0	1	2	3	4	More than 4	Total
No. of years in which x outbreaks occurred	65	35	6	4	0	0	110
Years in which x outbreaks 'should' have occurred [a]	64.3	34.5	9.3	1.7	0.2	0.0	110.0

Note: [a] Obviously the actual number of outbreaks must be a whole number. The 'theoretical' number, however, need not be, though there is no meaning to the notion of, say, 0.3 of a war.
Source: Richardson 1960b

periods. However, if there were no such factor at work and no systematic connection between the starts of wars so that the lengths of the intervals between them were random, wars would not be evenly distributed through time. There would still be some clustering due to chance. If we look at the actual statistical record, how do we tell whether any clustering is due to chance or whether it is sufficiently marked to require another explanation?

I shall give the detailed discussion of the problem in terms of Richardson's data and analysis and then look at some other studies. Richardson's analysis was conducted on wars of severity (in his terms, 'magnitude') 3.5 to 4.5 in the period 1820–1929. The number of wars of the appropriate magnitude in this period was quite large, namely 110, so a meaningful statistical analysis could be performed.

The first stage in the analysis was to find in how many years no wars started, in how many just one war started and so on. It turned out that in no year did more than three wars actually start. As he was concerned only with the cause of a war and not with for how long it went on, he did not worry about how many were being prosecuted in a year. Table 8.5 gives the result of this classification

The next stage was to consider the chance hypothesis to see what the theoretical distribution given by this would look like. This was refined to the following hypothesis: there are a great number of occasions on which wars could occur, but on only a very few of these does a war in fact start. If this were the case, then it would produce a *Poisson distribution* of years classified according to the number of wars which started during them. This theoretical Poisson distribution is then compared with the observed distribution. The results are shown in table 8.5 and figure 8.4, where they correspond closely and simple visual evidence alone seems sufficient to conclude that the probabilistic processes which generate the 'real' data are the same as those which generate the 'theoretical' data. There are formal tests for this, as we mentioned in the last section. The formal tests consist of finding the probability that the discrepancy between the observed and theoretical distribution is due to chance.

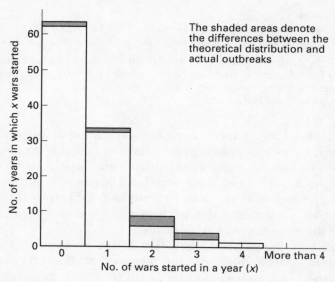

Figure 8.4

What does this analysis show? The distribution of the data is consistent with the hypothesis that wars could have occurred on a large number of occasions but actually happened only in a small proportion of possible circumstances, on account presumably, of some chance element or configuration of elements being present. However, although the statistics are consistent with this conclusion, it does not mean that we can affirm it for certain. Other assumptions might have given not very different results. It is interesting in what it excludes. In particular it has ruled out as very improbable the *a priori* plausible hypothesis suggested above that the outbreaks of war followed some periodic pattern.

The analysis supports what is a fairly conventional historical view of the causation of war. States, by and large, exist without fighting, but now and again events take an unusual turn which results in war. It may not be the same turn of events every time, and this analysis is

Table 8.6   *Outbreaks of war, AD 1500–1931*

No. of outbreaks per year (x)	0	1	2	3	4	More than 4	Total
No. of years in which x outbreaks occurred	223	142	48	15	4	0	432
Years in which x outbreaks 'should' have occurred	216.2	149.7	51.8	12.0	2.1	0.3	432.1

Source: Wright 1947

consistent with the view that the cause of each war is unique. A uniqueness theory would require a Poisson-type process.

This result is based on only a sub-set of the data available and is therefore relatively restricted. However, Singer and Small carried out the same tests on the longer period 1816–1980, and without the top cut-off point of severity 4.5. Their analysis also showed no evidence of periodicity in the starting of wars in their somewhat longer period of 165 years, which encompassed that looked at by Richardson.

Richardson applied this approach to the data collected by Quincy Wright covering the longer period 1500–1931. The data here are less reliable, partly because, as we go further back, things become more obscure, and partly because Wright had less of Richardson's care for definition and classification. However, the historical and the theoretical distribution shown in table 8.6 likewise show a close correspondence.

This last demonstration of the theory obscures one feature of the starts of wars which again shows that further tests for randomness or patterns may be necessary. If one takes averages over long periods of time – in fact 50 years – then there does appear to be a suggestion of periodicity. Still using Wright's data, if one takes three 100–year periods centred on 1625 (that is, 1575–1675), 1775 and 1800, the average numbers of outbreaks of war per year were 0.91, 0.24 and 1.15 respectively. These figures vary radically – the average in the final period is almost five times that of the second. The probability of this being fortuitous is infinitesimal. Nor can it be due to errors in the data. No doubt there are some errors – but not so many!

While the pattern (or lack of pattern) of outbreaks of war is interesting, it is not the only feature of the warlike behaviour of the international system. The same questions can be asked about wars in progress, measured in terms of nation-months. Here the answers are somewhat different. There was a clear periodicity in the amount of warfare going on in the international system after 1816, with cycles of between 14 and 21 years. Given the first result about outbreaks of war, this is surprising. However, it can be reconciled. Davis, Duncan and Siverson (1978) show that while war is not infectious in the sense that one war between two countries triggers off a war between two separate countries, it is infectious in the sense that when a war starts between two countries, others tend to join in, thus expanding the war. This would reconcile the observations.

Randomness does not imply ignorance of the processes which underlie the phenomena we are interested in. The above result does not demonstrate the impossibility of theory. We can show this with a simple (non-international relations) example. Suppose we have a hundred boxes of weak but volatile explosive laid out evenly in a large field so that if one box explodes it will not set off its neighbours. However, the volatility of the explosive is such that a fly landing on a box will make it explode. If we retire to a safe distance and watch the boxes explode as flies land on them, we will be unlikely to see any pattern in the order in which boxes explode. Thus, it is improbable that the boxes will explode in an orderly way along the lines in which they are arranged. If they did, we would look for some explanation other than the flies (that is, we would look for a systematic rather than a random explanation). Now, though the explosions are random, this does not mean that the process is not well understood – indeed we have an extremely good knowledge of the chemical processes involved and of the causal factor setting them off. However, we cannot predict when the cause will operate. If, having laid the gunpowder out, we had perfect knowledge of the initial positions of the flies and a highly deterministic theory of the directions in which flies moved, then, presumably, we could predict the order in which the boxes would explode. However, even if this were (implausibly) possible, it would still mean that the boxes were exploding without any pattern, and a knowledge of the past explosions alone would not help in any sort of prediction. A similar process might well be true in the case of war causation. We could derive a theory which would show when a situation was volatile and even predict the factors which would upset a precarious equilibrium. This would be consistent with there being no discernible pattern through time of outbreaks of war.

In this section I have discussed some of the features of the inter-national system which are of interest if one wants to get a view of the general patterns which operate in it. However, I have also asked why one should believe them. The crucial reason for believing in a pattern is that the probability of such a pattern arriving by chance is sufficiently small to justify the positive belief. We will occasionally adopt false beliefs – how many depends on how small we require 'sufficiently small' to be. At least, using these principles, we know how reliable the belief is, and hence have criteria for determining how much risk of error we are prepared to adopt.

9 ARMS AND ARMS RACES

1 THE SIGNIFICANCE OF ARMAMENTS

Wars are fought with weapons. If there were no weapons, presumably there would be no wars. However, if some people have weapons and some do not, then those with weapons can impose their will on those without. Put rather crudely, this is a crucial dilemma of the way the world is run, without any easy or obvious ways out of it. The relationship between armaments and war is still controversial, though research is being done which is beginning to shed some light on the problem.

Crudely there are two polar views about the relationship between arms levels (not arms races) and war. The first is that the crucial thing about arms levels between two states or alliances is that they should be balanced, so that there is, in Bull's terminology (1977), a simple balance of power.[1] In its extreme form this can hold that the level of arms is unimportant; what matters is the balance. This is the view held by many traditional strategists. The other view is that what is important is the total quantities of arms held by the two countries, where the more there are, the greater the risk of war. The distribution between the two is unimportant. Richardson held this view, and it was oddly one of the few propositions which he asserted without testing. It is the classical pacificist position. Clearly a composite view arguing balance is important, but that lower balances are safer than higher ones is perfectly tenable. The relationship of arms levels to war is not the same as the balance theories, but they are related. In general we can assume that if there is an arms race, there is an attempt to achieve balance. There is a presumption, though it is only a presumption and it needs testing, that, if there is an arms race, then on the balance theory this

---

[1] A simple balance of power obtains when there are two states or alliances with approximate parity of military power. The complex balance of power, or the balance of power system, involves several states which form alliances so as to achieve an overall balance of power (see chapter 11, section 2).

should not in general provoke war. However, on the aggregate arms theory we can be more confident and assert that it would be related to war. On both the balance and the aggregate arms theory we would expect a unilateral build-up of arms to lead to war.

There is also disagreement as to whether arms in themselves make wars more likely by increasing tensions, or whether they are merely the consequence of tensions which would exist in any case and are neutral as far as exacerbating the danger of war is concerned. Again a combined position is possible. The basic causes of warlike tensions can be independent of arms, but they can be exaggerated by a high level of arms.

While the evidence for deciding between these various hypotheses is not conclusive, it is suggestive. If balance were the overriding factor, then one would expect there to be no relationship between the military power of a nation and its participation in war. Observation of its military power would give no insight into whether it fought or not. However, Bremer (1977) shows that there is a strong correlation between national capability for war and participation in war. This militates against the balance hypothesis, unless further qualifications are to be found, and suggests that the more arms there are in the system, the more likely is war.

Whatever theory of arms and war we adhere to, even the most neutral, it is clear that there are great amounts of arms in the world at the moment and that there usually have been. At best, they are an enormous economic drain, and if we could be as secure without them as with them we could be a lot better off – this, at least in its cautious form, is uncontroversial.

However, it is not just the level of arms which concerns people, but the fact that there are frequent phases where levels steadily increase. Most countries seem to have experienced such a phase since about 1948. The term 'arms race' is used to describe situations where two or more countries increase their armaments in apparent response to increases in the other country's arms, because of the threat they believe to be involved. This is a positive feed-back process in which the actions of one country cause a reaction in another, which induces the first country to extend the scale of its actions, and so on.

Arms races have constantly troubled people who are interested in the problems of peace and war. The reasons for this are not hard to find, for their relevance to the study of peace and war is obvious. That arms races are a real phenomenon and not just a figment of the pacifist's imagination is clear. One classic example is the so-called 'Naval Race' between Britain and Germany in the period before the First World War. Britain and Germany were enlarging their fleets, at times rather dramatically, by building, among other things, the large Dreadnoughts; and the explicit motivation in the case of both countries was the naval build-up of the other power. In more recent times, the Soviet Union and the United States have been increasing their nuclear armaments and accompanying delivery systems in response to the armaments of each other. There have been many other cases.

What is the function of a theory of arms races? The basic idea is to be able to specify the relationship between the armaments programmes of two competing countries. If we can do this, then we can go on and analyse the implications of such relationships. It is tempting to suppose that the process would go on indefinitely, and that the nations would build up to progressively larger and larger levels of arms. We shall see that this is not necessarily true. The analysis of even simple relationships gives us an insight into some curious features of arms races which are by no means self-evident. It can, though it need not, lead us into some understanding of when and how armaments races stop and, if we are lucky, into considering theories of disarmament, which, to a limited degree, is the reverse process.

A 'true' arms race is essentially an interactive process where the cause of one country's increase in the level of arms is that of the other. However, it is sometimes argued that the motivation for arms build-ups is not the arms of a rival but the self-interest of pressure groups such as military and industrial concerns which benefit either economically or in power and status with increases in military expenditure. The specification of explicit forms of the relationship between the arms levels of two countries provides us with a tool for distinguishing between 'true' arms races in the sense that the primary motivation is fear of the arms level of some opposing power, and arms build-ups which are made for some different purposes such as in response to pressure-group interests. This is not easy, but we have a few results (and a few puzzles), which are discussed below.

While arms races are clearly relevant to war, and are a proper part of the analysis of the causes of war, a theory of the arms race is not by itself a theory of the causes of war. To connect it with these causes, we need a separate theory relating the level of armaments to the probability of war. This involves other questions, which we discuss below.

2   THE RICHARDSON THEORY OF ARMS RACES

While there has been much discussion of arms races in various contexts, particularly since the First World War, there was initially little attempt to theorise about them. Particular arms races were described historically or, at the other extreme, were the subjects of dogmatic and inadequately substantiated assertions as to their effects. This was remedied by Lewis Fry Richardson (Richardson 1960a) in work which was initially done in the inter-war years, though it was scarcely recognised until the 1950s. It has been followed by a great outpouring of work in the tradition he pioneered. It is still the only major example of deductive thinking which has originated in the study of international behaviour, as distinct from being borrowed from other fields, such as economics.

In this section, I shall describe a simplified version of the Richardson theory of the arms race which illustrates its important characteristics.

Suppose two countries, Alpha and Beta, consider each other to be military rivals. Thus, each country views the arms of its opponent as requiring some response.[2] Initially, assume that the sole factors which influence the government of Alpha in setting its armaments level are the level of arms held by Beta and an innate suspicion factor which means it wants a certain quantity of arms even if Beta has none at all. The higher Beta sets its armaments level, the more arms Alpha requires above this point. These are rather simple assumptions and only in a crude sense can they be regarded as a rational actor model, though it is possible to formulate more specific assumptions about the choice behaviour which would make such behaviour the consequence of maximising assumptions. We can draw a simple graph of the level of arms which Alpha regards as the minimum acceptable in the face of any level possessed by Beta. Figure 9.1(a) illustrates a situation where Alpha requires at least £5 billion worth of arms plus 80 per cent of

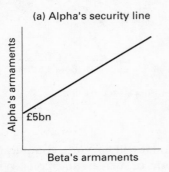
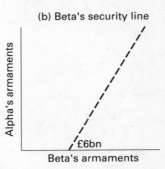

(a) Alpha's security line
(b) Beta's security line

Figure 9.1

---

[2] The use of the anthropomorphic view of the state apparently implied in such phrases as 'Alpha (or France or Bolivia) thinks that ...' is one of the cardinal sins in the analysis of international relations. More appropriate wording would be 'The decision-makers of Alpha think that ...'. However, it is convenient to use the anthropomorphic version for brevity, while drawing attention to its dangers.

Beta's arms. Any point on or above the line which is drawn will mean that Alpha is satisfied, and regards itself as safe.

We also assume that Beta reacts in the same way and, being cautious, regards it as necessary to have at least £6 billion worth of arms plus 70 per cent of Alpha's arsenal. Beta's security level can similarly be represented as in figure 9.1(b) by the broken line: Beta feels secure if it is either on its security line or to the right of it. In figure 9.2(a) I have superimposed the two security lines on the same graph.

These two lines divide the diagram into four areas, labelled P, Q, R and S. In areas P and Q, which lie to the left of Beta's security line, Beta will be dissatisfied and will increase its arms level. This is represented in the figure by a move towards the right. In areas Q and R, Alpha will be dissatisfied, and the consequent increase in its arms is represented by a move upwards in the graph. So, in area Q both parties are increasing their arms, and the general direction is therefore diagonally upwards. On these assumptions, both sides are content in area S and there is no alteration in the arms level. In P, the move is, of course, simply horizontal, as Alpha has no desire to increase its arms levels. Correspondingly, in area R the move is vertically upwards.

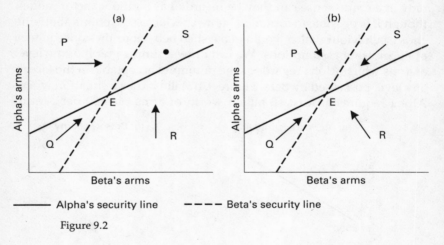

Figure 9.2

This is a very simple situation, and it will be worth complicating it a little before analysing the implications of such assumptions. While the quantity of an opponent's armaments is clearly a significant factor in determining a country's arms level, it is equally clearly not the only one. Thus, money spent on armaments cannot be spent on anything else. This pulls in the other direction, as a country which is arming is therefore poorer in terms of what it can consume than it would have been otherwise. There are now two factors, cost and security, pulling in opposite directions and suggesting opposite courses of action. This brings about a significant modification to the model. In the earlier version, Alpha did not really mind if it was above its security line; this just meant that it had some superfluous arms. However, Alpha is now conscious of the added cost involved, and wishes to maintain the level it needs, and no more. If it is above its security line, it will reduce its level of arms. This is illustrated in figure 9.2(b). If the arms levels are in area Q, both Alpha and Beta will be dissatisfied and will increase armaments – there will be an arms race. In area R, Alpha feels insecure and increases its arms; Beta, however, has too many and, finding them too costly, will cut back. In area P the converse is the case. In area S, both will find the level of armaments too expensive and both will reduce them.

The treatment of rearmament and disarmament as reverse processes, each of which is equally likely, might seem glib. Disarmament rarely seems to come gradually but in periods of traumatic change, such as after a major war, or as an aspect of big and rapid political change such as is being experienced in the Eastern bloc, particularly since 1989. Some caution is required, however, in interpreting the meaning of 'disarmament'. Although disarmament sometimes takes the form, usually as a result of an agreement, of actually scrapping useful items of equipment and cutting down armed forces, there can be *de facto* disarmament simply by not replacing old and obsolete equipment. In this inconspicuous and rather negative form, disarmament is probably more common than is realised. Rearmament involves positively acquiring equipment or expanding forces (and spending more money), and is therefore more likely to attract attention. The theory regards the two processes as symmetrical. This is a simplification, but it is a more reasonable one than it might appear at first sight.

This picture of an armaments race is still absurdly simple. Despite this simplicity, it is worth analysing the implications of the assumptions we have made, as the results, in certain cases, are somewhat surprising.

The first question is whether there is some level of armaments at which neither country would want either to increase or decrease its amount of arms. This would be the 'balance of terror' point. Such a situation exists where the security lines of the two countries intersect (figure 9.2, point E). At that point, each country is on its own security line, so the situation stays stable until some other factor alters. This point is called the *equilibrium arms level*.

What happens when the level of armaments is not at the equilibrium arms level? This has been loosely considered in figure 9.2(b), but needs amplifying. Take point F in figure 9.3, between the security levels and below the point of equilibrium.

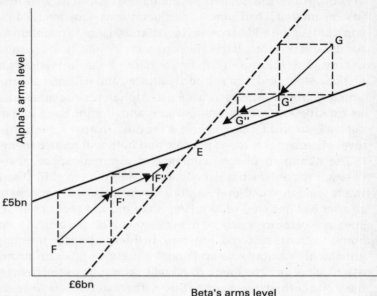

Figure 9.3

Each country is below its security level and therefore wants to increase its arms, Alpha by moving upwards in the diagram, and Beta by a move to the right. Let us assume for convenience that Alpha ignores the fact that Beta is also out of equilibrium, and increases its arms to its security level, assuming that the level of arms held by Beta will remain constant. Let Beta reason similarly. If they then simultaneously increase their arms by the appropriate amount, they will find themselves at point F', which is nearer the equilibrium but which still leaves them both dissatisfied. If the process is repeated, they will move successively to F'', F''', and so on, until they reach the equilibrium point. Once there, of course, they will stop. If the hypothesis about the way the two countries decide on the arms increase in each year is correct, then the arms race will decrease in momentum year by year as the equilibrium is approached. However, not to allow for the rival's movement until it has occurred presupposes some naïveté on the part of the rulers of the countries concerned. In practice, the error is more likely to be in the opposite direction, consisting of an overestimate of the rival's hostile actions. However,

170

the basic point, that the arms race will move cautiously towards the equilibrium, is unaffected by this; the only change is in the path by which it moves there and the speed at which it approaches equilibrium.

Now let us take point G, which is also between the two security levels but is above the equilibrium point. In this case exactly the reverse process will take place. Because of the cost, both parties will move down towards their security level, and assuming that both sides ignore the possibility of the other decreasing its arms level, they will arrive at point G'. At the next stage, they will move to point G'', and so on, until they reach the equilibrium level. Thus, although they will have mutually disarmed, this will not lead to a general and complete disarmament. A similar argument shows that the countries will move to the equilibrium level of armaments from any other point on the diagram.

This sort of system, which moves to an equilibrium level no matter from where it starts, is said to possess a point of *stable equilibrium*. This is not the same as saying that there is no arms race, but the fact that it is limited (albeit possibly at a high level) is important.

Now let us look at another set of security curves permitted by our overall assumptions which are illustrated in figure 9.4. The critical difference between these lines and those in the first example is that

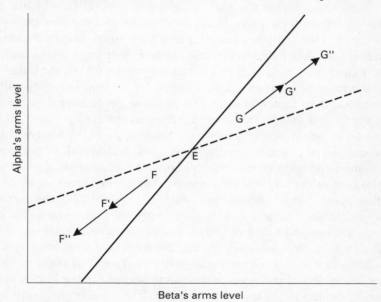

Figure 9.4

171

Alpha's security line intersects the horizontal axis and is steeper than Beta's, which cuts the vertical axis. In the previous case, the reverse was true.

This is not as implausible as it might appear at first sight. The government of Alpha is aware that Beta has various ends in view other than an attack on Alpha. For example, it may have internal security problems for which it requires arms. Consequently, Alpha is content to be completely disarmed providing Beta does not have armaments in excess of £5 billion. However, if Beta goes beyond this level, then Alpha reacts sharply. Thus an increase of, say, £1 billion in Beta's arms provokes an increase of about £1.5 billion in Alpha's (figure 9.4). An equivalent assumption is made about Beta's reaction behaviour. In this new situation, as in the earlier case, there is an equilibrium level of arms indicated by point E.

Now consider what happens when the arms levels are at a point F. Here, Alpha is above its security line and Beta is to the right of its line. Thus, both parties are anxious to reduce their armaments. By an analogous argument to the one conducted earlier, we can calculate that they will get to F'. This puts them both in a position even further away from their security levels. Consequently, they will reduce their armaments again, continuing in this way until they reach a completely disarmed state.

Now let us repeat the analysis, starting at point G, which is above the equilibrium position. Here, both Alpha and Beta are below their security level, and want to increase their arms. Again making our naïve behaviour assumption about how they arrange their arms levels, it is clear that, with each move that they make (to G', etc.), they both fall further below their security levels. In consequence they will both increase their armaments again and move yet further from the equilibrium, and there is no reason for the process to stop. They get into a runaway arms race which has no limiting point, at least within the assumptions of the theory. Perhaps it will end in war, or perhaps in a dramatic revision of their conceptions of adequate security levels on the part of the countries concerned. The theory gives us no help on this point. Similar arguments can be carried out for the remaining areas, though with a qualification. For any point north-east of the equilibrium point, but outside the area we have already considered, the arms movement would go into the explosive area. From any point south-west of E, it will move down to zero. From any point north-west or south-east of the equilibrium point, it could move into either area and possibly to the equilibrium point. The equilibrium point has no particular attraction in this area, and the arrival of the arms system at this point would be pure coincidence. Systems such as this second one, where the equilibrium does not act as an attractor but, indeed, for most of the time as a repeller, are known as unstable systems and their equilibria as *unstable equilibria*.

It is unsatisfactory to leave the model with armaments increasing to infinity. Empirically it is absurd. We have to bring in some further assumption or assumptions to restore reality. There are two obvious possibilities, war and economic impoverishment. War is clearly a possibility, and one which Richardson seems to have assumed was the norm in such cases. I defer a discussion of that until section 5. For the moment we shall consider the alternative.

As the costs of armaments grow, their dampening effects would be expected to increase more than proportionately after some point (see figure 9.5). There is likely to be an upper ceiling on the proportion of the national income which a country will spend on arms, unless it is actually at war. This may be short of what could reasonably be called impoverishment. This suggests that the instability of the explosive arms race may, in certain cases, be localised by the existence of some upper stable equilibrium to which it would ultimately tend – though this might, of course, involve a high level of arms.

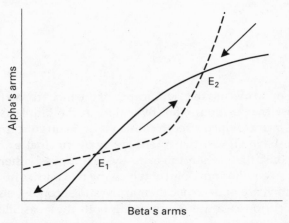

Figure 9.5

In both the cases of the Richardson model we have discussed, it has been assumed that an equilibrium level of arms actually exists. There is no particular reason for this, however. For instance, the two security levels could look as in figure 9.6, the lines intersecting at a point where the armaments of the two powers are negative. This has no meaning on our present definition of the variables.[3] However, the situation poses no severe problem from the point of view of analysis. The two countries will disarm completely, and so approach the equilibrium point as closely as possible.

The fact that the equilibrium is unobtainable does not mean that we cannot use the model in the analysis of those points which are obtainable. Indeed, the argument from which we derive the propositions about the behaviour of arms could be stated in terms which never mention this equilibrium at all. However, it is more convenient to state the issue in a general form and to regard all the situations as special cases than to have a whole set of *ad hoc* situations.

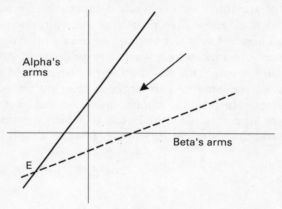

Figure 9.6

Before going on to discuss the significance of the Richardson theory, let us summarise the position so far. By making some simple assumptions about the factors which affect a country's decision concerning its arms level, we have shown that there are two principal groups of possible situations: first, when the arms system moves either up or down towards an equilibrium point at which the two parties no longer want either to increase or decrease their arms; and secondly, a system which has the curious feature of admitting both the possibility of a fully fledged, unlimited arms race and, alternatively, complete mutual disarmament. We arrived at these different conclusions on the basis of assumptions which were not radically different from one another.

[3] Richardson interpreted 'negative armaments' as 'negative hostility', that is, friendliness. He measured this by trade, which is, unfortunately, a dubious indicator. In my view it is easier to interpret the model as that of an arms race rather than the more amorphous hostility race as far as the international system is concerned. In principle, it can apply to any interactive system for which these basic relationships are appropriate.

They merely reflected different degrees of response to the rival's activities.

These conclusions are significant and would be unlikely to emerge from a purely verbal analysis of the problem. Our ruthless simplification of the world's complexities has already begun to pay some dividends, and, in the next section, we shall see to what extent these turn out to be illusory.

3 SOME IMPLICATIONS OF THE RICHARDSON THEORY

Social systems are always in a state of flux, so we would not expect the security lines depicted in the Richardson model to remain stationary indefinitely. The lines on the graph will move around, and the suitability of the model as the basis for a theory of arms races depends on how severe and frequent such movements are. If the lines are continually moving, this is an indication that there are other factors whose neglect limits the usefulness of the theory. If, however, the movements are relatively small, the model can form a suitable basis for a theory, and we can begin to analyse the problem in those terms.

Suppose, for the moment, that the world is such that the model accurately represents real arms races, but that there are some small variations in the lines over time.

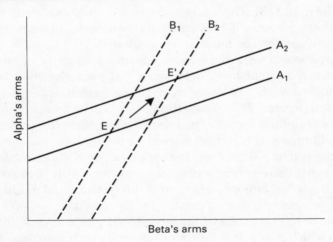

Figure 9.7

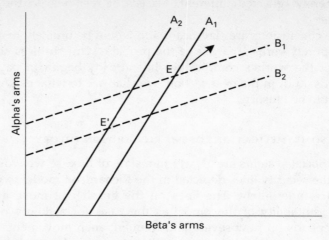

Figure 9.8

As far as the stable case is concerned, the model is quite well behaved (figure 9.7). Suppose that an arms system with security lines A_1 and B_1 exists, and that the system is at the equilibrium point E. Now imagine that, for some reason, the two countries become more sensitive to each other's level of arms and the former pair of security lines, A_1 and B_1, are replaced by A_2 and B_2, where A_2 is above A_1 and B_2 is to the right of B_1. These establish a new, higher equilibrium point at E'. The arms levels will move towards the new equilibrium, and the general situation will be more or less unaltered.

In the unstable case the increase in the sensitivity of the two countries is represented by similar shifts in the security lines, but the new equilibrium, E', is lower than before, which appears a little paradoxical (figure 9.8). Suppose the system is in its original form and is at the equilibrium level E. The increased sensitivity occurs and the new equilibrium is at E', which is *below* the original one and the actual level of the system's arms. From the basic analysis of the unstable case, it follows that there will be a runaway arms race. This demonstrates again that relatively minor alterations in the system could produce this effect – or, indeed, the opposite. In an unstable system, small variations in the constants of the system can produce very different results – which is why it is called 'unstable'. In such situations policy decisions have to be made with great caution, as an action might have quite dramatically unexpected consequences.

The overall implications of the model are rather disturbing. The basic model in both the stable and the unstable case is essentially the same – that arms are stimulated by the arms of a rival, dampened by a cost factor and all influenced by a rather more stable grievance or friendliness factor. However, for different relative strengths of these factors we predict radically different behaviour, which may lead to stability or great instability. Further, intuition is a bad guide in this. Only by careful analysis can we show these different possibilities. We also know that this is a very simple model and unlikely to mirror reality accurately (I present evidence below to support this conjecture). However, there is no reason to suppose that a more realistic model will be more stable. In other words, neither stability nor instability can confidently be perceived by intuition. Realistically we can only deduce them from accurate theories. But we know that social scientists are not very good at providing accurate theories at this stage, or perhaps for many years to come.

4   DIFFICULTIES AND EXTENSIONS

The real world does not look much like the world depicted in the model of arms races – it is much more complicated. What, then, is the point in analysing it as if it were similar? There are two points to make in response to this, both of them negative. First, we have shown that intuition is a poor guide to reaching an understanding of a certain sort of situation. Without formulating a model and putting it into simple mathematical terms, it is unlikely that we should have come across the division of possibilities into stable and unstable systems, where the latter in particular have such peculiar characteristics. At its weakest, this model has demonstrated that unstable systems are possible and that small variations in the initial conditions can have large consequences. This theory, though undoubtedly much too simple, has a measure of plausibility. That instabilities can occur in such simple systems destroys one's confidence in the stability of more realistic and complex ones. Complexity by itself does not make the system any more stable; in fact, the reverse may be true. There may be more balancing factors, but there may also be more destabilising ones.

The second response, which is implicit in what was said in the second chapter of this book, is that many events which are affected by a large number of factors can, nevertheless, be largely explained by a few. The tests on arms races are still inconclusive. The Richardson theory could be deficient either because it is too simple, or because it identifies the wrong variables. We still have to be open-minded. However, the claim that because the theory is simple it is worthless is

177

invalid. Some types of social event are much simpler on examination than they appear at first sight, and the arms race may be one of them.

The theory of the arms race has been analysed in mathematical terms. The point of doing so is not, as is sometimes hinted, to make it more difficult to understand. It is frequently easier to work out a theory initially in mathematical terms, even though it may subsequently prove possible to express it in natural language. Mathematical analysis also makes it easier to see the precise consequences which follow from some assumption. A set of plausible premises might turn out, on investigation, to yield extremely implausible implications. It is often much easier to see this in highly disciplined mathematical language than in verbal discussions, which, being more prone to ambiguity, are not always suitable for expressing complex logical arguments.

The value of a mathematical argument is seen in the extension of the Richardson theory to an arms race between several states. The two-state case is, of course, a great simplification, as arms races often involve several countries. Natural language is inadequate to describe the complexities involved, and mathematical forms have to be resorted to. There are many ways in which an arms race might involve more than two parties, and a general theory of arms races must be able to make provision for this.

Another variant of the arms race system occurs when there are several countries divided into two blocs. If all members of each bloc feel the same way as their partners, the problem can be dealt with as if it were a two-country arms race, blocs taking the place of countries. However, such similarity of interest is not likely to exist for long. An approximation to this situation existed in the late 1940s and early 1950s between the Western and Eastern alliances. Normally, though, a country in an alliance is unlikely to regard its allies' weapons as quite the equivalent of its own, not simply out of prejudice, but because it knows that there might be occasions when an ally would refuse to go to war, even if there were a general similarity of outlook between the two nations. Furthermore, countries feel threatened to different degrees by the rival alliance and are likely to react differently to their armaments. However, these problems can be treated as modifications of the two-party arms race. A greater complication is the fact that the various countries in the blocs have interests elsewhere which also influence the level of arms they require. Thus, Britain in the earlier post-war period wanted arms for a variety of imperial purposes unconnected to its fears of the Soviet Union. One cannot explain the British arms level purely in Cold War terms.

The extension of the Richardson theory to arms races involving many countries is complicated, but it does not collapse beneath the weight. The theory can be broadened to encompass situations more reminiscent of the real world than the basic theory which has been dealt with here, in a manner which still retains its essential characteristics.

A problem in any theory of this kind which depends on measurement is how to carry out the quantification necessary. The basic conclusions of the theory, that an arms race can be either stable or unstable, are true given a wide variety of different measures. Failure to find an appropriate one would not weaken its value as a cautionary tale, but, if we are to test and apply the theory, we need to find a suitable way of measuring the level of arms.

In the description of the theory, the level of arms was measured in terms of money spent on them. This is very crude. As a measure of cost, the percentage of the gross national product devoted to arms provides a more appropriate indicator of the strain on the economy. However, as we are concerned with arms as devices for threatening other states, it would be more appropriate to take military effectiveness as the measure of the size of arms levels. Cost as a criterion conceals the fact that some forms of weapons are much more to be feared than others, in a manner which may not be closely related to cost.

The difficulties of formulating an effectiveness measure for arms levels are compounded when we recognise that it is not only the weapons which a country has already which are of significance, but also those which it could acquire in the near future. The image of a completely disarmed state is more ambiguous than it appears at first sight. It seems legitimate to regard a disarmed country which could produce a nuclear bomb within a year as being 'less disarmed' than one which is not capable of producing such a weapon within the foreseeable future. Similar conditions apply to countries which are not in a completely disarmed state.

Once again, the measurement problem is both serious and difficult to solve. It is not, none the less, a problem which invalidates the exercise, for even crude measures embodied in crude theories can, in many cases, be illuminating as guides to the behaviour of the world.[4]

5 ARMS RACES AND WAR

A major reason for being interested in arms races is their alleged relationship to war. They have often been blamed as a cause of

[4] I discuss the problem in greater detail in my *Formal Theories in International Relations* (Cambridge: Cambridge University Press, 1989).

war and, if the charge can be sustained, then we ought to take the problem of their control very seriously. Earlier studies, such as those of Gray (1971) and Bull (1961), have expressed scepticism about any relationship between arms races and war, but these were content with very loose definitions of the phenomena and did not examine the data in any systematic way. They were primarily anecdotal accounts. The studies recorded below are part of the movement towards treating data with care, and for the systematic testing of hypotheses.

It is difficult to determine conclusively whether arms races cause war, in that an association of the two variables does not of itself imply a causal relationship. It is rather easier to refute it, as this is implied if there is no association. However, we can offer relevant evidence. An important study was done by Wallace (1979 and 1982) using the data from the Correlates of War study. He considered the ninety-nine cases of 'serious diplomatic incidents' catalogued by Singer and Small in the period 1816–1965 and classified them according to two criteria: (a) were they preceded by an arms race or not, and (b) were they followed by a war or not? The resulting table came out as:

Serious diplomatic incidents

	Preceded by arms race	Not preceded by arms race
Followed by war	23	3
Not followed by war	5	68

Source: Wallace 1982

This looks fairly compelling. On these data, wars are markedly more likely to result from a serious incident if there has been a prior arms race than if there has not. It will not be a surprise to find that the figures pass all statistical tests of significance with flying colours. However, let us examine it more carefully to see what it means. It demonstrates an association without much doubt. However, while it is consistent with the hypothesis that arms races cause war, it is consistent with a number of other hypotheses also. Thus, there could be another factor which is responsible for them both. It is argued that arms races are merely symptoms of hostility, which derives from more fundamental causes. Hence, the arms race is caused by the hostility and the wars are likewise caused by the hostility. This would explain the association as much as a view that the arms race caused the war. There would be an intermediate hypothesis that the underlying hostility is the basic cause but that the arms race aggravates this.

180

Unfortunately it is impossible to discriminate between these hypotheses on the basis of these data. It would require a much more detailed study of the individual cases to determine who felt hostility about whom and why. It is not, of course, idle curiosity which prompts our desire to make such a discrimination. If arms races are serious aggravating factors which predispose states to war, then we should pay great attention to trying to contain them. If, however, they are merely symptoms, then trying to halt an arms race will not do any good and we shall be deluding ourselves that success meant anything as far as war is concerned (though it would save money). Clearly this has very important policy implications. However, we can say that the association is so powerful and clear that, if an arms race develops, we should get very worried, as this is a powerful indicator that a crisis might spill over into war.

We should also look at the significance of the figures themselves and see how sensitive they are to the particular definitions of the various terms involved. There are three issues of concern: first, a definition of 'serious international incident', secondly the definition of 'arms race' and thirdly the definition of 'war'. Clearly a definition of 'serious international incident' is arbitrary. However, it is not totally without foundation, and it is improbable that different definitions would alter the numbers by more than a few percentage points. There is no reason to suppose that if the number were pushed up or down by say ten – which is fairly generous – they would be particularly biased in favour of any of the categories. Even if we are to be pessimistic and assume that ten were to be subtracted from just one of the two categories which permit it, the basic conclusions would be a little weakened but still stand fairly solidly. Hence there is a presumption that the general conclusion would remain unchanged because of differences in definition of this factor.

Now consider 'arms race'. All that we can entertain here, of course, is that both sides increase their arms together. As is shown in the next section, the evidence for genuine interaction is ambiguous. Wallace was careful to define 'arms race' to exclude some doubtful cases. There are some technicalities, but the definition is roughly that each country must increase its arms by at least 10 per cent per year for at least ten years. This is a fairly strict criterion and means that the study, in effect, considers only severe arms races. It is quite possible that mild arms races differ in their consequences. The final point is the definition of war. As we pointed out in chapter 8 this is not as easy as it sounds, because of possible contagion effects. It is here that a proper caution has been raised (Weede 1980). To what extent are the wars referred to genuinely independent wars? To a degree, of course, they are not. However, Wallace reworked his data to allow for this. Clearly again there is a judgement involved in assessing contagion, but, excluding the downright eccentric, the ranges of figures which different judgements will produce is likely to be small. The results came out as follows:

Serious diplomatic incidents

	Preceded by arms race	Not preceded by arms race
Followed by war	11	2
Not followed by war	4	63

Source: Wallace 1982

Though slightly weaker (particularly in the top left-hand cell), the result is still very clear. There appears to be a very marked association between arms races and war.

However, even this is not sufficient. Diehl (1983, 1985) has argued that Wallace still underestimates the degree of contagion involved in the definition of war in that Wallace treats the states involved in both the First and Second World Wars as if they were a collection of independent dyads. Thus, during the early years of the century, the arms race between Britain and Germany and that between France and Germany were counted as two instances of arms races and war. This, Diehl argues, is misleading. There is a problem nevertheless, and this reverts to the definitional issues involved in a definition of 'a war' which were broached in chapter 8. It is misleading both to regard these events as totally independent and to aggregate them and simply treat them as one single arms race. Only further disaggregation can give a 'fair' picture.

However, Diehl approaches the problem by excluding these particularly contentious and difficult cases. Extending the figures to 1970 but excluding the periods 1915–20 and 1940–4 in order to avoid these complexities, he produces the following table:

Serious diplomatic incidents

	Preceded by arms race	Not preceded by arms race
Followed by war	3	10
Not followed by war	9	64

Source: Diehl 1983

This set of data shows a much less clear-cut relationship. Admittedly the number of crises resulting in wars preceded by an arms race to those not preceded by an arms race (that is, 3:10) is greater than the equivalent ratio of crises preceded by an arms race and not followed by a war to those neither preceded by an arms race nor followed by war (9:64). However, neither the size of the figures nor the clarity of the relationship really enables us to draw conclusions with any great confidence. The data are perfectly consistent with the view that there is no relationship between arms races and war.

Diehl then went on to examine the cases of unilateral build-up in the same period. Conventional wisdom, as expressed in the balance theory, suggests that where there is a unilateral build-up of arms, there is a greater likelihood of war as the stronger state can beat the weaker state with greater ease. Diehl finds the following:

Serious diplomatic incidents

	Unilateral build-up	No unilateral build-up
Followed by war	3	7
Not followed by war	30	34

Source: Diehl 1985a

This suggests that there is no relationship between the unilateral build-up of arms and the onset of war, which is surprising.

It is hard to draw an unambiguous conclusion from these data – except that the above table seems to show fairly convincingly that there is no relationship between unilateral arms build-ups and war. The data do not really support any of the favoured hypotheses with any degree of conviction. The only conclusion which can be drawn with any degree of confidence is that the relationship between arms races and war is still obscure. The difficulty comes in the definition of the units. When is an arms race one arms race, two arms races or more? This is unclear. More salutary is that the same problem applies to war, which is a central concept in our analysis. Clearly the issues we raised in chapter 8 on this score were not just pedantic.

There are other reasons besides their relationship to war why we should be interested in arms races. They are very expensive. Resources which could be used for many other purposes are used in building arms. Arms races are not found only between rich countries which can afford them: Less Developed Countries (LDCs) pursue arms build-ups just as enthusiastically, and use much the same proportion of their gross national product on military expenditure. Further, a high proportion of the scarce technical skills of the LDCs go on maintaining and operating armaments, so it is possible that the burden in terms of potential growth is greater than the statistics indicate. Whether this is true or not, the sheer cost of arms, which in some sense do nothing and are there only because another country is heavily armed, is immense. There must be cheaper ways of doing things.

6 ALTERNATIVES AND TESTS

The analysis outlined so far has been explicitly that of a model which is a severely simplified picture of the world. However, this does not mean it is immune from testing. It is widely argued that tests are better construed as competitions between two alternative theories rather than as a competition between a particular theory and total agnosticism (Lakatos 1970). In the case of arms races, there is a challenger to the type of interactive model of which the Richardson model is an exemplar in what I shall call the 'autistic model'.

Proponents of the autistic model argue that the 'race' element in arms races is misleading. The arms build-up in a country is much more dependent on internal factors than it is on threats from another country. While in the Richardson theory the cost of the arms is regarded as a cost and a drawback, in fact it might be the opposite. The manufacture of arms is very profitable to many people in both money and prestige. Most organisations, whether commercial or not, have a strong tendency to increase in size and to empire build. Military organisations are no exceptions to this. It is suggested, only half facetiously, that if there is an arms race in which the United States participates, then it is between the different branches of the US military, who all want the latest and most elaborate weaponry, rather than between the US and the USSR or anyone else. Claims are made that this is a characteristic only of capitalist societies, stemming from the desire for profits on the part of the capitalist makers of arms. There is little reason to assume that socialist societies are immune from this. Financial reward does not come only in the form of profits. The senior posts in the military and military procurement organisations in the USSR provide congenial rewards in terms of economic benefits and social prestige which make their occupants anxious to retain and expand them. Thus, it is argued, two countries such as the US and USSR are not really racing. They are simply building up arms in response to internal factors. The external threat is not a major factor.

184

An analogy is the way both states are building up large numbers of domestic airliners. They are not doing this in competition with each other: it is unlikely in either case that the number of airliners operated by one is a factor in the decision-making processes about the procurement of airliners of the other. Apart from referring to the rival's arms as an excuse for their own activities, the same applies to armaments.

The problem is how to distinguish between the 'autistic' and the 'racing' hypotheses. If two countries steadily increase their armaments, this would be consistent with either hypothesis. We must search for signs of interactions by looking for some relationships between deviations from some steady rate of growth. Thus if one country's arms blip upwards, we would expect the other's to do so also, presumably with a lag. Rattinger (1975) looked at the arms race between the Warsaw Pact and the European members of NATO in essentially this way. He took an underlying trend attributable to 'Bureaucratic Politics' and then took out deviations from this trend. An interaction mechanism would have shown a relationship between these deviations on both sides, and it would therefore be a test. Unfortunately for the interaction hypothesis, there was very little relationship. Both because of its methodological and substantive interest, the Richardson model must be one of the most widely tested in international relations. A number of arms races have been examined statistically with great care with the theory in view. Similarly, decisions about armaments have been studied to see how far the rival's arms have been a major factor in the expansion of the armaments budget.

The results are mixed. The interaction factor plays a smaller role than one (than I, at least) would have expected. In a large number of cases, hostility, of which arms might be thought to be some sort of measure, seems to be internal to states, and the internal factors are predominant. This is not universally true. The Middle East is one case where there do seem to be clear interactive elements, and where the Richardson model appears to fit. Similarly, in the classic naval arms race between Britain and Germany in the years prior to the First World War, cited whenever arms races are discussed, the Richardson model appears also to apply. The 'racing' element may, of course, have been an excuse to some degree, particularly for the German government, but on the British side, at least, the increase in naval strength was primarily reactive and in response to the activities of Germany. While the evidence is open to reinterpretation and reanalysis, as it stands at the moment the Richardson model does not provide the general theory of armaments which we might have hoped for. Given the unsettling conclusions which arise from this, it would have been a reassurance were the alternative theories not equally bleak. However, the model does apply to certain situations. Further, if the theory is interpreted more broadly to include other sorts of hostile interaction besides armaments, then it may have yet wider applicability.

The most spectacular and significant arms race in the world since 1945 has been that between the super-powers. It has attracted much attention amongst arms-race modellers, but despite many ingenious efforts it does not fit into the Richardson theory particularly well. However, if we take conventional weapons between the Warsaw Pact (headed by the Soviet Union) and NATO (the North Atlantic Treaty Organisation, headed by the United States), the model does provide a modest but respectable fit. On reflection this does not seem too surprising. With conventional weapons, it can rather crudely be said that the more one side has, the more the other needs. Thus, if one side increases the number of its battleships, the other will have to respond by increasing the number of its battleships in order to preserve the original balance. This was at the heart of the Anglo-German Naval Race of the pre-1914 era. This form of behaviour is an underlying assumption of the Richardson model. However, with nuclear weapons the situation is rather different. The essence of the nuclear deterrent is that if one side attacks the other, the first can still respond, that is, it can use its 'second strike capacity'. However, if the putative attacker increases the number of its weapons, the second strike capacity can still exist and the threat remain what it was before. There may be some relationship in that if the putative attacker increases its weapons by an enormous factor it could weaken the possibility of the second strike, but it is not likely that this is a sensitive relationship. Thus the interactive element in a nuclear arms race can be much looser and barely exist. Hence the Richardson model is less likely to be significant.

What, then, is the significance of the Richardson model? It illustrates clearly that intuition is a bad guide to the behaviour of systems of any degree of complexity – after all the Richardson system is a simple one, but its analysis still gives counter-intuitive results. The model does appear to give an appropriate description of some arms races, and for these it is very useful. However, it does not seem to apply to many others and is not, as it stands, a general theory of arms races. It is possible that some new insights (though not necessarily complications) will add to its range, though the vast amount of effort which has been required to get it to its present level of development and testing might make us sceptical of further major developments.

10 ECOLOGY AND THE FREE-RIDER

1 THE ECOLOGICAL PROBLEM

It is now clear that various changes in the global environment, caused by human agency, will seriously and adversely affect the conditions in which we live. There are a variety of different but related problems involved. The consequences of industrial production and consumption have created a large number of secondary products and resulted in pollution. Some of this is temporary, but some of it may have permanent or at least very long-run effects on the global environment. A prominent example is the possibility of global warming caused by the build-up of carbon dioxide and other gasses, with its accompanying threats of climatic changes and rising ocean levels. Other problems are the extinction of various forms of living matter due to over-fishing or over-hunting or simply the destruction of the animal's habitat through the expansion of production and the world's human population, which are still increasing rapidly. The extinction of various species of whales, and the threatened extinction of more, are examples in this category. Population is growing rapidly, and somewhere there is a limit to what is supportable on the globe. There is little doubt, even amongst optimists, that there are significant harmful consequences of mass wealth production which are not directly taken into account in economic decisions. There are also advantageous side-effects of mass production, though there seems to be consensus that the negative effects predominate. However, the seriousness of the negative effects is controversial, with views ranging from those who think it is mildly disadvantageous to those who think the potential problems are catastrophic, involving, in particular, severe and deleterious climatic consequences.

Some of the problems involved are scientific. The physical consequences of many events are still not unambiguously predictable. The cutting down of the tropical rain-forests has the net effect of increasing the level of carbon dioxide in the atmosphere. This is

187

particularly significant as far as the greenhouse effect is concerned. But the significance of the reduction of some given amount of forest is still hard to evaluate. We know only roughly what the alternatives and their consequences are. Even the directions of some changes are not clear. Global warming will result in more clouds, which will trap more heat in the lower atmosphere and aggravate the process further (that is, it is positive feed-back). However, the clouds will also reflect away more sunlight, which will have a cooling effect – that is, it is a negative feed-back process. How these two processes will balance off against each other and what the net effect will be are simply unknown.

However, some of the problems, perhaps the most significant, are political. Suppose we knew exactly what the consequences of various alternative courses of action were: there is still the problem both of deciding which is the most appropriate course of action and then taking and carrying out any relevant decisions. There is no person or body to take them. While this in itself might be surmountable, there are conflicts. Suppose that all states were restrained in their fishing policies except for one. The one state on its own would not eliminate the fishing stocks. It gets the benefits of other states' restraint, which permits it to enjoy its profligacy. As this applies to all states, there is a continuous tension between, on the one hand, the restraint necessary for the mutually beneficial policy and on the other, individual self-interest. The problem seems to have some of the characteristics we noted in chapter 4. The prisoners' dilemma on a grander scale comes to mind. The problems are global in that on these issues everything is interlinked and the consequences of actions in one country are felt in others. Consequently the solutions must also be global.

The interest in and awareness of the problems have accelerated since the early 1970s. A major step in this was the work on *global modelling*. Complex computer models of the global system were developed. An early set of models, which created much debate (some of it heated), was developed by Forrester and Meadows into the various 'World Models', and in particular the model called *World3* (described in *Limits to Growth* in 1972 and written 'World3' and not 'World 3'). The Forrester/Meadows models presented a very pessimistic view of the world if present production and population trends were to continue – incomes would fall, pollution would rise, and the global economy would in general be in a bad way. It is this which caused the controversy. I shall now describe the principles of global modelling and, broadly, the results obtained.

188

2   THE 'LIMITS TO GROWTH' AND GLOBAL MODELLING

With computers it is possible to simulate the behaviour of very large and complex systems, including social systems. The principles are the same as with simpler models. For example, in the case of the arms race model (chapter 9) we made some assumptions about the behaviour of states with respect to armaments. From this we deduced the sort of arms race patterns which would be observed, and the consequences of various different assumptions about behaviour. If we had gone beyond giving a qualitative account of their behaviour and traced the detailed patterns of the arms build-up, then this could have been a *simulation* of the behaviour of the arms-race system. To do this on a large scale it would be convenient to use a computer, though for a simple model, patience and an adequate supply of paper would do instead. Because of the simple nature of the system a qualitative account of its behaviour tells us as much as is useful, and to plot time paths – with or without a computer – is really unnecessary. However, with more complex models, time paths of some of the variables are the most appropriate forms of output. The virtue of computer models is that they can generate output for extremely complex models – much more than could possibly be worked out by manual computation.

World3 is a very complex model of this type: it can be handled only on the computer. It is a model of some of the aggregative features of the global economy. In the model, there are five broad sectors – population, capital, agriculture, non-renewable resources (for example, oil), and pollution. To give some idea of the nature of the assumptions, I shall take the population factor. It is assumed that the birth rate is pushed down by an increase in pollution, a decrease in food-intake and an increase in crowding. However, these effects do not operate in a proportional or *linear* manner. Thus a decrease in food-intake in the case of fairly wealthy populations will initially have no effect, will then have a slight effect, and at some point have a large effect. The other relationships are similarly *non-linear*, that is, not proportional. Birth rates decline with an increase in incomes per head. This is a well-attested phenomenon, if superficially surprising. Death rates decrease with food-intake and increase with crowding. The birth and death rates are also influenced by the age distribution of the population. The change in population over any period of time, such as a year, is the difference between the births and the deaths. Some of these factors are affected by other elements of the model. An increase in production increases the income per head, but also the pollution. But just as 'population' represents a complicated array of relationships, so do 'production' and 'pollution'. In consequence, what we have is an extremely complicated set of interacting relationships which include feed-back processes and long and irregular time-lags. The aim of the model is then to find out what these interacting relationships produce in terms of population movements, food output per capita, pollution, population and so on. It gives trends of these movements over time, and the 'output' of the model is then a set of time series of the different variables. It is this output, of course, that we are interested in.

The assumptions as described are very general. For example, we assume that birth rates decline with an increase in crowding without specifying the rate of decline. The model can be adjusted to run with a whole variety of different rates of decline so that the consequences of different levels can be examined. One advantage of using computer modelling is that it can be readjusted easily to run under a whole range of modified assumptions.

The results of the World3 model were not particularly encouraging. On the basis of the model, the designers concluded that, if the same trends of production and reproduction which existed in the 1970s continued, some crucial aspects of the world economy would move into a critical stage about the second or third decade of the twenty-first century. Thus food per head of world population would decline, industrial output would decline and overall pollution would go up. This is not a cheering prospect. However, by running the model and altering the various rates of increase (for example, decreasing the rate of increase of industrial production), it was shown that stable levels of world per capita income at about the same level as average European incomes during the 1970s was possible. Thus not everything was gloom and doom, and the pessimism which is associated with this model is perhaps exaggerated.

The Forrester/Meadows work provoked a great deal of controversy, but also much work on other models of the same general sort aiming either to confirm or refute their results. Thus, a team led by M. D. Mesarovic and E. Pestel devised another model in the same tradition. In qualitative terms this gave similar results, in particular stressing that there are eventual limits to growth. A more sceptical approach was adopted by a team from the British Department of the Environment, which produced a model essentially based on the assumptions of perfect competition in the economy. Their scepticism was directed partly at placing much confidence in the results of such models, though they did this by building one of their own, the SARU model. Even this, if more cautiously and sceptically, pointed in the same direction. Other models are avowedly normative, such as the BARI-LOCHE model devised by a group of South American mathematicians and economists, who argued that the gloomy outlook that the other models predicted for the twenty-first century already existed in South America in the twentieth. Their explicit goal was to make recommendations about what to do, whereas the others had just described what they expect to happen under certain conditions. Other models are based on the economic technique of 'input–output analysis', including a United Nations-sponsored model devised by W. Leontieff and a Japanese model called FUGI. President Carter commissioned a study by Barney called *Global 2000*. Others are more restricted in their scope, such as a Dutch model called MOIRA which deals with food supplies. All, nevertheless, though with different degrees of confidence, give results which confirm the dangers of uninhibited growth rates.

A weakness of this world-modelling tradition is that the models are a-political and overlook the often crucial feature that many outputs are the consequence of conflictual or collaborative processes. The significance of this varies according to the factor under discussion. It is of primary significance in the case of the levels of armaments, which are clearly determined by an often complex conflict process. It is of rather less significance in the case of overall demographic growth.

There is a rather different tradition of global modelling which emphasises the political element. In origin, these pre-date the models described above, and their aims were originally to investigate the more conventional problems of international relations. The first major attempt in international relations was the Inter-Nation Simulation (INS) devised by Harold Guetzkow in 1959 and his associates at Northwestern University (Guetzkow 1981). This was a large mixed computer–human game of considerable complexity which owed some of its inspiration to the complex management games devised around that time in management education. This was a 'game' in the sense that human beings took part in it and made decisions, though a large part of the background in terms of the economic structure, effects of the level of income on popular support and so on was given by the computer model. A significant development of the INS was the International Processes Simulation (IPS) designed by Paul Smoker (1981), which took heed of the many criticisms of the INS models to make what is generally conceded to be a more realistic model. Another development was by Stuart Bremer; he took the basic INS model and replaced the humans who had taken part on the gaming version of the model with computer models of the decision-taking units.

Initially the political models were developed separately from the 'world-modelling' tradition, which seemed to leave substantial weaknesses in both camps. However, this is partly bridged by the GLOBUS model, an all-computer model devised at the Wissenschaftszentrum in Berlin under the inspiration of Karl Deutsch and the leadership of Stuart Bremer. In ambition the model aims to provide a simplified replication of the whole world system, rather conventionally using the state as the basic social unit. The model has 40,000 variables and parameters and simulates the behaviour of twenty-five states, corresponding to real states in the international system plus an 'all other states' member. As the real-world analogues of these computer states cover 80 per cent of the world's gross national product and 74 per cent of its population the degree of simplification is not excessive. The overall model is divided into six sub-models, one for each of the following sets of processes: domestic economic processes, domestic political processes, demographic processes, government budget processes, international economic processes and international political processes.

Most of the model is a complex interacting decision-making model. Thus there are sub-models of decision-making groups who take decisions according to certain admittedly simplified principles, with states as the primary decision takers and the organisers of sub-decisions. The underlying theory is that the actors are constantly trying to move from their present state to some desired state and that their behaviour can be seen as a consequence of this. Different parts of the model, however, reflect decision-making theories to different degrees. The demographic model is a pure process model in which there are no decision-making actors. By a process model I mean a model in which the decision maker is not identified, and population just grows according to specified rules. In this, the demographic model is markedly different from the other aspects of the overall model. Further, it does not involve any feed-back loops to other parts of the model and is an exogenous variable. The justification for the lack of a feed-back loop is that the time span of the model is relatively short. Not all behaviour in the rest of the model is derived from goal-seeking principles. Thus the variables in the 'international political processes' model deals with such things as the sending of 'hostility', 'friendliness' and so on, where these are regarded as the attributes of various actions measured on various (inevitably subjective) scales.

The *standard run* of the model goes from 1960 to 2010 and the time paths of a large number of variables are plotted for that period. From 1960 to 1978 the data are real data; the rest are projections. Various assumptions are made about the post-1978 period as part of the purpose of this sort of modelling is to provide quasi-experimental test-beds. The model depends on the existence of the large quantity of data which now exist, and on political as well as economic variables, which have been accumulated over the last two decades and which have been mentioned in chapter 8. Its feasibility is not due to the expansion of computational power alone.

The model produces some interesting results. The most cheering of the projections is that economic and environmental catastrophes are not generated in this model, certainly not prior to 2010, the end of the standard run, and probably not later either. The year 2010, of course, is earlier than even the earliest dates predicted for the decline in world per capita incomes. Bremer (1987) suggests that the short projection time plus the lack of feed-back loop in the demographic model helps to make the projections of the model relatively benign as far as the long-run environmental prospects for the world are concerned. The relatively small part played by other environmental variables in this model is presumably another factor. This more optimistic portrait of the future is consoling even if a broader group of variables might make it less so. Other consoling features of the model are the projections which suggest that the income differences between the richest and the poorest nations will decrease, not increase, which most people would find ethically pleasing, and which conflicts with some brands of conventional wisdom.

It would be rash to assume that these models have 'proved' anything – they are projections from the present to the future, and no more. Likewise it would be rash to assume there is no problem. At the very least, there is a case to answer.

3 THE SOCIAL MECHANISMS OF POLLUTION

The underlying social mechanisms which brings about this state of affairs can be illustrated by the following examples. Consider a manufacturer whose production involves smoky furnaces. The factories emit the smoke and cause other people distress. This is a cost for them. However, the manufacturer does not have to pay for this and, unless they are in a position to insist or persuade the manufacturer to adopt a less messy form of production, he will continue to produce smoke as well as the product. These costs are called 'external costs' in that they are above and beyond the costs which are directly borne by the principals. There is, needless to say, a large literature on the problems of externalities.

Another version of this occurs in what is known as 'the tragedy of the commons'. Suppose there is some common land which is suitable for grazing cows where everyone has the right to put a single cow on it. Suppose that initially ten cows graze (implying ten owners), producing a certain quantity of milk. If an eleventh cow is added, milk production goes up proportionately, that is by a tenth. This assumes therefore that there is adequate land to provide good feed for the eleventh cow without affecting the supplies for the other ten. This might go on for a while, as more cows are put on the commons, but at some time the grazing is going to prove inadequate and, say, the twenty-first cow will not find enough feed for her to produce the same increase in the quantity of milk as her predecessors. Moreover, as the grazing is general and the new cow is not restricted to the worst bit of grazing but has the same chance as any other cow, all the cows will suffer a reduction in milk production. Hence the total increase in milk production is even less than the production of the added (or marginal) cow. If further cows are added, the net increase in production will get smaller and smaller and in the end become negative. That is, though the marginal cow will still produce some milk, the effect of her grazing on the same piece of land will be to cut down the milk of the others by more. For the sake of the argument, we suppose this arises at the thirty-fifth cow. This is shown at the point M (for 'maximum') on figure 10.1A. This would be the optimum number of cows to have on the commons from the point of view of maximising milk production. However, the owner of the thirty-sixth cow will still want to put the cow on the commons as, though the aggregate amount of milk will go down, the cow will produce some milk, which is all the owner is concerned with. Similarly with the addition of subsequent cows, right up to the point where a further cow will produce no milk at all because of the paucity of feed. Unfortunately, at this stage, none of the cows will produce milk and milk production will have been reduced to zero through the attempt to feed fifty cows. As long as a new cow added to the commons continues to produce any milk at all it is clearly profitable to the owner of the cow to keep her there, even if it reduces overall milk production. Notice that this is a consequence of the perfectly rational decisions of the individual owners of cows – no one has been foolish or rash; they have merely tried to get as much milk as possible for themselves. This is illustrated in figures 10.1A, B and C.

Figure 10.1A represents the overall milk production; figure 10.1B represents the milk production of a cow added to the existing stock without taking any account of the effect of her grazing on the milk production of other cows (the production of the marginal cow); figure 10.1C represents the net effect on production occasioned by the

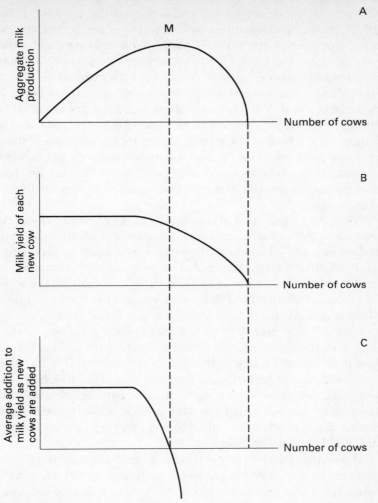

Figure 10.1

marginal cow, taking into account the effect on the existing cows of adding another. As long as the curve in figure 10.1B remains positive, it is rational for the individual cow-owner to put his cow on the commons. There is no particular reason for people to stop at the maximum point which can be regarded as a social optimum. This is another case in which, when the individual members of a social system adopt rules of individual rationality, the consequences for the system as a whole are malign.

The essentials of this simple story are repeated in many contexts. If

195

the general processes of industrial production produce pollutants which make the global environment worse, it is still perfectly rational for the polluter to continue. The private benefits are greater than the private losses even if the global environment as a whole is harmed. What is rational and sensible conduct for the individual, or even the individual state, involves considerable costs which are borne by the rest of the world. While some of these problems can be considered in the contexts of a single state, most cross state boundaries, and indeed concern the whole of the planet, giving us the problem of the global commons. It centres round the issue that there are costs incurred as a result of many economic and social activities which are not borne by the principals in the process but which are cumulatively very damaging.

While the simple story of the tragedy of the commons does catch the essence of the ecological problem, there are three features in particular it does not, and which make the political and practical problems much more difficult. First, the global system is very complex, with a multitude of feed-back processes. It is difficult to know how it functions in all its interactions, and hence what the consequences of various actions might be. Even if we know the general direction of events, the significance of some factor is often difficult to determine. The 'greenhouse effect' will probably increase the level of the sea; but just how far, and hence with what consequences, it is impossible to say with present techniques. The problem of predictability is obviously important in its own right. It has a further implication in that uncertainty can be used as a tool for political debate by arguing that, as we are not sure what the consequences of a particular course of action are, we should do nothing.

The second problem is that it is not a 'pure' tragedy of the commons problem in that some people will benefit from global warming. Thus, while the wheat producers of the USA will lose, higher grain yields in the USSR are predicted. There are two separate sub-issues. First, will global warming bring a net harm or a net gain? This is partly a factual issue about the consequences, concerning which there is a great deal of ignorance. It is also partly an issue of how we trade off the benefits and the losses. There is no unambiguous trade-off between the loss of large parts of Bangladesh under the sea and improved agriculture in Canada. The general assumption is that the harm is likely to be so significant that it easily outweighs the benefits, but it brings up difficult scientific and moral issues and cannot be dismissed glibly. The second of the sub-issues concerns the costs of change as such. If southern England were to acquire a Mediterranean climate, it would

196

be regarded as a distinct improvement by many. However, the costs of this shift in terms of altered agriculture, buildings, the loss of parts of eastern England under the sea or, alternatively, their horrendously expensive preservation may mean that the improvement is absurdly costly. In the world as a whole a new equilibrium climate somewhat warmer than the present might be just as good as the present world climate, but the costs of adjustment are immense in terms of both resources and social dislocation and unhappiness.

The third problem is that the consequences of actions carried out today are spread over time. The immediate consequences of some polluting acts may not be particularly noticeable, but their long-term consequences when it is too late to do anything may be large. Suppose, in the tragedy of the commons, that the result of too many cows on the pasture is to diminish the productivity of the land in the future (a frequent enough type of problem). In the short run the milk production might be at an optimum, but at the expense of production in times to come. If we combine our uncertain knowledge of the system with the fact that the consequences are spread over the future, perhaps the distant future, the political temptations for doing nothing are obvious. Why sacrifice a certain present gain for a problematic loss in the future when in any case a 'technological fix' may have come to our assistance? These lagged effects are probably already in operation. No matter with what speed and determination we attack the problem of global warming, some will probably take place because of past actions.

Problems of pollution and the environment are not new, though the widespread concern is. People have been aware that species such as the buffalo have been hunted to or near to extinction, and that human factors have been involved in the fogs and smogs which have affected many industrial cities. In the nineteenth century one of the reasons for Parliament not sitting was the smell of the Thames, which was the direct consequence of activities which were all too human and recognised as such. There are three reasons why people are now concerned about environmental problems. A century ago it seemed that there was nothing much one could do about them. Though caused by human beings, there was no political way in which they could be solved. However, some environmental problems were essentially local and, if behaviour could be altered on a local scale, then the benefits would be clearly felt also at that local level. Action was taken in cleaning up cities. Pittsburgh in the 1940s and 1950s is a classic example of a dirty town being transformed into a clean town by political effort. It was realised that political actions were possible which would achieve the goal. The same is true to a lesser extent of London, where political actions altered the atmosphere, primarily by cutting down fossil fuel emissions. Once such actions are seen as practicable even on a local scale, it is natural to conclude that they may be possible on a larger scale and that the passivity of our ancestors over their local problems need not be repeated by us today over global problems. Accidents with severe environmental consequences such as Chernobyl or the sinking of oil tankers also make it clear that human behaviour is involved; and human behaviour can be modified. The second factor is the development of technology which, in some respects, has led to cleaner methods of energy production. The cleaning up of London involved the prohibition of the burning of coal for heating and the diminution of coal-burning in industry and on the railway system. This would not have been possible if other methods of energy production had not been available. Whatever the political will in the nineteenth century, nothing could have been done without the technological developments of the twentieth. The final reason for the awareness of environmental problems is the development of our knowledge of environmental factors, which has required a development of advances in the physical sciences. There is concern about the effects of the destruction of the ozone layer. However, to be concerned, one has to know of the existence of an ozone layer in the first place, and to have the ability to detect holes in it and the knowledge to realise the probable adverse effects of such holes on humans, animals and plant life. This is all relatively recently acquired knowledge. Similarly, the concern over the 'greenhouse effect' requires a sophisticated (and still by no means finally established) theory of the behaviour of the climate and its long-term consequences. Casual observation of the weather system gives one few clues.

While the formal problem of combating pollution on the national scale is the same as for the international, the political problem is rather different. Cities have been cleaned up because the social systems were hierarchic in the sense that they had authorities or governments which could impose their will on polluters. There were considerable political problems since the individual actors were very powerful; but ultimately, once the nature of the problem was appreciated, it could be solved through the hierarchic system, which could organise the appropriate remedies. However, the international system is not hierarchic in this sense; there is no government, as is often remarked. Yet decisions have to be made on a global scale where there is no really effective mechanism for making decisions.[1]

Individual rationality will produce collectively irrational results. In the relevant respects, the international system is a negotiation system – the power elements of it are largely irrelevant for dealing with this sort of problem. How such a negotiation system might work and the problems facing it are the core problems of this chapter.

4 THE FREE-RIDER

Let us reconsider the 'tragedy of the commons' as described above but where, instead of each farmer having the right to put one cow on the commons, a smaller but still significant number of farmers can keep several cows on the pasture. This model is a little closer to the problems we face in the international system. Without any agreement between the farmers we would get the same result. If all farmers pursued their self-interest, the result would be that the aggregate milk production would sink to zero. However, this might be avoided by a negotiating system, which, with fewer actors, is more likely to work (Olson 1971).

Suppose the number of cows on the pasture is such as to produce the maximum amount of milk. Can this optimum be preserved? The difficulty is this. While it is better for everyone if they can agree to keep the number of cows at the optimum, it is always in the interest of the individual farmer to cheat and have one or two extra cows. Though overall production will decline, the defector's share of it will increase more than proportionately. The same argument applies to all the farmers, which makes the agreement an insecure one. This problem is very like the one which faces the fishing industry. We can estimate the level of fishing which, over time, will enable the maximum number of fish to be caught without depleting the stocks. However, it will normally be profitable for a single fishing vessel to exceed the limits set down. This is a perennial problem in fishing control.

Consider the following (hypothetical) instance of the tragedy of the

---

[1] A great deal of ingenuity has gone into trying to devise forms of property rights and negotiation principles so that these sorts of problems could be coped with by market mechanisms. Whatever their relevance in domestic economies, it is not clear that they are particularly helpful for the problems we are discussing.

commons.[2] There are ten farmers putting cows out to pasture. If they all use the collaborate or C strategy, then they will produce the attainable maximum of 1,000 units of total milk production. Each might produce a little more (the 'defect' or D strategy) and gain more than those farmers who do not defect. If they all defect, the total milk production will be 750 units. The total milk production which results will depend on how many farmers defect; the production of the individual farmer will depend then on how many of the others defect and how many collaborate and also on whether the defect or collaborate strategy is used. We can pose the problem from the point of view of farmer A. In matrix 10.1, the columns represent the number of the remaining nine farmers who defect. Thus D(3) indicates that three farmers defect and therefore that six collaborate. The rows indicate whether farmer A joins the collaborators or the defectors. The first number in brackets denotes the gain or pay-off to farmer A; the second is the pay-off to those who adopt the opposite strategy to his. Thus, in the top row, the second number is the pay-off of the defectors, whereas in the bottom row the second number is the pay-off to the collaborators. Thus, in the top row, where farmer A collaborates, the entry under D(7) indicates that seven farmers defect and get 90 units each, while two farmers plus farmer A – that is, three in all – collaborate and get 65 units each. However, farmer A can defect, and hence increase the pay-off to 85 units while that of the co-defectors decreases to 85. The new pay-off to the collaborators is denoted by the second number in the box and is given as 60.

[2] The example and matrix 10.1 are derived from the more general table below:

No. of Cs	No. of Ds	Milk per head to Cs	Milk per head to Ds	Total milk to Cs	Total milk to Ds	Total milk to all
10	0	100	—	1,000	—	1,000
9	1	95	120	855	120	975
8	2	90	115	720	230	950
7	3	85	110	595	330	925
6	4	80	105	480	420	900
5	5	75	100	375	500	875
4	6	70	95	280	570	850
3	7	65	90	195	630	825
2	8	60	85	120	680	800
1	9	55	80	55	720	775
0	10	—	75	—	750	750

Matrix 10.1

	No. of defectors				
	D(0)	D(1)	D(2)	D(3)	D(4)
Collaborate	(100, —)	(95,120)	(90,115)	(85,110)	(80,105)
Farmer A Defect	(120,95)	(115,90)	(110,85)	(105,80)	(100,75)

	D(5)	D(6)	D(7)	D(8)	D(9)
Collaborate	(75,100)	(70,95)	(65,90)	(60,85)	(55,80)
Defect	(95,70)	(90,65)	(85,60)	(80,55)	(75, —)

The nature of the problem becomes clear. No matter how many of the others collaborate or defect, it is always to the benefit of farmer A to defect. As all farmers are the same, an identical argument applies to them all and, without some extra factor, we can expect all of them to defect, promising a poor solution for them all.

This problem, which is found in many different contexts, is known as the *free-rider problem*. The crucial feature is that 'free-riders' get the benefits from everyone else's restraint but profit from their own lack of restraint. This is the first aspect of the free-rider problem. Another feature is that, if there are a large number of people in the group, everyone is tempted to be a free-rider because the global advantages of restraint are negligible. Thus the commons will be vastly overworked and any agreement will be insecure. This is at the heart of the ecological problem. There are many global commons. Apart from the more obvious ones such as the sea, the atmosphere of the world is a common good. However, it is destroyed by many forms of human activity, and there will be severe consequences from its over-utilisation. However, no single actor bears the responsibility for very much pollution, and it is rational for any individual actor to ignore the pollution effects. This is exactly the same problem as we faced with the cows on the commons, and we can consider the simple model as a guide to our analysis of possible solutions.

In the case of the commons, the problem is to find some means of restraining each farmer from increasing the production of milk, which, from each individual farmer's point of view, is the rational thing to do.

Consider matrix 10.1 again. Assume that all the nine farmers other than A act together, so that they all either collaborate or defect together as a single player and only farmer A may deviate. We can derive from the matrix another, more compact, matrix in which the first number in each pair of brackets denotes A's pay-off; the second denotes the pay-off to each of the other farmers.

Matrix 10.2

		Other farmers	
		Collaborate	Defect
Farmer A	Collaborate	(100,100)	(55,80)
	Defect	(120,95)	(75,75)

This is a mixed game. Farmer A might think that defection would be relatively safe as the 'other farmers' group can defect and punish, but only at substantial cost to themselves in the classic chicken manner. However, if the 'other farmers' defect, improbable in any case, it will be to farmer A's advantage to respond in the classic prisoners' dilemma manner. Thus, the situation appears to favour farmer A strongly, and there is a powerful argument for trying to get into this position. Unfortunately this applies to all the other farmers, who likewise want to act alone. Hence the coalition of the 'other farmers' is likely to be frail. By singling out this smaller number of options we can see clearly that only disadvantageous solutions are possible. We shall now consider how to dissuade actors from being free-riders.

In a strictly hierarchic system, an authority which can pass rules and insist that they are obeyed can simply prohibit the farmers from bringing more than the optimum number of cows to pasture. It is not absurd to suppose that such a system could exist. A town council or some organisation of farmers could be in a position to impose its will authoritatively, as did the freemen in medieval towns who could allocate grazing rights on common ground. In general, in ecological problems which are confined within the boundaries of a state, an authoritative solution can be imposed, though often there are difficulties where powerful interest groups are involved. However, in situations which transcend state borders, such authoritative solutions are not normally possible.

In principle it is clear that we arrive at the same result in a negotiation system in which people agree to coordinate their conduct. In the case of the farmers, the game might be regarded as one in a series of iterated games, one being played every year. In this case the 'other farmers' might be ready to respond if farmer A defects. Knowing this, farmer A might be deterred, and the general cooperative solution prevail. However, this possibility does not normally apply to the more general global commons. Many of the environmental problems are irreversible or reversible only after a long time. The rise in the level of the sea due to global warming is in this category of being reversible only over a very long period. Hence the game is essentially a one-shot game and, inasmuch as it is a chicken game, it is a game of severe chicken. Hence, the repeated game escape route is blocked to us.

However, there is a way in which the deterrent to farmer A might be effective. Suppose the coalition of 'other farmers' is not perfectly disciplined, so that one or two are ready to break ranks and defect if they see farmer A defecting and getting away with it. If one or two leave the coalition and defect, this will weaken the resolve of others, who now become prone to defection and so on as more defect. It is quite plausible to suppose that, while a genuinely unitary actor would not defect, there may be a general defection which results from a sequence of particular defections. Farmer A will know that defection will result in this general defection, and will then be deterred from initiating the move. This version of the model is quite plausible in environmental problems, particularly if we are looking at states as the relevant decision-making bodies. Some are clearly much more committed than others to environmental issues and are unlikely to defect, whereas others are quite likely to. Paradoxically, then, the existence of the weakly committed will strengthen the system and deter possible defectors from breaking away. Clearly if all parties were committed to environmental issues, there would be no deterrence necessary. The global equivalent of farmer A would not exist. The point of this argument is that, if there are any weakly committed states, it is useful to have some even more weakly committed states to make the deterrence credible. In the absence of genuinely weakly committed states, the strongly committed might try to pretend to be weakly committed – a strategy which runs into the problems discussed in the chicken version of deterrence.

Another possible way of achieving cooperative behaviour arises if the actors become convinced that the systemic goals are of importance in themselves. That is, they voluntarily forgo individual optimisation for the benefit of systemic optimisation. This could be for idealistic reasons such as the preservation of the planet, or because of some feeling of 'community' – that is, the feeling that the social unit whose goals are relevant becomes broader than the goals of the original actors. Before the cynical retire too rapidly into their cynicism, they should reflect that, if any social group bigger than the individual is optimising its goals, it requires the members of the group to have this

203

feeling of community for some group or another. States, for example, seem to be able to induce strong feelings of loyalty amongst their members which clearly transcend the individual goals of the members. It is difficult to argue that people are members of a group only for the self-interested benefits they can get out of it and will leave the group if some better prospect offers itself. Further, people's behaviour in the group is not solely in support of this self-interest. Counter-examples abound to the thesis of total self-interestedness. However, if individuals or smaller groups feel a sense of community in one group (and it is hard to dispute that they do), it is not being particularly idealistic to assume that they may shift their loyalities to another, possibly larger, group. If people are willing to subordinate personal self-interest to the state, there is no particular reason why they should not subordinate it to the planet.

5   CONCLUSIONS

Widespread concern about the global environmental problem is a recent phenomenon. Initially *Limits to Growth* was greeted with scepticism, following, as it seemed, in the gloomy Malthusian tradition. The Rev. Thomas Malthus, an Anglican clergyman, wrote the *Essay on the Principle of Population* in 1798; it was the *Limits to Growth* of his day. He argued that population would increase exponentially, that is, at a certain percentage each year, meaning that the absolute number of births would go up year after year. However, he suggested that food supplies would grow linearly, meaning that there would be a constant absolute increase in food each year, which would ultimately be constrained by the fact that the supply of land was limited. The constraints on population would then be 'famine, pestilence, and war' – none of which is a particularly appealing form of population control. His only suggestion for avoiding these was 'moral restraint', in which he had little confidence. Writing at the end of the eighteenth century, this seemed all very plausible, though it aroused furious criticism. However, it turned out to be wrong. Malthus underestimated the capacity for food supplies to grow, and this capacity has been underestimated ever since. That Malthus was wrong when he wrote – and concentrated only on population – does not invalidate the relevance today of a similar style of argument which has to be considered in its own right.

Despite the occasional complaints of the latter-day anti-Malthusians, there can be little doubt that the global system does not have a capacity for indefinite growth. Some limits on growth are approaching rapidly, viewed in an historical perspective if not the time perspective of an individual human being. While the recognition of a problem is half the battle, the other half is nevertheless formidable. There are two aspects, the scientific and the political.

First consider the scientific problems. We can isolate them from the political by assuming that we have a Rational and Benevolent Dictator (to be called the RBD), whose orders are in fact carried out and who has the best current available information. The RBD's problem is to find the 'best' decision. The political problem is to find how to carry out the decision of the RBD under the political arrangements which might more plausibly exist.

The RBD has to solve distribution problems as well as scientific ones, as some courses of action will favour some people more than others. Indeed, the competition for favourable distributions is at the heart of the problem of the commons. However, we assume that the RBD has some clear concept of an appropriate distribution of benefits and wishes to make the best possible decisions to achieve the highest sustainable level of income consistent with other requirements. What are the problems in doing this?

The scientific information is still uncertain in detail, even if the general trend is clear. How seriously should our RBD consider the limits to growth tradition? Is modelling sufficiently advanced for the results to be taken seriously? The SARU group, for example, was very sceptical of results derived from computer models. Also there was the suspicion that the modellers were professional pessimists. However, while the RBD would be cautious about accepting any particular results, the general trends which come out from too many different models and modelling traditions agree too closely to be ignored. This is confirmed by other, narrower, studies done on the environmental system which likewise suggest that significant changes will occur. This, at least, seems to be generally accepted and should be adopted as part of the corpus of rational belief of the RBD. Thus, while the detailed effects of increases in carbon dioxide may be a subject of controversy, it is widely believed that present emissions of the gas will have serious warming effects on the environment. It is therefore worth spending a large amount of resources, or forgoing considerable wealth increases, in order to cut down the present level of emissions. However, there is serious doubt about the significance of other factors, and our RBD has to work with a considerable measure of uncertainty and runs the risk of carrying out unnecessary acts while omitting some necessary ones. As knowledge is scanty, and the effects of relying on inadequate information costly, it would

205

be prudent to carry out very much more research into the scientific aspects of the problem.

The main concern of this book is with the social and political problems. Even if a hypothetical RBD could be quite clear about the proper course of action, in the real world there is no decision-making mechanism which would reach anything approximating to the same decision.

However, there are grounds for modest optimism. First, though the international system is anarchic, it is not chaotic. A relatively small number of states account for a high proportion of the pollution. Thus, in the case of carbon dioxide emissions, China, the United States and the USSR account for over half. If we add both Eastern and Western Europe, this goes up to 70 per cent. If these could be controlled, even if the rest of the world became free-riders, there would be a substantial improvement. A powerful sub-group such as the above might well be able to impose sanctions on free-riders and improve the problem further. It is likely that other pollutants show a similar sort of pattern, in which a small number of actors are responsible for a large part of the problem – indeed the usage of CFCs is even more concentrated than that of carbon dioxide emissions. There is a strong supposition that small groups can reach collaborative solutions much more easily than large (Olson 1971), and hence that some reasonable form of collaborative solution could be reached.

The difficulty with this is similar to that which an RBD would encounter. Though states might be ostensibly hierarchic systems internally, they are not so in fact. Sub-groups within them will suffer from attempts to control various forms of economic development and will force compromises on the leadership and move away from any solution which an RBD might have suggested. Thus, though a group of governments might agree that a tax on carbon emissions would be an appropriate way of controlling them, it is unlikely that people involved in the industries will agree. This is much the same sort of problem as getting generals to agree with disarmament. The predictions are uncertain (though less so with carbon dioxide emissions than with many other things – Grubb 1990). Given the long time scale involved in seeing any benefits, existing vested interests can point, often with great political effect, to the undoubted short-term costs involved in achieving a speculative long-term gain.

This is not the only problem about the global commons which needs decisions to be taken. The distribution between states of costs and benefits is by no means equal. Iceland, for example, is much more seriously affected by a ban on whaling than is Belgium. This problem is aggravated when we consider that in general LDCs are probably worse hit than richer countries. Rich countries became rich at the expense of polluting the atmosphere at a stage when it was a long way from saturation. Poorer countries are now wanting their share of the commons and look askance at richer countries saying that this is not possible as it has all been used up. It is probable that the most effective way of achieving rapid economic growth in the LDCs would be in environmentally costly ways. At some point, therefore, it will be necessary to accept that there has to be some equalisation of the costs. Resources must be transferred from those countries which will bear a lower part of the costs of environmentally sound policies to those which will bear a higher part. This will probably result in a net transfer from rich to poor countries, though this should not be confused with aid designed to help growth in those economies in general.

There is one encouraging factor in this problem. It does not involve violence. While tall smoke-stacks may look phallic, they do not seem to be taken as phallic symbols, and powerful emissions of noxious gasses (despite the unfortunate double duty of the word 'emission') are not associated with *machismo*. The difficulties which are involved when violence is a feature of the problem are largely absent, meaning that appropriate collaborative solutions become more of a possibility.

11 THE THEORY OF ALLIANCES

There are approximately one hundred and eighty states in the world, the precise number depending on the definition of 'state'. These states do not determine their mutual relationships in complete isolation from one another, but form alliances of varying degrees of strength and, on certain issues, decide policy together. The word 'alliance' is not used here in any technical sense, and still less in any legal sense; it is taken to mean any sort of coordination of policy. Thus there are strong alliances such as that between Britain and the US, and weaker friendships (here also called alliances) between, for instance, Britain and Sweden, where there are fewer formal agreements but a great deal of similarity of policy. Alliance formation is not restricted to state behaviour. Alliances are to be found in all walks of life. Within the domain which interests us here, alliances are made across state boundaries and, of course, between state and non-state actors. Business firms and states often work in league with one another against other states and other firms.

An alliance usually excludes some members who, in principle, could have been in the alliance but are not. We could conceive of an alliance in which every country was a member, and it would have some of the attributes of the types of alliances we are discussing. The United Nations was conceived of as such an alliance, though in fact various states such as South Africa are excluded, as China was earlier, while a few have excluded themselves, such as Switzerland. However, such alliances have other, different, characteristics, and we shall be more interested in those which not only include certain members, but also exclude others. Countries excluded from a particular alliance may form one or more of their own.

The purpose of a theory of alliances is to try to see why alliances form in the way they do, form in the sizes they do, and if possible why they break up when they do. There are many different sorts of

208

alliances, but we are basically interested in those in which some military component is involved. This may be a strong agreement to help out the other members in time of war, or it might be a very weak understanding not to do various things which could be interpreted as hostile.

Another classification of alliances is between the hierarchic as distinct from the egalitarian alliances. A completely hierarchic alliance is one in which the leader of the alliance virtually tells the rest what to do; in a completely egalitarian alliance there is no discernible leader. The Eastern European alliance, formalised in the Warsaw Pact, was close in its early years to being a completely hierarchic alliance. It subsequently became looser and is now (1992) in disarray. The NATO alliance, though more egalitarian, nevertheless had a clear leader in the United States, whose influence on the behaviour of the alliance was much greater than that of any other state. Pure instances of either type are inevitably hard to find except, perhaps, for short periods of time.

Apart from the different types of alliances which can exist, there are also different patterns of alliance structure into which the world can be divided. At one limit, there can be a Hobbesian 'Each against all' state of affairs, but this is not likely. Alternatively, the world could be divided into two alliances such that every country is a member of one or the other – this is a pure case of what is described as the tight bipolar system (Kaplan 1957). The world in the early 1950s consisted of two fairly tight alliances plus a large residual category of countries, the non-aligned, who were in neither alliance but who were also not in any real alliance with each other (though there were several sub-alliances amongst the non-aligned). Yet another possibility is of having several alliances in existence together with a bevy of neutrals. The present position of the world seems to fit into this pattern, which is, of course, extremely complex and changing. We have little reason to mourn the passing of the 'hard' Cold War days, but the tight bipolar system at least had the merit of being easier to understand (Kaplan 1957).

The difficulty with any theory of alliances is that the problem can become remarkably complex, as the number of ways in which even a few states can combine is legion. Suppose that ten countries can form any number of alliances (including the one where each alliance consists of a single member) and that the alliances can be of any size. The total number of patterns of alliances possible under such circumstances is 115,975 – or 115,974 if we exclude the single case of all being in one alliance (Nicholson 1989).

Table 11.1 *Number of ways in which ten countries can form into x alliances*

Number of alliances (x)	Number of alliance patterns
1	1
2	511
3	9,330
4	34,105
5	42,525
6	22,827
7	5,880
8	750
9	45
10	1
Total	115,975

Suppose the ten nations, called A,B,C ... J, form a bipolar world; that is, every nation is a member of one of two alliances. In this case there are five possible alliance structures, namely 1 against 9, 2 against 8, 3 against 7, 4 against 6, and 5 against 5. There are ten possible ways in which the structure of 1 against 9 can appear – A against the rest, B against the rest, C against the rest and so on. This is the simplest case, so it is not surprising that there are 511 different ways of forming a bipolar system out of ten actors.

A more realistic, but more complex, problem arises when there are two antagonistic alliances with a third bloc consisting of neutrals. The neutrals are not strictly an alliance in the sense that they have a common policy, but they do form a residual alliance, separate from the rest. Suppose that countries A and B form the central states of the opposing alliances. The remaining countries can go into alliance with A or B or join the neutral camp. Suppose it is possible, but not necessary, for either A or B or both to be left alone, and also that there is at least one neutral. In this case there are 1,221 possible alliance patterns.

A final variant of the problem is a division of the nations into five categories. Again there are two antagonistic powers, A and B, central to the two opposing alliances. We have another category of 'true neutrals', consisting of at least one country. If suitable inducements were offered, they might be willing to join either side. Italy, in the period before and during the early part of the First World War, was in this position. We then have two further categories of 'biased neutrals', each with at least one member. The first group of biased neutrals

210

might stay neutral or it might go into alliance with A. It would not, however, consider joining with B. The other group consists of states which might consider joining with B but not with A. Assuming that there must always be one representative of each type of neutral, but that either A or B or both can be alone, there are 5,418 different alliance patterns.

In formulating a theory of alliances we continue with the general assumption that states are self-interested and join alliances because they get something out of it. Thus, this is an exercise in the thin theory of rationality. Despite the potential complexities outlined above, it is possible to state something meaningful and useful about the problem.

2 THE BALANCE OF POWER

One of the most widely discussed theories in international relations is that of the 'balance of power'. It is the jewel in the crown of the realist theory of international relations. Crudely this states two things. First, if two opposing sides are of roughly equal strength, then this reduces the chance of war in that neither side can be certain it will win. Secondly, in a world with many actors, alliances will form so that a balance will tend to come about, resulting in stability. It is not argued that there will be no war, but that war of one sort or another will be relatively minor ('limited wars', in today's language) and will not threaten the essential structure of the international system. It is this second feature which is both the interesting and controversial feature of the theory.

It is generally agreed by scholars of widely different theoretical dispositions that expositions of the principles of the balance of power are usually imprecise (Wight 1966). It is possible to have a host of interpretations of its meaning and implications. There is often a lack of clarity as to whether it is a normative or prescriptive theory, advocating a set of rules which, if followed, will result in a stable international system; or a positive theory which describes how the international system in fact works. Some versions of the latter case imply that it forms the basis of a 'hidden hand' in which the system tends to some sort of balance (possibly an equilibrium, but this again is unclear) if states follow some principles of self-interest. Others seem to imply that it implies a broader view of self-interest which could, perhaps, be regarded as long-term optimisation. Of course, a theory can be both prescriptive and descriptive, and that is the most natural reading of some of the literature. There are those who hold that its imprecision is

211

precisely its virtue, but, as the reader will by now have gathered, this is not a view with which I have much sympathy.[1] I shall give an account of the balance of power theory which is, I believe, coherent, and assess whether such a theory can be justified either as normative (prescriptive) or descriptive.

The balance of power appears in two forms: the simple and the complex (Bull 1977). In the simple balance of power it is asserted that, in a two-party world, if each state has approximately the same level of arms, then there is unlikely to be a war. This is perhaps the form in which it is most generally understood at a popular level. As was shown on pp. 180–4 above, the evidence that this is so is far from clear. The more interesting case is the complex balance of power involving more than two actors where the actors can form alliances. In its positive or descriptive form this involves a theory of alliances, for it is argued that certain alliance patterns will be formed which, providing the actors follow certain rules of behaviour, will generate a stable international system. These two forms of the balance of power describe different situations and are not inconsistent with each other.

In statements of the complex balance of power, it is posited, in good realist tradition, that the actors are motivated by a desire for power. However, as power in this context is normally assumed to involve a zero-sum relationship, the more power one state has, the less the others have. Thus the actors are assumed to be as involved with the reduction of other actors' powers as they are in establishing their own. Hence, if one state or group of states begins to get more powerful and threatens to establish a hegemony, the other states will form a counter-alliance to balance the would-be hegemony. In more modern terminology (Riker 1962), they will form a 'blocking coalition', that is, a coalition which is not strong enough to defeat the other alliance, but which is strong enough to stop the other alliance from winning. Suppose there are two alliances, R and S, of approximately equal power, and some uncommitted states N. No one can prosecute a successful war. Now suppose that R begins to grow more powerful for whatever reason, thus threatening to become the victor in a war against S. The rules of the balance of power system suggest that members of the neutral group N will join S, the *weaker* alliance, and restore the balance. Alternatively, or in addition, members will leave the stronger alliance in order to join the weaker until the balance of power (in the simple sense) is restored.

---

[1] An early attempt to describe the balance of power rigorously was made by Zinnes (1967; Zinnes, Gillespie and Tahim 1978). More recent developments have been by Wagner (1986) and Niou, Ordeshook and Rose (1989).

What forms of behaviour are required for this system to work in the way described? Consider two versions. The first is where all members of the international system put its preservation as a major goal. Thus, while each actor wishes to expand its own influence, it does not want to do so at the expense of risking the destruction of the system in essentially its current form. In consequence, balance of power theorists argue that states in a balance of power system will not eliminate 'essential actors', a term left undefined but presumably meaning one of the more powerful ones. The preservation of the system is a dominant goal. The second version is where every state wants to be a hegemon, and to dominate the system. However, and necessarily, they also want to stop any other state becoming a hegemon. Thus, if a state which is a member of R becomes more powerful and threatens hegemony, its companions will become uneasy and defect to S while the uncommitted states will also join the S alliance. This need not conflict with a long-term desire to be a hegemon, though clearly the short-term task is to stop the more immediately threatening state.

For either of these versions to work it is clear that states have to regard alliances quite flexibly and be willing to leave and join alliances without too much ideological heart-searching. Each state has to be prepared to befriend or fight any other should the appropriate circumstances arise. It is claimed that the balance of power system worked reasonably well in the century which divided the end of the Napoleonic Wars in 1815 from the First World War in 1914. This was a period in which the European powers shared broadly the same culture, though Russia was perhaps at the limit of the common culture. More importantly, they shared a concern with the preservation of the system more or less as it stood in Europe, whatever their considerable ambitions to alter it in the rest of the world.

To what extent do these descriptions rest on plausible assumptions about behaviour? Remember, they are typically described as 'rational' in some self-seeking sense consistent with the 'thin' theory of rationality described earlier; but is this sort of behaviour consistent with such a concept of rationality? The crucial moves are made by a state which deliberately joins a weaker alliance in order to stop the march of a putative hegemon. However, a rational state intent on increasing its power might just as plausibly want to join the growingly powerful group in order to share in the fruits of the hegemony. Indeed if the system is viewed as a zero-sum game, this will often be the most 'rational' course of action. Suppose we have R as the stronger alliance, S as the weaker and a single neutral country who is a member of neither. Thus the total members of the system are R + S + 1. By joining

R, the stronger alliance, and eliminating S, the $R+1$ actors are now more likely to win any battles and they can divide the benefits of the international system heavily in their favour, though, realistically, not completely so. However, if by joining S the neutral actor manages to preserve the balance of power, the benefits of the system will now be divided amongst the $R+S+1$ actors, which means rather less for each. Therefore, there is the strong presumption that the uncommitted actor will go into the stronger alliance, in contrast to the principles of the balance of power. The members of alliance S could offer it some inducements which are larger than the ones which R would be willing to offer and, by playing each side off against the other, the uncommitted actor could do very well for itself. Further, members of S might be induced by R to switch alliances in order to gain more benefit. Any prediction about which alliances the actors will move into depends on the various bribes and inducements which actors will offer to others to build up a winning alliance. There is no presumption that this will always lead to a blocking alliance, as is implied in a 'hidden hand' version of the balance of power.[2]

The ambiguities of the problem can be illustrated by considering another case. Consider a neutral actor, called N, and ask whether it will join a blocking alliance in the following situations. Suppose that R is a single large power, but not large enough to defeat the coalition S if N joins in with S. However, N and S together cannot defeat R, so they form a blocking coalition. In this case one gets a balance. Suppose, though, that if N joined R, together they could defeat S and together divide the benefits of victory. However, with S out of the system, and in the new system of just N and R, N would now be dominated by R and the system could be primarily arranged in the interests of R as the hegemon. Thus if N has any long-term viewpoint, it will join in the blocking coalition, but if it took a short-term point of view, it would join R. The 'long-term', in this sort of context, means several years. There is no clear presumption either way, and what will happen can be determined only by empirical analysis. How people weigh the near against the distant future is an extra-rational consideration.

What is clear is that it is very difficult to say *a priori* which alliance formations and reformations will take place. The assumption that self-interested actors will always try to form blocking coalitions as

---

[2] It is common to assert that a balance of power system requires at least five actors for stability (Frankel 1988, p. 168). There seems to be no theoretical justification for this, and it is based on the observation of only one period where the balance of power was arguably in operation – Europe after the Napoleonic Wars – when, in fact, there were five actors. Wagner (1986), in a proper theoretical analysis, shows that a system with three members is quite sufficient.

suggested by the balance of power formulation does not seem very sound. They may sometimes do so, but not as a general rule. However, nor can we say anything general about the other forms of alliance formulation. We need rather more specifics in order to apply the theory of alliances, such as it is, at the moment. A 'hidden hand' is hard to justify, though many classical theorists such as Hedley Bull would be happy with this conclusion (Bull 1977). However, the theories of the balance of power are all based on arguments derived from prior assumptions about rational behaviour. We should note that balance of power behaviour involves very far-sighted behaviour on the part of the actors. This does not seem to conform with common experience. In most circumstances one would have expected states to join the alliance which was stronger, and hence more likely to win.

Whether the balance of power is in fact an operating feature of the international system is an empirical matter. It seems to require somewhat implausible behaviour. While the evidence is not conclusive, it is suggestive. It is discussed in the next section.

3   THE STATISTICAL TESTING OF THE ALLIANCE THEORIES

Testing a theory of alliances such as the balance of power is not easy. We have to be able to say what the alliance patterns will look like which are consistent or inconsistent with a particular set of principles for joining alliances. However, if we have a sufficiently large set of instances, we can use probabilistic models on the lines discussed in chapter 8. Consider a basic instance. Suppose we have a number of people who are gathered together. Initially they are all standing around on their own, but then groups begin to form. Let us look at two alternative ways in which people might form groups. First, suppose that people have a tendency to join small groups rather than large ones; alternatively we can suppose that people join groups independently of their size, so they are as likely to join a large group as a small one. In both cases these are general tendencies (that is, probabilistic hypotheses), and we would expect some individuals to go against the trend. After the whole process of group formation had continued for a while, we would expect these two processes to give rather different distributions of group sizes. In the case of the first principle, groups would be of roughly equal size; in the case of the second, there would be a spread of different sizes. Thus, if we wished to test which of these two hypotheses was valid, we could do so by looking at the distribution of group sizes after the process had

215

gone on for a while. This sort of analysis is standard in statistical testing.

Initially we shall consider the argument in terms of the formation of groups of individual people. In chapter 8 we made use of the principle of formulating a theoretical distribution of various attributes if certain random processes are assumed, and comparing these results with the actual events in question. If the actual and theoretical distributions coincide sufficiently closely, this is evidence in favour of the random process used to derive the theoretical distribution being the same as that which is operative in the real world. In a crude sense this is what we did in the last paragraph.

Consider an imaginary example of the number of people talking together at a cocktail party. At any given time, there will be a number of groups of two, a number of groups of three, and a smaller number of larger groups such as six. There will also be a number of people standing on their own, in transition between groups and so on. These are the isolates, or the 'groups' with only one member. If we take a number of snapshot counts of the groups in the party, counting on each occasion the number of groups of any given size, and if we tabulate our results, we will get a distribution in the same way as described in chapter 8. We would then be able to see what probabilistic process generates a similar distribution of group sizes.

The size of any group is determined by the rate of entry into and exit from the group. We are not attempting to discover why one particular group is bigger than another particular group, or why Sally joined the group which had Peter in it; we just want to obtain some general principle which governs entry into and exit from groups. Any theoretical distribution is unlikely to fit perfectly. Now a theoretical distribution which is relevant must be deduced from particular probabilistic rules of entry and exit. Let us consider two of these. The first such rule is that entry into a group is independent of its size, while the rate at which people leave is proportional to the size. Put slightly differently, this means that people join groups without taking any particular notice of how big the group is, since they are as ready to talk with just one other person as with a group of five. Similarly, they stay as long with a small group as with a large one. So, because more people are in it, a group of six is more likely to lose a member in any given five minutes than is a group of two. This is one of many intuitively plausible hypotheses in a context such as a cocktail party. This particular case gives what is called a *truncated Poisson distribution* of group sizes. This is the Poisson distribution (see chapter 8) with no

216

Table 11.2 *Number of states on either side in wars greater in size than severity 3.5 (3,160 deaths), 1820–1939*

Number of states [a]	1	2	3	4	5	6	7	8	9
1	42	24	5	5	2	1	2	0	1
2		3	2	1	1	0	0	0	0
3			0	1	0	0	0	0	0

[a] There was also one war of 15 versus 5.
Source: Richardson 1960a.

zero values, as, in the present context, the notion of a group of zero size is meaningless.[3]

An alternative assumption is that people are positively attracted to large groups, and having got there, stay in the group until the party ends. Such behaviour will give a *Yule distribution*, which is derived by assuming that new entrants to a group come in at a rate proportional to the size of the existing group, while, once in, members do not leave (or very rarely). Exit occurs only when the group disintegrates and all the members simultaneously revert to the status of isolates – that is, the party ends.

Let us now leave the world of hypothetical cocktail parties and go to the world of real alliances between states. The data we shall use are given in table 11.2 and relate to the number of states on each side in wars fought during the period 1820–1939.

Table 11.2 shows, for instance, that there were 2 wars between an alliance of three members and one of two members. Also, of the 91 wars reported here, 42 were between single nations on both sides and therefore did not involve alliances (except in the limiting sense of an 'alliance' of one member). This is perhaps a larger proportion than might have been expected.

With some qualifications discussed below, the balance of power theory would suggest that the number of states on each side in a war would be approximately equal. Even a casual examination of the figures shows this to be incorrect. Another fairly obvious test is then to see whether they follow the Yule distribution. In table 11.3 the

[3] In an empirical study (Horvath and Foster 1963) of various groups of individuals formed in non-violent circumstances such as those which appeared at swimming pools, in play groups, in the street, and so on (but not actually at cocktail parties, though the groups might be expected to have similar characteristics), the group sizes followed the truncated Poisson distribution very closely, which is evidence in favour of the entry and exit rules posited being the correct ones. It would be unwise to generalise very far from this study.

Table 11.3 *Number of states on either side in wars*

No. of states in an alliance	1	2	3	4	5	6	7	8 and over
No. of alliances of size x	124	34	8	7	4	1	2	2
Theoretical (Yule) distribution	128	29	11	5	3	2	1	2

numbers of alliances of various sizes are computed from table 11.2 and contrasted with the theoretical Yule distribution for the same numbers of alliances.[4]

It can be seen from table 11.3 that the figures for the theoretical distribution are close to the actual ones in such a way that one can plausibly assume that the same probabilistic hypothesis explains the hypothetical and the actual data – that, for warlike purposes, the number of states joining alliances is proportional to their size, and that alliances break up rather than lose members during the conflict. As this is a statistical hypothesis, it does not mean that alliances never lose members, only that it is comparatively unusual.

This is inconsistent with the balance of power principle. If the balance of power were to be a dominant feature of behaviour in the international system, then we would expect states to move from stronger alliances to weaker alliances and neutrals to join the weaker ones. We would expect a rough equality of alliance sizes. Even if we take just the number of states on each side in wars, as in table 11.2, we see that the number of occasions on which one nation fights two is much greater than when two fight two (namely 24 as against 3). More generally, there is a significant imbalance in the number of states on each side in wars, whereas there is a crude presumption that if states operated the balance of power principles, there would be an equal number of states on each side. Not only is this not the case, as the above distribution shows, but a very plausible alternative hypothesis, namely that states tend to join the larger of two alliances, fits the facts remarkably well.

[4] There are 91 wars. As we call a single actor an alliance of one and as all wars are fought between two alliances, there are 182 alliances. We can explain the derivation of table 11.3 by considering the 34 alliances of two states. From table 11.2 we see that there are 24 wars in which an alliance of 1 fought an alliance of 2; there are 3 wars in which two alliances of 2 fought each other, giving 6 alliances; then there are two, one, and one cases where an alliance of 2 fought alliances of 3, 4 and 5 respectively. These all add up to 34. The other figures are calculated similarly.

If states were all of equal power, then these data would be a damning criticism of the balance of power theory; but of course they are not. An unequal number of states in each alliance does not mean an unequal distribution of power and vice versa. This weakens the criticism, though it should still cause advocates of the balance of power as a description (as distinct from a prescription) of how the world works some discomfort. The strength of the figures in their support of the alternative hypothesis means that only some very special assumptions about the distribution of power in the system will validate the balance of power hypothesis. Another life-line for the balance of power enthusiasts is that these are figures of wartime alliances. The peacetime alliances may follow a different path, and no equivalent study on them has been done. However, even if the pattern is different, it is a significant modification of the balance of power theory as usually stated if there is a difference between peacetime and wartime behaviour in this respect.[5]

4 ALLIANCES AND WAR

A second, rather different, statistical problem concerns the relationship between alliance formation and the occurrence of war (Singer and Small 1968). The pattern of alliances and their membership is widely believed to affect the frequency of war. This may not be the case, but it is at least plausible. However, it is not very clear which alliance patterns make war less likely (or possibly less destructive), and which make war more likely. The theory is oddly undeveloped in any rigorous sense, as I have shown, but there are some interesting statistical results.

The investigations were based around the notion that the more alliance commitments there are in the international system, the less flexible it is and the more prone to war. The basic phenomenon to be measured, therefore, was the reduction of independent units in the international system. Two separate but related variables were used: alliance aggregation and the tendency of nations to form into two hostile camps (bipolarity). Both propositions were tested with a time

---

[5] Richardson examined the size of bandit gangs in Manchukuo in 1935, and the size of Chicago gangs. These too followed a Yule distribution. This suggests that individuals in face-to-face relationships and states in anonymous relationships both join alliances for violent purposes in similar ways. I hypothesised above that behaviour might be different depending on whether violence was or was not involved, and this is consistent with the views expressed in chapter 1. However, in this case the behaviour of political and face-to-face groups seem to be similar, in contrast to the speculations earlier. I stress that this evidence is slim, and even if reliable, concerns just two situations. It suggests a speculation but no more.

lag (three years emerged as the best), as one would not expect any reaction to an alliance to be immediate.

In both cases, the results were markedly different in the nineteenth and the twentieth centuries. In the twentieth century there is a clear positive relationship between alliance aggregation and the onset of war, and between the degree of bipolarisation and the onset of war. However, in the nineteenth century the reverse is the case. These results hold even if different measures of war and of alliance aggregation are used, and do not appear to be artefacts of the particular indices.

The empirical evidence is rather hard to interpret in the framework of alliance theories, whether ancient or modern. What we have is a phenomenon in search of a theory. Until the phenomenon is explained by more than casual suggestions, we are deceiving ourselves if we think we have a theory of alliances.

The results are clear but surprising. However, as one of the functions of a statistical test of informal theoretical notions is to discover the unexpected as well as the expected result, the study is important. We are left without any adequate explanation of the relationship between alliance formation and war, which represents a major challenge for further theorisation.

PART IV
CONCLUSION

The approach of this book has its critics, opponents and detractors. There are those who believe that social behaviour conducted by conscious, thinking beings is so different from the behaviour of the non-human world that any 'scientific' pretensions are illusory. Others regard such analysis as proper in some fields, such as economics, but not in others, such as the study of violence. Some of the problems are problems in the philosophy of science and must be discussed as such. However, there are also serious confusions amongst those who deny the legitimacy of a social scientific approach but who still want to develop theoretical concepts and use theories involving generalisations. For example, why have the classical balance of power theorists who deplore social science evaded the strictures of the Popperian philosophers of science?

Theory is not developed for its own sake. War poses one of the most severe moral problems facing humankind. The relation between morality and social science is at times subtle and requires careful analysis.

12 THE CRITICS

1 INTRODUCTION

The approach taken in this book has been criticised on many different counts. These range from basic differences in the philosophy of knowledge to simple misunderstandings and confusions, with serious but answerable difficulties somewhere in the middle. The differences which come from different philosophies of knowledge are basic and not resolvable here; perhaps they are not resolvable at all at present. However, many of the other disagreements are due to a lack of consistency on the part of some scholars of international relations, who seem to be able to hold one set of methodological views when it comes to international relations and conflict analysis, and another when it comes to anything else.

Underlying much of the criticism is the doubt whether the study of international conflict can be approached as a social science. There are two levels of criticism. One I shall refer to as the 'radical critique' ('radical' meaning 'fundamental', not, in this case, 'left-wing'), and the other I shall refer to as the 'limited critique'. The radical critique involves an assertion that a social science in the sense of sets of testable hypotheses about human behaviour of any sort is not possible; the limited critique involves an assertion that, while some forms of human behaviour, such as economic behaviour, can be analysed in this way, international behaviour is excluded from the normal precepts of the social sciences.

If the limited critique were to hold up, it would invalidate one of the primary themes of this book, that conflict is a general phenomenon which can be looked at profitably in its many manifestations, and where it is useful to analyse one form of conflict in terms of another. Such a criticism is serious and has some curious implications. International relations are conducted by human beings in much the same way as other interactions. If we can make generalisations about human behaviour in one of its manifestations, it is hard to see why we

223

cannot in another. There may be practical difficulties making it more difficult to study some forms of human behaviour (perhaps international relations) than others, but it is hard to see why the *principles* of understanding human behaviour in one context should be totally different from those which apply in another. It may be that people behave rather differently in their 'international relations' behaviour – this is, of course, quite possible, and is an empirical issue. However, even if this were so, there is no reason why this behaviour should be of such a totally different nature that the principles and procedures which prove effective for analysing other forms of human behaviour do not apply to international relations. It is difficult to see how this position can be justified.

The radical critics hold that a social science as discussed in chapter 2 is not possible as a description of any form of human behaviour, particularly social behaviour. There is a powerful case for this point of view (Winch 1958). Because I have discussed it elsewhere (Nicholson 1983), I shall not repeat my arguments. While I think it is wrong, it is not part of my purpose to dismiss it as trivial. However, it has a serious implication which is faced by only a handful of authors (Louch 1966). The methodological principles I advocate are widely held in many other social scientific disciplines. Amongst most economists, and such newer areas of social research as organisational theory, my approach would attract little comment. Amongst psychologists and even more so, sociologists, there is not universal acceptance, but it would still be seen as a proper approach by many. It is standard social scientific methodology. If the general principles I deem applicable to the study of international conflict were not to apply to economics, then most of the modern discipline of economics would simply collapse. There is a non-trivial argument which would result in this conclusion (Winch 1958) and which, if it is correct, means that you, gentle reader, will have wasted your time in reading this book. Not all the critics of the social scientific approach are clear which form their criticism takes. If the critique of conflict analysis is the radical one, then social science in this empiricist mode is impossible. No matter what form of social behaviour is under review, this is a very fundamental critique, and it is surely reasonable to require the critics to analyse it fully with all its fearsome implications for academic politics. However, if the limited critique is the relevant one, some rather more precise analysis of why international conflict should be subject to this curious special rule should also be laid out in detail.

2   THE APING OF THE NATURAL SCIENCES

A prominent social scientific analyst of international relations once remarked, in a mood of self-deprecation, that social scientists all suffer from physics-envy. This would be eagerly agreed to by the critics who suggest that social scientists are too prone to look at the successes of the natural sciences and seek to gain equivalent successes and respectability by improperly aping their methods and principles. In its fullest form this is the radical critique. It is implied by Adam Roberts, referring to the view that increasing formalisation of knowledge of human behaviour might contain and control violence (*New Society*, no. 441 (11 March 1971), 409), when he remarks: 'Critics might argue that such a hope springs from an irrelevant analogy with the natural sciences.' In response one might reasonably remark that if a method has worked well in one area, it makes perfectly good sense to try it out in other areas. It may not be successful, but it would seem foolish not to try. However, there clearly are differences between the social and the natural sciences, as most social scientists are perfectly well aware. Here I briefly summarise arguments which I deal with in much greater detail in Nicholson (1983).

We must distinguish between 'methods' and 'principles'. The principles of a science, both natural and social, are that a science consists of empirical generalisations, testable, at some stage, by confrontation with data. Generalisations, taken together, logically imply other generalisations, and the whole structure of generalisations forms a theory. If we can have testable generalisations in social affairs, then the rest seems to follow. The crucial issue is whether we can make generalisations. Suppose we cannot. In an extreme form it is difficult to see what this would mean. Psychologically we understand the world by fitting things into categories – that is, classifying and generalising. We could not use common nouns – words like 'cat', 'novelist', 'government' or 'war' – if we were unable to do so. This does not mean that all members of these sets are alike; it means that they are alike in some interesting respects, so we can make some statements about novelists or wars which would not apply to non-novelists or non-wars. It is possible, however, that what can be generally said about social units is weak and uninteresting. Once we define 'interesting', which involves making a value judgement, this is a factual issue and cannot be determined *a priori*.

Suppose, then, that the generalisations we can make are weak to the point of not being worth making. It follows that we cannot make any

225

sensible statements about policy, for this requires generalisations. If I assert that the unilateral reduction of troops in Europe by NATO countries would have increased the likelihood of war, I can meaningfully do this only by having some theory about the relationship of war to the relative number of troops on two sides, and I can really believe this only if I know of various instances to confirm it. Of course, the instances are not identical, and the evidence may be less than totally compelling, but nevertheless it must be strong enough for me rationally to hold that one consequence rather than another will follow from the actions. If we cannot say this, then our principles of rational action evaporate and the holder of such methodological views should refrain from prescription. Such modesty is rarely to be found.

Now it may be the case that we cannot make such statements as the one above because the basic criticism I am intending to refute is true. But, in that case, policy advice and policy itself may as well be decided by tossing a coin. However, those academics who hold such philosophies are rarely inhibited in recommending policy. If they seriously hold the point of view they express, then either (a) their advice is equivalent to coin-tossing, though it looks more acceptable if it is leaked to the press, or (b) they are inconsistent in that the basis for making non-random suggestions for policy is also the basis for recognising the legitimacy of the scientific analysis of the international systems.

The use of simplified models and mathematical and statistical methods is considered with particular disdain by many critics, who hold that this is a particularly unfortunate form of imitation of the natural sciences. Statistics are discussed below. The function of models as ways of coping with complexity has been discussed earlier. It is odd that, while glorying in the complexity of international relations, the classicists should scorn such a helpful tool. Thus, Bull remarks of modelling that 'However valuable this technique may have proved in economics and other subjects, its use in international politics is to be deplored.' Unfortunately he does not say why, other than that it simplifies reality, which is, of course, the point. The reason for the use of mathematics is somewhat different. Mathematics is a powerful tool in which complex deductive arguments can be expressed. Further, we are compelled to define things clearly, and the possibilities of ambiguity are fewer. However, its use is a convenience (in the highest sense of the word). The relationship of a mathematical expression to the world and a natural-language sentence to the world involve the same sorts of principles. They are not more stringent in the case of mathematically asserted phrases than in others – contrary to widespread belief. I refer those who doubt this assertion to Nicholson (1983 and 1989) and Körner (1960).

3 SOME SUPPOSED SINS OF THE SOCIAL SCIENTIST

I shall now state six of the commonest objections to the social scientific approach to the analysis of conflict,[1] along with my responses. These objections are not all mutually exclusive, but they appear in one form or another as I have stated them. I state them in my own words, but in serious forms. I do not intend them as straw men.

Sin 1

The social scientist does not realise that the occasional insights come from stepping outside the social science and using intuition. The social science itself adds nothing or very little.

Hedley Bull makes an assertion similar to this about Thomas Schelling (Schelling 1960), whose conclusions he admired but whose methods he deplored. It was a curious assertion in 1966, and has not improved with age. The ambiguities of rationality implicit in such games as chicken are made clear in Schelling's book, *The Strategy of Conflict*. Bull regarded it as 'amusing and perhaps profitable to pursue these illustrations', but he does not seem to recognise that there was practically no awareness of such conundrums prior to this sort of analysis. They are hard to see, except in crude terms, without these 'illustrations', and harder yet to discover.

The intuition which Bull so values is a valuable but dangerous weapon in the analysis of social life. A social scientist differs from the natural scientist in that the social scientist is a human being observing human beings. A social scientist can reason 'If I were in that situation, I would do such and such', whereas an astronomer cannot say 'If I were a star, I would do such and such.' It is a useful device for the preliminary selection of hypotheses, but it has grave dangers. Human beings differ. It seems 'obvious' from introspection that the possibility of execution will deter people from murder. Statistical evidence does not bear this out. Similarly, when people achieve positions of great

---

[1] In this section, I frequently cite Hedley Bull and, to a lesser extent, Joseph Frankel in order to criticise them. I choose them as particularly sophisticated members of the school I attack. That I attack them despite their relatively recent deaths – Bull's tragically early – should be taken as a tribute, as I am sure they would accept. I only hope people will be bothered to attack me when I am dead.

power, such as becoming the Prime Minister of Britain or the President of the USA, they frequently act in ways which appear inconsistent with their previous stated attitudes. They may be hypocrites, and doubtless some are, but they are also subjected to pressures which are hard to imagine without having experienced them. Introspection and intuition frequently give the wrong answers. The social sciences are full of faulty hypotheses derived from over-confident introspection.

Sin 2

The social scientist forgets that statistics require the over-simplification of data, and the forcing of events into common classifications, when it is the differences which are most conspicuous.

Of course, this is partly true, but it is true of many applications of statistics where their use is generally accepted. All road accidents are different, and the result of a complex set of interrelated general and specific circumstances. However, the attempt to relate the frequency of accidents to alcohol consumption is perfectly proper and gives useful results because it applies in a whole range of different circumstances. The relationship between alcohol consumption and road accidents is derived from observation.

This sort of problem arises constantly in the social sciences. Apart, perhaps, from population, there are hardly any measures which appear in any reasonable sense to be 'natural' or 'obvious'. Economic measures such as gross national product (GNP) are based on arbitrary procedures by which we add up such diverse things as ice-creams, machine-tools and package holidays. The aggregations are very useful, indeed vital, for any theory of economics, and for the most part they work quite well. This is their justification, and not any supposed quality of 'naturalness'. They work particularly well in comparing different relatively close years with each other. Statements asserting that the GNP has gone up by x per cent per year over a number of years are useful and meaningful, for the relative proportions of the different constituents are likely to be fairly constant. They are less useful over a hundred years or between two very different economies such as those of the USSR and Zambia. In the study of conflict we can devise plausible measures for such things as 'hostility', 'cohesion', 'agreement' and so on, which are in principle neither more nor less soundly based than the economists' measures.

228

Sin 3

The social scientist forgets that social science is a-historical. Human society is a constantly developing entity, and events do not repeat themselves as is required for a social scientific analysis. Thus 'war', 'diplomacy' or 'alliance' mean different things in the eighteenth and the late twentieth century.

The last sentence is true, but theories can involve theories of change as well as of stasis, as with the theory of evolution, or indeed any dynamic theory. This is just a particular version of the view that 'similar' events are never similar enough in international relations, a view concerning which I have already expressed scepticism. Most of the work in the social scientific approach of international relations uses data taken from the world since 1815. If we assume that human beings are much the same now as they were in 1815, then the differences lie in the different social structures. But theories of how people behave in different structures are precisely what the social scientist is aiming at and, with sufficient knowledge, one can project from one set of social structures to others which are not directly observed. If the differences are marked, then the writers of the past such as Machiavelli, Clausewitz and Thucydides have nothing much to offer us either. They are a comment on their own times and nothing else. Martin Wight's (1979; Butterfield and Wight 1966) illustrations from his vast knowledge of the past are likewise of feeble assistance in understanding the present. Thus, the statistical historian is indicted with a strange set of bedfellows.

Underlying my position (and, I would suggest, that of anyone who takes any of the above authors as being relevant at all for the understanding of today's behaviour) is the view that there is a universal 'human nature' which changes only on the time scale of biological evolution and that the different behaviours of human beings which we see are due to different societal conditioning. I certainly think this true over periods of a few centuries. This is part of a more general argument which I cannot see how to settle definitively. David Hume comments: 'Mankind are so much the same, in all times and places, that history informs us of nothing new or strange in this particular.' Many subsequent historians and philosophers of history such as Collingwood have opposed such a view. The Freudians, like Hume and the social scientists, clearly believe in the relative constancy of human nature (Gay 1985).

Sin 4

The social scientist forgets that while, in principle, social behaviour can be analysed scientifically, in practice it is too complex.

Complexity is, of course, a problem, but the explicit attempts to deal with this sort of issue have yielded rich dividends (see Simon 1962). The computer has helped the social scientist a great deal in this. Complexity is a problem in an analysis of the social world which does not disappear with the use of imprecise language.

Sin 5

The social scientist forgets that our perceptions of international relations are inherently subjective, and hence that agreement about whether something is or is not 'similar' to something else is often lacking. Further, agreement about whether some observations are appropriate evidence for a proposition is also scarce.

Joseph Frankel (1988) refers to his own book as 'no more than a statement of subjective perceptions of reality by the author, aspiring to come as close as possible to the perception of many actual participants in the process of international relations' (pp. 4–5). From this, Frankel would appear to be a radical critic of the social sciences. If there is a high degree of subjectivity about our perceptions of some phenomena, this is a warning to be especially careful about our definitions. Suppose we are concerned with the hostility expressed between two countries. Initially two people might have different views depending on what sorts of evidence they considered. If they share their evidence but the disagreement persists, we could conclude that a discussion in terms of hostility is impossible (which is a tenable point of view, though not often held). Alternatively, the definition of the concept of hostility can be redefined, carefully and as publicly as possible. The disagreement might reduce to two people's differences as to what counted as hostility. We are then in a better position to work on these two different definitions and see, to their mutual agreement, what effects the different definitions have on other relevant variables. The very subjectivity of the initial concept should force us into more careful definition and back to a point where we can get agreement on cause and effect even if we still disagree about what we mean by hostility.

Notice also that Frankel pursues the goal of finding what the actors' perceptions are and by implication sees this as international relations.

It is a perfectly proper activity, but by no means all the problems of international relations can be seen in this way. Relations between alliance formation and war, for example, are not the intended result of conscious goal-directed activity. Our earlier analysis of the unconscious motives would also be irrelevant on this narrow and limited view of the field.

Sin 6

The social scientist forgets that the results of scientific international relations are trivial and necessarily so.

This view is expressed by many writers including Frankel; 'I think that only minor phenomena are amenable to "scientific" analysis.' This is readily refuted by pointing to a phenomenon which, by common consent, is important, and which has been illuminated by 'scientific' methods. I suggest that the finding on pp. 219–20 above concerning the relationship of alliance patterns to war meets these criteria. There are many others. I would add two further points. First, the definition of 'minor' is an extra-scientific judgement. On one set of value judgements issues might be considered minor, whereas on another set they would be major issues. Secondly, if any propositions, whether minor or major, in international relations are susceptible to scientific analysis, it is unclear why others should not be also. If any propositions, however trivial, can be scientifically made about the problem, why cannot more be?

4   CONTRADICTIONS AND THE COYNESS OF CRITICS

The critics of social science methodologies have always been more vociferous in Britain than the USA, though even there prominent critics exist. Even in its early days, the 'behavioural approach' in political science in general has been less eagerly received in Britain (Crick 1959). Why this should be is unclear, though there have been many speculations from both sides of the methodological divide. I do not propose to add to this aspect of the debate, but instead to discuss some aspects of the sociology of criticism.

The critics of social sciences seem unwilling to turn their wrath on the older versions of international relations theory, as if their very antiquity means we should treat them with a proper respect. It leads them into methodological contradictions, for the assumptions on which their own theorising is based are in fact the very ones they reject

231

in their criticisms of modern methodologies. Unfortunately much of the classical theory is not expressed in testable form. (In Machiavelli's time, concepts of testability were not well understood.) However, they are now, though it would appear from writers like Hedley Bull and Joseph Frankel that the absence of testability is a feature of classical work which is to be positively commended, and they see no reason to change it in modern work in that tradition. According to them we have something which is inherently subjective, and perhaps desirably so. However, generalisations are still made. One of the major modern contributions to the classical tradition is Hedley Bull's own *The Anarchical Society*. In this he makes many generalisations. Consider his analysis of the balance of power. He asserts, for example, that 'The existence of local balances of power has served to protect the independence of states in particular areas from absorption or domination by a locally preponderant power' (p. 106). There is then a question why we should believe (or disbelieve) such a proposition. Unfortunately Hedley Bull does not consider this. I would argue that there must be evidence in the sense of cases of observations of local balance of power situations where there is domination and an absence of a balance of power. Indeed, the conditions should be found in matrix 12.1.

Matrix 12.1

	Balance of power	Non-balance of power
Domination	No (or few) cases	Many cases
No domination	Many cases	Few cases

The hard-line critic of social sciences would argue that such a matrix would be impossible to construct because of the heterogeneity of the data. This is a consistent position, and one which is not totally refuted by modern empirical analysis, if one maintains that the supposed data are spurious because of the false assumptions of homogeneity. However, such a critic, to be consistent, would have to argue that the original statement was meaningless, for it is, in form, and presumably intention, an empirical statement. Thus, if Bull's statement is to be meaningful it must be testable by observations of the form described above. These, however, contradict the methodological principles which Bull adheres to in his earlier essay which I cite and from which, so far as I am aware, he did not recant.

This is a general problem for many of the classical school. In fact statements are made which are meaningful only if, however vaguely, they are intended as empirical generalisations. The significance of this is missed, however. Concern is lacking both for identifying the nature of statements (such as identifying them as empirical, moral and so on) and for specifying, and if all goes well, finding, the evidence on which we can base rational belief in those which are empirical. These features characterise social scientific work but are absent in other traditions. This is a major weakness of the classical position.

An interesting question is why these characteristics of the classical tradition do not attract criticism from outside the international relations field for their methodological deficiencies. This stands in marked distinction to psychoanalysis, where the ferocity of the attacks on psychoanalytical methods of analysis is at times quite surprising, far surpassing the attack on behavioural methodologies, which is conducted more in sorrow than in anger. A major criticism of psychoanalytical methods is that they are untestable, and because of this do not measure up to the proper canons of scientific theories. The claim that psychoanalysis is scientific was strongly urged by Freud and is still held by many in that tradition. The criticism is serious, though mistaken, and is one to which psychoanalysts have left themselves wide open. This has been discussed elsewhere (Farrell 1981; Nicholson 1983).

An oddity is that classical 'power politics' in international relations theory has not been subject to similar criticism. It is open to all the objections which can be raised against psychoanalytic theory. It can be made consistent with any form of behaviour of the actual world. Thus, it is unclear what a refutation of the view that states aim to maximise power would consist of. When it is formulated in testable form, the adherents of the theory simply say that statistical methods are inappropriate to the testing of such theories, in much the same way that statistical analyses are dismissed by the methodological conservatives of the psychoanalytical movement. Just as the methodological conservatives in international relations theory resist any attempt to formulate their theories in testable form, so their counterparts in the psychoanalytical movement resist such attempts at restatement. Yet while psychoanalysis has been assaulted by some schools of the philosophy of science, notably by Karl Popper and his followers, classical international relations has been spared this treatment. We cannot even say that, while psychoanalysis deals with important things, international relations deals with issues which are less substantively important. International relations deals with world peace. Without some success in this area, psychoanalysis, along with everything else, will become irrelevant.

I have no real answer to this conundrum. Perhaps some theory of the psychology of intellectual development will be able to help one day. A tentative answer is that both psychoanalysis and behavioural theory leave the way open for, and indeed positively invite looking at, the prospects of change. Thus they are in some sense optimistic doctrines in that they offer the hope that the sufferings of the world can be alleviated.[2] The attacks come from essentially a conservative standpoint, though not conservative in a particularly political sense. Scepticism about psychoanalysis and scepticism about the possibilities of a science of social behaviour are essentially pessimistic doctrines. Fundamentally they stem from the view that the sufferings of the world are with us and that a modest alleviation is all that we can expect.

Psychoanalysis is in some way threatening and is disruptive of order. Similarly, notions of the balance of power are conservative and are essentially doctrines of order made by very respectable people, whereas the social scientific method hints at a world which is disorderly, uncertain, but more capable of improvement. While this view is vague and tenuous, I cannot help feeling that to be opposed to psychoanalysis and to be a believer in the sanctity of the balance of power is somehow more respectable, certainly in Britain, than to be involved in statistical international relations and a serious consideration of psychoanalysis.

[2] Not that Freud was much of an optimist. He claimed that he told patients 'you will be able to convince yourself that much will be gained if we succeed in transforming your hysterical misery into common unhappiness. With mental life that has been restored to health you will be better armed against that unhappiness' (Freud, 'The Psychotherapy of Hysteria', in *Studies in Hysteria* (first German edn, 1895; Pelican Freud Library vol. 3, Harmondsworth: Penguin, 1974)). Nevertheless, I think that my characterisation of psychoanalysis is essentially correct.

13 SOCIAL SCIENCE AND VALUES

1 SOCIAL SCIENCE AND ETHICAL NEUTRALITY

While some aspects of social investigation are carried out from intellectual curiosity alone, an underlying motive is often a desire to improve the way in which we live. Conflict analysis involves the study of how people behave with respect to conflict – in particular, war. Many scholars consciously and explicitly work in the discipline in order to reduce the amount of warfare in the belief that a fuller understanding of the phenomenon is a prior condition for effective action.

Social scientists who step out of the scientist's role and become advocates are automatically involved in a world of values and political commitment. One course of action is recommended in favour of another, which means evaluating the costs and consequences of the actions against each other in a moral sense. This view, which I accept and elaborate in this chapter, has unfortunately led to much confusion about the relation of values to science. In particular it is asserted that it is impossible to have a value-neutral social science in the sense (presumably) that the social science we produce and the propositions we believe in differ according to our values. I shall try to resolve these confusions in order to discuss more effectively the relationship of values to decisions.

I shall illustrate the problem initially in terms of an example from the natural sciences to keep the issues as clear as possible. Newton's laws of motion are accounts of how the world actually behaves, and carry with them no connotation either of approval or disapproval. In themselves they are undoubtedly value-free. However, the act of asserting a scientific statement is an action which may have consequences, and may therefore involve moral issues. Thus a discussion of Newton's (value-neutral) laws of motion with somebody who is about to drop a bomb is a moral action, as it will help them aim more effectively. For a physicist to discuss the laws of motion with the crew of a bomber at such a time implies that this particular act of bombing is regarded as an appropriate thing to do, though this does not destroy the value-neutrality of the laws of motion themselves. The nature of the statement – whether it is logical, empirical, moral, aesthetic, or even whether it is correct or not – is irrelevant to the fact that if, in uttering it, we have reason to think that this will affect someone's actions, then such an utterance is a moral act.

The same applies in the social sciences. In drawing attention to some findings of the social sciences, social scientists are often trying to persuade someone to act differently. They are therefore engaging in moral acts. This is very clear in the case of analyses of environmental problems, both in their natural and social science aspects. Similarly, psychologists attempting to explain to a government how perceptions of opponents alter in times of tension hope that the members of the government will act on their suggestions. The statements about the changes in perceptions in themselves are, or should be, value-neutral. The confusion between the epistemological nature of scientific propositions (which are value-free) and the act of asserting the propositions (which does involve values) is at the heart of the controversies over the ethical neutrality of the social sciences. They should be distinguished.

The interconnection between values and scientific statements does not stop here. Not only the assertion of a set of scientific propositions, but also the initial decision to work on one line of investigation rather than another is a choice and hence involves morality. The decision of a social scientist to pursue one line of investigation rather than another implies a belief that the line pursued is in some sense more important, though this may be from a personal rather than a social point of view.

Again to take an example from the natural sciences, it would be hard for a scientist to claim that, in choosing to work on the effects of toxic gases on the human body, there was not a moral judgement involved if the work was to be used in concentration camps. However, moral problems are not always so clear-cut. Work on the effect of certain viruses on the human body may be used for beneficial purposes in medicine, or for germ warfare. A scientist working in such an area is thus in a genuine moral dilemma – a dilemma in which social scientists also constantly find themselves, particularly if they are working on problems such as conflict, where the results of investigations might be used for a variety of widely different purposes. Work on the conditions under which passive resistance works effectively will be of use to rebels who dislike violence, but will also help the authorities defeat such strategies. One may wish to help the rebels but find one has inadvertently helped a repressive regime.

236

That there are moral problems involved in some scientific work is thus clear. This is especially true in the social sciences, where research is often close to policy and decision. Scientific propositions are value-free, and a scientific argument is not an argument about values. However, it is not correct to conclude from this that the making of scientific propositions is not a moral act.

2 POLICY, SCIENCE AND VALUES

From time to time social scientists are consulted on issues of policy, and their statements frequently have importance in the determination of what choices are taken. This is most obviously true in economics. The relevance of the study of conflict to policy is also very clear. The discipline is now emerging with a body of theory and suggestive, if not totally compelling, data to augment the 'wisdom' of intuitive analysts. This raises some important questions. Can social scientists, operating purely in their professional capacity, recommend one policy rather than another?

Suppose two economists agree on the effects of a factory moving out of one area and rebuilding elsewhere (and in such a case they probably would achieve a high level of agreement). They might still disagree over what they would recommend. Should a firm be allowed the freedom to act according to its own perceived interests, or is it proper to constrain it if its actions hurt other people, who are unable to participate in the decision? This disagreement is not one of economics but of moral and political values where there is no general consensus on the relevant values. An agreement on the factual and theoretical analysis indicating the most appropriate way to achieve some specified goal in no way implies an agreement that the goal is a desirable one. They may have different views on what the goals of the government should be, stemming from their respective visions of the 'Good Society'.

Consider a more extreme example. Two sociologists might be in complete agreement that capital punishment would reduce the amount of sheep-stealing. One might recommend that capital punishment for the crime should not be instituted, believing that the sanctity of human life is more important than the reduction in the amount of sheep-stealing. The other might recommend that it be introduced, on the grounds that property rights should be firmly asserted. They agree on that part of the problem which is within the province of social science, but differ radically on the values involved. Few people would accept the values implied by the second proposal today, but two centuries or less ago, they were widely held.

237

In almost any complex problem, a choice involves advantages and disadvantages according to most sets of moral principles. If a road is to be built which has enormous advantages for traffic flow, it will incur costs in displacing people who live in its path and resent being moved. Politics is often the choice of whom to benefit at whose expense with – at least in some societies – the attempt to compensate those who bear the costs. Ecological and environmental problems provide many cases of this sort, and, as we earlier argued, this is the source of many of the difficulties. The same is true in conflicts where there is a violent component. A conflict may be resolved more to the benefit of one party than another. It is sometimes, perhaps often, the case that two parties in conflict can mutually increase their security as the spiral of arms and tensions reduces. However, the manufacturers of arms do not benefit from this, and are apt to try to persuade the rest of us that the security is illusory.

This would be less of a problem if the social sciences consisted of a larger body of tested hypotheses which were generally assented to. Clearly this is not the case for the most part. Theories are provisional and in their early stages reflect the investigator's prejudices as much as science. The selection of the variables to be studied in relation to a particular problem and the way in which these variables are treated are dictated by the scientist's present view of the world. As social scientists can rarely abstract themselves from their value-laden human condition, their choice is likely to correspond to their ideology.

In the long run, of course, the theories will be subject to tests, and that which most successfully survives the tests will be preferred to the one which is most reassuring to the scientist. However, most theories in the social sciences at any given time are provisional, and are asserted partly because they conform to the preliminary assessment of the facts, and partly because they conform to the social scientist's values.

In making recommendations, scientists, whether social or natural, should make their values clear. All they are professionally competent to do is to analyse the effects of policies, and not to evaluate them except in a purely technical sense. After that, their values are to be respected neither more nor less than those of other citizens. Members of governments usually select, as their senior advisors, people who agree at least broadly with their own values, so that there is less need for constant reconsideration of value questions. Social scientists, acting as advisors, are then put in the position of giving technical answers to problems.

The moral of this is that social scientists must be careful not to let their values creep in surreptitiously under the guise of science. Their analyses of social issues are of interest to the general public, but their values can claim no special hearing. The public, in their turn, should beware when something is urged as 'economically necessary', or 'sociologically desirable', for such recommendations are based on values as well as science, and should be recognised as such.

Some problems seem so horrific that it appears immoral to consider them – the problems raised by weapons of mass destruction such as nuclear weapons can be thought of as belonging to this category. The act of totally destroying a society is so morally repugnant that even to engage in an analysis of it, which might appear to give it some sense of legitimacy, is prohibited. I disagree with this point of view, as is implied by my earlier analysis of deterrence. The extreme consequences of the use of nuclear weapons make it all the more necessary that the whole business is looked at with more, not less care. There is an acute moral paradox which the deterrence theorist has to face. Nuclear deterrence involves making an outrageous threat. However, its very outrageousness means that it succeeds, and the benefits are considerable. Is it moral to threaten immoral acts for moral ends if the threat is certain to succeed? More problematic is whether such a threat is moral if it will almost certainly succeed but not quite certainly. The solutions to these moral problems do not seem to me obvious, and therefore I think it proper to work on both the logic and the ethics of nuclear deterrence even at the risk of appearing to accord it legitimacy.

3   CONFLICT AND VIOLENCE

Most, though not all, of this book has been concerned with violent conflict, either its reality or its threat. It is a widespread value judgement, which I share, that violence is a bad thing, at least when it results in death. However, it is easy to slip from this into assuming that conflict, whether violent or not, is always to be deplored. Without going into great detail about the role of conflict in the development of society, there are some forms which are beneficial which illustrate the point. Thus it is widely believed that competition is desirable in the political arena. A multi-party system in which the various parties are in conflict is particularly highly thought of in 1992 as a means of running a polity. Likewise law courts are often based on an adversarial principle while economic competition is often thought to be beneficial and effective in producing a wide variety of goods and services. Conflict has its drawbacks even when there is no question of its

239

becoming lethal, and it is not surprising that there are significant differences of opinion on the appropriate balance between competition and cooperation in any society. It is rare, however, to find anyone who holds that a totally conflict-free society is desirable.

Violence, however, is different. Machiavelli in *The Prince*, his famous advice to rulers, shows that a moral ruler will be a dead ruler. Machiavelli's charm is his lack of moral humbug in the way he argues the case for ruthless self-interest. However, this is a very pessimistic doctrine and, though its pessimism is not grounds for assuming it to be false (or, as a pessimist might argue, grounds for assuming it to be true), it suggests that we should try hard to find alternative and more satisfactory ways of running the world which, ideally, would avoid violence altogether or at least reduce it, while enabling us to enjoy other moral goals such as independence, liberty and so on.

Clearly, whether one regards warfare as having a use or not depends on one's moral judgements. Few codes of ethics would give warfare no redeeming features. The issue seems to be whether the redeeming features are worth the enormous costs. Total pacifism, in the sense that its adherents hold there is no situation where violence is justified, is relatively rare, though there are prominent cases of this view being held – for example, by the Quakers. However, the word 'pacificism' has been used (possibly initially by A. J. P. Taylor – Ceadel 1989) to denote the view that while war is occasionally justified, it is rarely so. How the benefits of war are to be balanced against the costs depends on the attitudes of the individual person – it is a moral matter, and people make different moral judgements. However, it is possible to be a Clausewitzian pacificist. This is someone who believes in the instrumental use of violence on occasion, such as in defence against a despotic adversary, but thinks it rare for violence to be worth the cost (this is my own position). Indeed, one might argue that all true pacificists would be Clausewitzians in this sense. Bertrand Russell could reasonably be placed in this category (Ryan 1988).

4   SOME FURTHER PROBLEMS OF POLICY ADVICE

Decisions have to be made in social life, and some of the most crucial concern violence and war. However, the study of conflict as a social activity by means of the methods of the social sciences is still in its relative infancy. Its findings are tentative, and applications to decision making can be claimed only with diffidence. Is it then of any practical help, and can one responsibly advocate its application to real-world decisions?

To look at this, we must examine the nature of a decision more closely. A decision maker must have some expectations about the various consequences of choosing the different alternatives. They will not be predictions made with certainty (one would be concerned about the wisdom of a decision maker who was confident about the future). To have such expectations and beliefs, the decision maker must have made some predictions about the future, however cautious and provisional. This implies the existence of an implicit theory about how the world works. If there is no such theory, then, as I suggested earlier, we might as well choose by throwing dice. Whether we like it or not, we are faced with the problem of formulating rational beliefs about the future. For this, we clearly need all the help we can get. Now, while I am very cautious in recommending confidence in our social scientific knowledge of the international system, I am even more cautious about the knowledge derived from more intuitive analyses. Social scientists have looked rigorously at the propositions of traditional beliefs, and in many cases found them wanting. Arguments about balance of power, arms races and so on are empirical propositions, and in principle (and often in practice) testable. If they are not, then their meaningfulness is suspect. While anyone who took advice from a social scientist on the future of the international system should do so only with scepticism, it is no more than they should be willing to bring to the advice of a traditional scholar. While policy makers might at times be over-impressed by tools in the form of computer models and elaborate statistics into letting their scepticism lapse, they seem just as ready to be seduced by the ambience of an Oxbridge college into accepting propositions on the basis of plausibility rather than evidence. Admittedly, the use by governments of some of the theories which have been described in this book has not been such as to generate a great deal of confidence. The theory of games has been well digested in strategic circles, particularly in the United States, but sometimes with sad consequences, as in Vietnam. This is not so much because the theory is wrong as because of its premature application to problems where both theory and data were inadequate, and where ideological predilections to accept certain interpretations and reject others triumphed over rigorous and sceptical analysis. However, the record of the intuitive analysts cannot bear much scrutiny either: there are many parallels between the interventions in Vietnam and in Afghanistan, where the latter was made without any reference to the theory of games or any of the other scientific approaches to the study of behaviour.

241

5 CONCLUSION

Conflict analysis is a primitive though developing discipline. It is rather like medicine in its early stages, when incorrect theories sometimes led to doctors doing more harm than good. However, by the nineteenth century, doctors, with their still primitive scientific background, probably did rather more good than would have been done by the application of traditional remedies based on a very selective observation of their past effects. The formalisation of the sciences did much to advance the reliability of their results.

Conflict analysis, viewed as the social scientific analysis of conflict, and in particular violent conflict, likewise emphasises the need to be self-conscious about our grounds for belief. If it is believed that the balance of power favours stability and, perhaps, peace, then the theory must be posed in testable form and systematic evidence produced which rationally justifies such a belief. We must further identify what conditions would cause us to abandon the belief. Traditional work has frequently lacked rigour in indicating why we should adopt general beliefs, too often basing them on the evidence of a few selected, and often ill-defined, instances. Besides a concern for the grounds for rational belief, we must also consider the nature of rational action and be aware of the ambiguities of such concepts in conflict situations. Finally we should be self-conscious about our attitudes to violence and try and steer through the powerful emotions which beset us in trying to think about such subjects. War is not likely to disappear in the near future as a human institution, but clarity of thought and careful, objective analysis might speed it on its way.

REFERENCES

Achen, Chris H. 1989. 'Rational Deterrence Theory and Comparative Case Studies'. *World Politics*, XLV, 143–69

Allison, Graham T. 1971. *Essence of Decision: Explaining the Cuban Missile Crisis*. Boston: Little, Brown

Anderson, Carl R. 1976. 'Coping Behaviors as Intervening Mechanisms in the Inverted-U, Stress Performance Relationship'. *Journal of Applied Psychology*, vol. LXI, no. 1, 30–4

Ashford, Oliver M. 1985. *Prophet or Professor: The Life and Work of Lewis Fry Richardson*. Bristol and Boston: Adam Hilger

Axelrod, Robert. 1984. *The Evolution of Cooperation*. New York: Basic Books

Ayer, A. J. 1986. *Voltaire*. London: Weidenfeld & Nicolson

Banks, Michael. 1985. 'The Inter-Paradigm Debate'. In A. J. R. Groom and Margot Light, *International Relations: A Handbook of Current Theory*. London: Frances Pinter

Beer, Francis A. 1981. *Peace Against War: The Ecology of International Violence*. San Francisco: W. H. Freeman

Bennett, Peter. 1977. 'Toward a Theory of Hypergames'. *OMEGA*, V, 749–51

Bennett, Peter and Malcolm Dando. 1979. 'Complex Hypergame Analysis: A Hypergame Perspective of the Fall of France'. *Journal of the Operational Research Society*, vol. XXX, no. 1, 23–32

Blair, Bruce G. 1985. *Strategic Command and Control: Redefining the Nuclear Threat*. Washington, D.C.: Brookings

Boulding, Kenneth. 1977. 'Twelve Friendly Quarrels with Johan Galtung'. *Journal of Peace Research*, III, 167–91

1988. *Conflict and Defense: a General Theory*. New York and London: University Press of America (1st edn, 1962)

Bracken, Paul. 1983. *The Command and Control of Nuclear Weapons*. New Haven and London: Yale University Press

Braithwaite, R. B. 1953. *Scientific Explanation*. Cambridge: Cambridge University Press

1955. *The Theory of Games as a Tool for the Moral Philosopher*. Cambridge: Cambridge University Press

Brams, Steven J. 1985. *Superpower Games: Applying Game Theory to International Conflict*. New Haven and London: Yale University Press

Brecher, Michael. 1980. *Decisions in Crisis: Israel, 1967 and 1973*. Berkeley and London: University of California Press

Brecher, Michael, Jonathan Wilkenfeld and Sheila Moser. 1988. *Crises in the Twentieth Century*. Oxford: Pergamon

Brecher, Michael and Jonathan Wilkenfeld. 1989. *Crisis, Conflict and Instability*. Oxford: Pergamon

Bremer, Stuart. 1977. *Simulated Worlds: A Computer Model of National Decision-Making*. Princeton: Princeton University Press

    1980. 'National Capabilities and War Proneness', in Singer 1980, pp. 57–82

    (ed.). 1987. *The GLOBUS Model: Computer Simulation of Worldwide Political and Economic Developments*. Frankfurt on Main: Campus Verlag

Brown, J. A. C. 1961. *Freud and the Post-Freudians*. Harmondsworth: Penguin

Bueno de Mesquita, Bruce, 1981. *The War Trap*. New Haven: Yale University Press

Bull, Hedley. 1961. *The Control of the Arms Race*. London: Weidenfeld & Nicolson

    1966. 'International Theory: The Case for the Classical Approach'. *World Politics*, vol. XIX, no. 3, 361–77

    1977. *The Anarchical Society: A Study of Order in World Politics*. London: Macmillan

Butterfield, Herbert, and Martin Wight (eds.). 1966. *Diplomatic Investigations: Essays in the Theory of International Politics*. London: Allen and Unwin

Calvocoressi, Peter. 1987. *A Time for Peace: Pacifism, Internationalism and Protest Forces in the Reduction of War*. London: Hutchinson

Ceadel, Martin. 1989. *Thinking about Peace and War*. Oxford: Oxford University Press

Cioffi-Revilla, Claudio. 1990. *The Scientific Measurement of International Conflict: Handbook of Datasets on Crises and Wars 1495–1988*. Boulder and London: Lynne Riener

Clark, Ronald W. 1972. *Einstein: The Life and Times*. New York: Avon

Cohan, A. S. 1975. *Theories of Revolution: An Introduction*. London: Nelson

Cohen, John. 1972. *Psychological Probability: Or the Art of Doubt*. London: George Allen & Unwin

Cohn, Norman. 1967. *Warrant for Genocide*. London: Eyre & Spottiswoode

    1975. *Europe's Inner Demons*. London: Sussex University Press (in association with Heinemann)

Collingwood, R. G. 1956. *The Idea of History*. Oxford: Oxford University Press

Connell, Jon. 1988. *The New Maginot Line*. London: Hodder & Stoughton

Crick, Bernard. 1959. *The American Science of Politics: its Origins and Conditions*. London: Routledge & Kegan Paul

Curtis, Michael. 1959. *Three Against the Third Republic: Sorel, Barrès, and Maurass*. Princeton: Princeton University Press

Cyert, R. M. and J. G. March. 1963. *A Behavioral Theory of the Firm*. Englewood Cliffs, NJ: Prentice-Hall

Davis, William W., George T. Duncan and Randolph M. Siverson. 1978. 'The Dynamics of Warfare: 1816–1965'. *American Journal of Political Science*, vol. XXII, no. 4, 772–92

Diehl, Paul F. 1983. 'Arms Races and Escalation: A Closer Look'. *Journal of Peace Research*, vol. XX, no. 3

    1985a. 'Armaments Without War: An Analysis of Some Underlying Effects'. *Journal of Peace Research*, XXII, 249–59

1985b. 'Arms Races to War: Testing Some Empirical Linkages'. *Sociological Quarterly*, XXVII, 331–49

Diehl, Paul and Jean Kingston. 1987. 'Messenger or Message? Military Build-ups and the Initiation of Conflict'. *Journal of Politics*, XLIX, 801–13

Dillon, G. M. 1989. *The Falklands, Politics and War*. London: Macmillan Press

Douglas, Mary. 1975. *Implicit Meanings*. London: Routledge & Kegan Paul

Douglas, Mary and Baron Isherwood. 1980. *The World of Goods: Towards an Anthropology of Consumption*. Harmondsworth: Penguin

Edelson, Marshall. 1984. *Hypothesis and Evidence in Psychoanalysis*. Chicago: University of Chicago Press

Elster, Jon. 1983. *Sour Grapes: Studies in the Subversion of Rationality*. Cambridge: Cambridge University Press

1984. *Ulysses and the Sirens: Studies in Rationality and Irrationality*. Cambridge: Cambridge University Press

(ed.). 1986. *The Multiple Self: Studies in Rationality and Social Change*. Cambridge: Cambridge University Press

Eysenck, Hans. 1985. *Decline and Fall of the Freudian Empire*. Harmondsworth: Penguin

Farrell, B. A. 1981. *The Scientific Standing of Psychoanalysis*. Oxford: Oxford University Press

Feyerabend, Paul K. 1975. *Against Method*. London: New Left Books

Fischer, F. 1967. *Germany's Aims in the First World War*. London: Chatto and Windus (first published in German in 1961)

Fisher, Seymour and Roger P. Greenberg (eds.). 1978. *The Scientific Evaluation of Freud's Theories and Therapy*. Hassocks, Sussex: The Harvester Press

Forrester, Jay W. and Dennis W. Meadows. 1971. *World Dynamics*. Cambridge Mass.: Wright Allen Press

1972. *Limits to Growth*. New York: Universe Books

1974. *Dynamics of Growth in a Finite World*. Cambridge Mass.: Wright Allen Press.

Forward, Nigel. 1971. *The Field of Nations: An Account of Some New Approaches to International Relations*. London: Macmillan

Frankel, Joseph. 1988. *International Relations in a Changing World*. 4th edn. Oxford: Oxford University Press

Frei, Daniel. 1983. *Risks of Unintentional Nuclear War*. Beckenham: Croom Helm

Galtung, Johan. 1964. 'A Structural Theory of Aggression'. *Journal of Peace Research*, vol. I, no. 2, 95–119

1969. 'Violence, Peace and Peace Research'. *Journal of Peace Research*, vol. VIII, no. 2, 81–117

Gay, Peter. 1985. *Freud for Historians*. Oxford: Oxford University Press

Gray, Colin. 1971. 'The Arms Race Phenomenon'. *World Politics*, vol. XXIV, 39–79

Grubb, Michael. 1990. 'What to do about Global Warming. The Greenhouse Effect: Negotiating Targets'. *International Affairs*, vol. LXVI, no. 1, 67–89

Guetzkow, Harold and Joseph J. Valadez (eds.). 1981. *Simulated International Processes*. Beverly Hills and London: Sage

Hacking, Ian. 1975. *The Emergence of Probability*. Cambridge: Cambridge University Press

Halliday, Fred. 1990. '"The Sixth Great Power" on the Study of Revolution and International Relations'. *Review of International Studies* 16, 207–21

Hanson, Norwood Russell. 1962. *Patterns of Discovery: An Inquiry into the Conceptual Foundations of Science*. London: The Scientific Book Guild (first published in 1958 by Cambridge University Press)

Hargreaves-Heap, Shaun. 1989. *Rationality in Economics*. Oxford: Blackwell

Healey, Denis. 1989. *The Time of My Life*. London: Michael Joseph

Hermann, Charles F. (ed.). 1972. *International Crises: Insights from Behavioral Research*. New York: The Free Press

Hirsch, Fred. 1976. *Social Limits to Growth*. London: Routledge & Kegan Paul

Hobson, J. A. 1938. *Imperialism: A Study*. London: Unwin Hyman (1st edn, 1902)

Hollis, Martin and Steve Smith. 1990. *Explaining and Understanding in International Relations*. Oxford: Clarendon Press

Holsti, Ole. 1979. 'Theories of Crisis Decision Making'. In Lamer 1979

Horvath, William J. and Caxton C. Foster. 1963. 'Stochastic Models of War Alliances'. *General Systems*, VIII

Howard, Michael. 1983. *Clausewitz*. Oxford: Oxford University Press

Howard, Nigel. 1971. *Paradoxes of Rationality: Theory of Metagames and Political Behavior*. Cambridge, Mass. and London: MIT Press

Humphrey, Richard. 1951. *George Sorel, Prophet Without Honor: A Study in Anti-Intellectualism*. Cambridge, Mass.: Harvard University Press

Janis, Irving L. 1982. *Groupthink*. 2nd edn. Boston: Houghton Mifflin

Jervis, Robert. 1976. *Perception and Misperception in International Politics*. Princeton: Princeton University Press

Jervis, Robert, Richard Ned Lebow and Janice Gross Stein. 1985. *Psychology and Deterrence*. Baltimore and London: The Johns Hopkins University Press

Kahn, Herman. 1965. *On Escalation*. New York: Praeger

Kaldor, Mary. 1981. *The Baroque Arsenal*. New York: Hill & Wang

Kaplan, Morton A. 1957. *System and Process in International Politics*. New York: Wiley

Körner, S. 1960. *The Philosophy of Mathematics*. London: Hutchinson

Kuhn, Thomas S. 1970. *The Structure of Scientific Revolutions*. Chicago: University of Chicago Press

Kuper, Leo. 1981. *Genocide*. Harmondsworth: Penguin

Laing, R. D. 1960. *The Divided Self*. Harmondsworth: Penguin

Laing, R. D. and Aaron Esterson. 1964. *Sanity, Madness and the Family*. London: Tavistock Publications

Lakatos, Imre. 1970. 'The Methodology of Scientific Research Programmes'. In Imre Lakatos and Alan Musgrave (eds.), *Criticism and the Growth of Knowledge*. Cambridge: Cambridge University Press

Lamer, Paul C. 1979. *Diplomacy: New Approaches in History, Theory and Policy*. London: The Free Press

Lebow, Richard Ned, and Janice Gross Stein. 1989. 'Rational Deterrence Theory: I think, therefore I deter'. *World Politics*, vol. LXI (January), 143–69

Lenin, V. I. 1939. *Imperialism: The Final Stage of Capitalism*. English edition, London: Lawrence & Wishart, 1939 (first edn, 1917)

Louch, A. R. 1966. *Explanation and Human Action*. Oxford: Blackwell

Luce, Duncan and Howard Raiffa. 1957. *Games and Decisions*. New York: Wiley

March, James, and Herbert Simon. 1958. *Organisations*. New York and Chichester: Wiley

Marx, Karl. 1950. 'Theses on Feuerbach XI'. In Karl Marx and Friedrich Engels, *Collected Works*. London: Lawrence and Wishart

Masterman, Margaret. 1970. 'The Nature of a Paradigm'. In Imre Lakatos and Alan Musgrave (eds.), *Criticism and the Growth of Knowledge*. Cambridge: Cambridge University Press

Maynard Smith, John. 1982. *Evolution and the Theory of Games*. Cambridge: Cambridge University Press

Meadows, Donella, John Richardson and Gerhart Bruckman. 1982. *Groping in the Dark: The First Decade of Global Modelling*. New York and Chichester: Wiley

Moran, Lord. 1966. *Winston Churchill: The Struggle for Survival 1940–65*. London: Constable

Moses, John A. 1975. *The Politics of Illusion: The Fischer Controversy and German Historiography*. London: George Prior

Most, Benjamin A. and Harvey Starr. 1989. *Inquiry, Logic and International Politics*. Columbia, South Carolina: University of South Carolina Press

Nicholson, Michael. 1970. *Conflict Analysis*. London: English Universities Press

1983. *The Scientific Analysis of Social Behaviour: A Defence of Empiricism in Social Science*. London: Frances Pinter

1989. *Formal Theories in International Relations*. Cambridge: Cambridge University Press

Niou, Emerson M. S., Peter C. Ordeshook and Gregory F. Rose. 1989. *The Balance of Power: Stability in International Systems*. Cambridge: Cambridge University Press

North, R. et al. 1963. *Content Analysis*. Evanston, Ill.: Northwestern University Press

Olson, Mancur, 1971. *The Logic of Collective Action: Public Goods and the Theory of Groups*. 2nd edn. Cambridge, Mass.: Harvard University Press

Ordway, Frederick I. and Mitchell R. Sharpe. 1979. *The Rocket Team*. London: Heinemann

Osgood, Charles E. 1962. *An Alternative to War or Surrender*. Urbana: University of Illinois Press

Popper, Karl R. 1959. *The Logic of Scientific Discovery*. London: Hutchinson

1963. *Conjectures and Refutations: The Growth of Scientific Knowledge*. London: Routledge & Kegan Paul

Rapoport, A. 1966. *Two Person Game Theory*. Ann Arbor: University of Michigan Press, 1966

Rapoport, A. and A. M. Chammah. 1965. *Prisoner's Dilemma: A Study of Conflict and Cooperation*. Ann Arbor: University of Michigan Press

Rattinger, Hans. 1975. 'Armaments, Détente, and Bureaucracy: The Case of the Arms Race in Europe'. *Journal of Conflict Resolution*, vol. XIX, no. 4, 571–95

Reuck, A. V. S. de and Julie Knight (eds.). 1966. *Conflict in Society*. London: Churchill

Reynolds, Charles. 1973. *Theory and Explanation in International Politics*. Oxford: Martin Robertson

1982. *Modes of Imperialism*. Oxford: Martin Robertson

1989. *The Politics of War: A Study of the Rationality of Violence in Inter-State Relations*. Hemel Hempstead: Harvester Wheatsheaf

Reynolds, P. A. 1971. *An Introduction to International Relations*. London: Longman

Richardson, Lewis Fry. 1948. 'War Moods'. *Psychometrica*, vol. XIII, part 1, 147–74; part 2, 197–232

1960a. *Arms and Insecurity*. Pittsburgh: Stevens

1960b. *Statistics of Deadly Quarrels*. Pittsburgh: Stevens (privately produced on microfilm in 1950)

Riker, William H. 1962. *The Theory of Political Coalitions*. New Haven: Yale University Press

Roberts, Jonathan M. 1988. *Decision-Making during International Crises*. London: Macmillan Press

Russell, Bertrand. 1967. *The Autobiography of Bertrand Russell*. Vol. II. London: George Allen & Unwin

Ryan, Alan. 1988. *Bertrand Russell: A Political Life*. London: Allen Lane

Salter, Stephen. 1984. 'Nuclear Disarmament'. *Nature* vol. 308, 490

Savage, Leonard J. 1972. *The Foundations of Statistics*. 2nd edn. New York: Dover Publications

Schelling, Thomas C. 1960. *The Strategy of Conflict*. Cambridge, Mass.: Harvard University Press

Schlesinger, Arthur M. 1965. *A Thousand Days: John F. Kennedy in the White House*. London: Deutsch

Schmid, Herman. 1970. 'Peace Research as a Technology for Pacification'. *International Peace Research Association: 3rd Proceedings*, 20–69

Scientific American. 1989. Special issue, September. *Managing Planet Earth*

Sen, Amartya. 1981. *Poverty and Famines: An Essay on Entitlement and Deprivation*. Oxford: Clarendon Press

Shubik, Martin. 1982. *Game Theory in the Social Sciences*. Cambridge, Mass.: MIT Press

Simon, Herbert A. 1962. 'The Architecture of Complexity'. *Proceedings of the American Philosophical Society* no. 106, 467–82

1976. *Administrative Behavior: A Study of Decision Making Processes in Administrative Organisations*. New York: Free Press

1982. *Models of Bounded Rationality*. Cambridge, Mass.: MIT Press

Singer, J. David (ed.). 1980. *The Correlates of War: Testing some Realpolitik Models*. New York: The Free Press

Singer, J. David and Melvin Small. 1968. 'Alliance Aggregation and the Onset of War 1815–1945'. In J. David Singer (ed.), *Quantitative International Politics*. New York: The Free Press

1982. *Resort to Arms: International and Civil Wars 1816–1980*. Beverley Hills and London: Sage

Skagestad, Peter. 1975. *Making Sense of History: The Philosophies of Popper and Collingwood*. Oslo: Universitetsforlaget

Smart, Ninian. 1986. *Concept and Empathy: Essays in the Study of Religion*. London: Macmillan

Smoker, Paul. 1981. 'The International Processes Simulation'. In Guetzkow and Valadez 1981, pp. 101–33

Snow, C. P. 1967. *Variety of Men*. London: Macmillan

Sorensen, Theodore C. 1965. *Kennedy*. London: Macmillan

Stern, J. P. 1975. *Hitler: The Führer and the People*. Berkeley: University of California Press

Taylor, A. J. P. 1965. *English History 1914–45*. Oxford: Oxford University Press

Taylor, Michael. 1987. *The Possibility of Cooperation: Studies in Rationality and Social Change*. Cambridge: Cambridge University Press

(ed.). 1988. *Rationality and Revolution*. Cambridge: Cambridge University Press

Vasquez, John A. 1983. *The Power of Power Politics: A Critique*. London: Pinter

Von Neumann, John and Oskar Morgenstern. 1944. *The Theory of Games and Economic Behavior*. Princeton: Princeton University Press

Vroom, V. H. 1964. *Work and Motivation*. New York: Wiley

Wagner, Harrison. 1986. 'The Theory of Games and the Balance of Power'. *World Politics*, vol. XXXVIII, no. 4, 546–76

Wallace, Michael. 1979. 'Arms Races and Escalation: Some New Evidence'. *Journal of Conflict Resolution*, XXIII (March), 3–36

1982. 'Arms and Escalation: Two Competing Hypotheses'. *International Studies Quarterly*, vol. XXVI, no. 1, 37–56

Washburn, S. L. 1968. 'Conflicts in Primate Society'. In A. V. S. de Reuck and Julie Knight (eds.)

Watson, James D. 1970. *The Double Helix: A Personal Account of the Discovery of the Structure of DNA*. London: Weidenfeld & Nicolson; Harmondsworth: Penguin

Weede, Erich. 1980. 'Arms Races and Escalation: Some Persisting Doubts'. *Journal of Conflict Resolution*, XXIV (June), 285–7

Weiss, Herbert K. 1963. 'Stochastic Models for the Duration and Magnitude of a "Deadly Quarrel"'. *Operations Research*, vol. XI, no. 1

Wiegele, Thomas C. 1976. 'Decision Making in International Crises: Some Biological Factors'. *International Studies Quarterly*, vol. XVII, no. 3

Wight, Martin. 1966. *Diplomatic Investigations*. London: George Allen & Unwin

1979. *Power Politics*. Harmondsworth: Penguin

Wilkinson, David. 1980. *Deadly Quarrels: Lewis F. Richardson and the Statistical Study of War*. Berkeley and London: University of California Press

Winch, Peter. 1958. *The Idea of a Social Science and its Relation to Philosophy*. London: Routledge & Kegan Paul

Woodham-Smith, Cecil. 1962. *The Great Hunger: Ireland 1845–9*. London: Hamish Hamilton

Woodward, E. L. 1938. *The Age of Reform 1815–1870*. Oxford: Clarendon Press

Wright, Quincy. 1947. *A Study of War*. 2 vols. Chicago: University of Chicago Press

Zagare, Frank C. 1987. *The Dynamics of Deterrence*. Chicago: University of Chicago Press

Zinnes, Dina. 1967. 'An Analytical Study of Balance of Power Theories'. *Journal of Peace Research*, IV, 270–88

1980. 'Three Puzzles in Search of a Researcher'. *International Studies Quarterly*, vol. XXIV, no. 3, 315–42

Zinnes, Dina, J. V. Gillespie and G. S. Tahim. 1978. 'A Formal Analysis of Some Issues in Balance of Power Theories'. *International Studies Quarterly*, XXII, 323–53

INDEX

Achen, C. 88
actors
  essential 213
  model of 56
  unitary 52, 56
acts 11
Africa 21
  South 29
  Sub-Saharan 29
aggression 105f.
agreement 228
airline pilots 129
alcohol 131
alliances 25, 35, 59, 164n, 208f., 229
  formation of 145
  and war 219f.
Allison, Graham 56
ambiguity 132, 133
ambivalence 108f., 115, 116
America (see USA)
analogy 14
analysis 26
  rational 3, 4–5
  statistical 17
anthropology 25, 35
anti-missile systems 68, 69, 70
Argentina 12, 109, 118
armaments (arms) 35, 116, 147, 164f., 238
  baroque 109
  control of 23, 72
  level, equilibrium of 169f.
  level of 25, 34, 35, 36, 164f.
  manufacturers of 238
  measure of effectiveness of 179
  nuclear 166
  and war 164f.
arms race 3, 30, 164f., 241
  Anglo-German Naval 165, 185, 186
  autistic 184, 185
  definition of 181
  model of 189
  Richardson theory of 166f.
  super-power 186
  unilateral 165, 183, 184

  and war 180f.
Asquith, Lord 120
astrology 49, 50 and n, 139
attitudes, psychological 22
Axelrod, R. 58, 67n
Ayer, A. J. 51

balance of power 3, 211f., 217, 218, 219,
    227, 231, 234, 241, 242
  complex 164n, 212f.
  simple 164, 212
  system of 164n
balance of terror 169
Bangladesh 196
bargaining 13, 14
Beer, F. 18
behaviour 3
  non-rational 139
  normal 43
  psychological 106
  rational 3, 4–5
  social, of animals 106
  social, of humans 106
Belgium, 1, 206
benefit 104, 105, 106, 206
Bennett, Peter, 98
Benthamism 111
biology 58, 105
bipolarity 219
births 146, 189
Blair, Bruce 56, 87
bodies, astronomical 11
Bracken, Paul 56, 87, 140
Braithwaite, R. B. 32, 60n
Brams, Steven J. 69n, 86
Brandt, Willi, 137
Brecher, M. 122n, 123, 135, 136
Bremer, S. 165, 191, 192, 193
Britain 12, 13, 29, 109, 118, 148, 165, 178,
    182, 208, 234
Buddhism 110
Bueno de Mesquita, Bruce 111
Bull, Hedley 3 and n, 164, 180, 212, 215,
    226, 227 and n, 231